HILLTOPS OF THE HONG KONG MOON

John Crook

MINERVA PRESS

LONDON
MIAMI   RIO DE JANEIRO   DELHI

ISBN 1 86106 566 3

MINERVA PRESS
315–317 Regent Street
London W1R 7YB

Printed in Great Britain for Minerva Press

HILLTOPS OF THE HONG KONG MOON

To Yiu Yannang, JP, MBE

Contents

Preface

During my year as a National Service officer in the Royal Artillery in Hong Kong (1953–1954) I wrote regular letters home. In these writings I explored many aspects of my fresh experiences. I was twenty-two, had completed a degree in Zoology at University College, Southampton and had gained a place for future doctoral research in animal behaviour at Cambridge. The army was an obligatory interlude between two periods of academic training. Yet that year was to be perhaps the most influential of my life.

National service opened up my character and widened my horizons in a way an uninterrupted entry to my profession as a biologist could never have done. To that year I have owed my fascination with Eastern life and thought and my gradual turn towards social anthropology, psychology and Buddhist studies, to which I eventually came late in my career. Yet to that time I owe something more, as will be apparent in this work – the beginning of an insight into Zen, a capacity for cross-cultural relationships and the exploration of deep friendship itself.

Hong Kong, at the time of the Korean War, had barely recovered from the ravages of the Japanese occupation which remained vivid in the minds of old China hands. The place was overflowing with refugees from Communist China, who included, among their number, intellectuals and brilliant businessmen who were to bring wealth and fame to the colony in years ahead. Talking with these people was a rich source for understanding the problems of the Chinese at that time, beset by ideological conflict, poverty and the anxieties of war. Few of my friends in the Army took a personal interest in the Chinese and, by the time I left, I was considered the regimental expert on the Chinese way of life! In fact, had it not been for Communism, I may well have taken up the study of China in later years had I been able to visit that country in an unimpeded manner.

The letters home explored all these matters and my parents carefully preserved them. My gratitude to them for their kindness and care remains deep. Intuition told me I might use the letters for some sort of writing but, in the event, although they were worked on for a few months after my return, they were then, due to a developing career, put safely in a bank to await attention. Forty years later I took them out and began to edit them for this book. The text is very close to the original writing, as I wish to preserve my manner and the register in which I wrote at the time, for that is already part of history.

With certain obvious exceptions, the material here all comes from those letters. The remaining portions (particularly Chapter Six) were written as letters but never sent. Chapter Twenty-six was written at a desk, on the troopship returning home, with tears falling on the blotting paper.

This work is in some sense an archive, providing a picture of Hong Kong colonialism, at a time when the British presence provided a freedom from tyranny for countless Chinese. Sino-British relations were nonetheless restrained, polite, with a mutual sort of surface respect hiding the native arrogance of each people. In fact, the relations between simple soldiers and ordinary Chinese may well have been the closest in the colony in spite of appearances. My closeness to my men on Brickhill gave me a considerable understanding of exactly what this relationship was. There was a certain mutuality deriving from the soldiers' loneliness far from home and the desperation and isolation of so many refugee people. While a degree of exploitation existed, there were also many relationships in which kindness and even love flourished. It was a rough world full of many rough diamonds.

My own public school origins (Sherborne) and education in the late imperial period of British history accounts for the mildly paternalistic attitude I sometimes show in these writings, both towards my own men and the Chinese. I have not attempted to edit this out, following some misconceived notion of contemporary political correctness, for it was a truth of the period which I do not wish to deny. As a national serviceman I had a critical attitude towards the army in which I served and this is often apparent. Nonetheless, I owed the whole experience to the army and to my training as a young lieutenant which brought out a certain confidence that was perhaps strongest in me at that time.

I learnt much from being given the command of the RHQ troop of my regiment, during the last months of service, an appointment normally given to a regular officer with the rank of captain. At the time I did not know that my work was well appreciated but my Commanding Officer finally gave me a generously worded recommendation to potential employers when I left. This touched me deeply because, in the end, in spite of its frustrations, I developed a soft spot for military life.

I have often not given names or else I have changed them when I give a critical account of someone's actions. Even after this lapse of time, I have no wish to embarrass those who have been my past companions. Other names are true history. I am especially grateful to Yiu Yannang, JP, MBE, at his retirement Deputy Commissioner of Labour in the Hong Kong Government and now active in a consultancy role, for his agreement that I may use his name throughout this text. Our friendship has continued through these long years and I am indebted to him for his reading of this work and correction of Chinese terms.

Brickhill is now the site of a huge modern marine aquarium dug deep in the hillside. The old officers' mess is still there and also the bunkers, now used as stores for gardening implements. In the eighties I visited the deserted gun site. A pack of wild dogs inhabited the place, the ghosts of departed soldiers!

John H Crook

Chapter One

The Longest Voyage

Outward Bound, June 1953

Two days after the Queen's coronation, with Mount Everest climbed and the Korean war showing signs of waning, I sailed from Southampton on a sunlit high tide bound for Hong Kong.

The preparations had been hectic, yet we were all so enthusiastic and caught up in excitement that any regrets at leaving home were pushed well into the background. Newly-fledged from Officer Training at Mons, my friends and I were preparing to make the most of our time as National Service subalterns. A Second Lieutenant at last, a glorious rank, an inflated sense of importance went with the new single 'pip' on the shoulders of our uniforms; the outward show of a successful passage through wearisome months of training – or else good bluffing. I had been trained as a Gunner officer in the Royal Artillery and was proud to belong to my regiment. We rather despised the blasé youths who besported themselves in tanks around the Aldershot moors, the smooth, sleek-voiced types, with predictable classy careers ahead of them. We gunners did not attempt to ape the pseudo-aristocratic manners of the cavalry but went our own way, less flashy and proud of our solid regimental achievements taught to us in history classes. Of course, there was no real dislike of the cavalry boys; they were charmers and good company. It was simply that already we were conditioned to a different loyalty.

The training at Mons had been effective and we were aware of the forceful confidence that had grown upon us, during our last month or so at the establishment. Out of my platoon, four of us were bound for the Far East. I had applied for Hong Kong after reading Han Suyin's book, *A Many Splendoured Thing*, love in Hong Kong that is, and spent my time dreaming of the fabulous adventures that, doubtless, awaited me on the far side of the world. I came third in the Passing Out Parade list and this permitted me to select the posting of my choice. Some of my friends with family attachments or girls in tow, were loath to leave home but I had no such limitations. The Canal Zone was too dusty. The Far East had it all. A month's leave had been spent putting together tropical equipment, sewing on the 'pips' and purchasing 'blues', formal dinner uniforms with their tropical 'monkey jackets', cummerbunds and other frivolities to be worn on elegant regimental mess nights.

On that momentous morning, I stood finally on deck watching the oily, green water widen between the ship and the quay, the military bands playing, rather sadly it seemed, and the telephone cables cast ashore as contact was broken. Below, on the quay, stood my father and mother; two small figures dwarfed by the huge cranes and the immense bulk of our ship; two figures, motionless, amid the portentous bustle of military police, hurrying officers, and the thumping, martial beat of the band; small and still and then waving, waving, as the ship detached itself from the quay and I waved in return. It was not an easy moment. The old, the stable, the secure, was being torn away, jettisoned on the quay, with the small grey figures diminishing, as the quay diminished, becoming dots, and then merging into the diffuse eddy of the waving crowd. The new, the unknown, the distinctly alarming lay ahead, together with the picking up of frightening little responsibilities. For a few moments I was near to tears. My friends had moved away from me as the departure approached and I was grateful to them.

Yet, for me, this farewell was not so poignant as for some. Most of the troops on board were bound for Korea and, although the festive mood of our departure had all the glory of a tattoo, there was already the grim undertone of that destiny awaiting some in the Korean hills. There was talk of peace but nothing was certain. The Far East was an active arena and, if for some of us, the distant prospect seemed remote, there was a flavour in the air of a crusade in which some must surely die.

Calshot Spit lightship, Cowes to port with slim yachts careering near us; some waved to us, others were grim at the race. We headed down the Solent, passed Hurst Castle and thence out into the Channel. So far, no duties, apart from constant attention to the raucous tannoy announcer and the fear of hearing our names called. I stood watching the sea with Chris. We had passed out together and had a common bond in our national service ineptitudes and a dread of being called upon to officiate in a task we knew nothing about. Chris was an intellectual and a musician with a wit as sharp as a compass point. We watched the sea and the gradual fading of England below a misty horizon. A cross-channel boat hooted us "Bon voyage" and the passengers were waving. A bell started clanging. Orders sprouted from the tannoy; our first lifeboat practice. We ran to our stations.

*

First calls

Gibraltar before dawn. Grey, misty, no sign of the Rock. A motor boat chugged out to us on sullen water. One man, ill, sent ashore. We did PT on the wet decks and wished for the sun.

Chris woke me up at 6.15 next morning. "Look – it's Africa!" I looked through the small porthole of our cabin and, sure enough, there, away on the horizon, stretched a long range of fawn-coloured hills with a pale golden mist shimmering above them, fading into the cool, unblemished blue of the sky. Patches of vapour covered the sea and the rising sun, touching them with gold, threw their long shadows slantwise over the waters, the whole air a dance of blue and gold.

Soon we were entering a broad bay, lined by shining white villas and other buildings, Algiers. White domes of mosques rose among the houses and crowned the tree-clad slopes in the foreground. In the distance yellow green hills, dry-grass colour, stretched away on either side. A white skyscraper dominated the town, tall and thin with flanges jutting out in a star-shaped plan. This was the Government Building and above it flew the Tricolour of France.

We were stopping here to take on fuel and water because trouble in the Canal Zone made such operations difficult at Port Said. I went ashore with a group of subalterns. A magnificent promenade was flanked by modern hotels, gleaming white and blinking with a myriad blind-covered windows. We passed the prefecture, a Credit Lyonnais and moved into a covered arcade, mixing with a jostling throng. Soon we were in the Kasbah where history seemed reversed. Hidden from the skyscrapers, bars and reception halls of the European world, we found ourselves in twisting, narrow streets, winding through a picturesque puzzle of squalid alleyways and tiny shops. The pavements were littered with huddled Arab figures selling fruit, watches, wallets and fake jewellery, while others begged holding little tins or cupped hands before us and cuddling their long garments around them to expose emaciated limbs and festering sores. A small boy passed us, led by a little urchin half his size. He was blind, his eyes blistered and closed, his skin peeling and sore. One young man had a white cyst projecting half an inch before one of his eyes. Most of the labourers, wearing red fezzes and dungarees, rushed busily up and down the little streets. Others, presumably merchants of some standing, draped in clean, white clothes, with turbans on their heads and carrying knobbly sticks, strode majestically through the mob. We were pestered unmercifully by scores of the prettiest little boys all wheedling in winsome ways. One likely lad of about ten years surprised us with "Messieurs, messieurs – mademoiselle vous attend – mademoiselle – très très bonne – vous venez?" It was eleven hundred hours.

Two of us penetrated more deeply into the maze of the market where there were no Europeans to be seen. We were the targets for many eyes, some friendly and kindly, a few clearly not. Most cast us a dignified glance and went on with their work. An Arab was playing the skirling music of the Islamic world on an ancient phonograph. The food looked clean and there were few flies. A chicken had just been slaughtered and the blood, spewing from its cut throat, sputtered all over the pavement and scattered feathers drifted about upon it.

We had taken a pound each ashore in Algerian currency and I was determined to try my hand at bargaining. I chose a pleasant-looking vendor of wallets and squatted down beside him. "Combien?" It was two hundred francs but, on remonstration, the price fell to one hundred and seventy-five, then one hundred and fifty and I finally took it at one hundred. By this time a crowd had gathered. A veritable gallery of robed and curious Arabs surrounded us, jostling each other and peering over one another's shoulders. The deal evidently pleased them for, as I stood up holding my wallet, they all grinned and smiled with friendly gestures and one old man patted me on the back. The seller also looked cheerful so, apparently, the "officier anglais" had been well rooked. Nevertheless we walked on feeling triumphant. I thought the Arabs singularly handsome, indeed proud-looking men and felt sure they would make interesting friends, if one began to understand and talk with them.

We sailed at 2 p.m. and cruised down the Algerian coastline. The sunshine was really wonderful!

*

Ship's Duty Officer

"Look at the porpoises!" exclaimed one of my fellow subalterns. Actually they were dolphins, leaping in curves of perfect symmetry from the waters, their bodies gleaming grey above, silvery in the sun, and white below on belly and chest. Their heads ended in long, pointed beaks, full, I knew, of sharp piscatorial teeth and the speed of their movement was like flying. Prancing up from the waters, they shimmered a moment in the light before plunging into a deep wave's side. There must have been thirty at least, cavorting and jumping from crest to trough aslant our bows.

I am tasting the joys of the Mediterranean for the first time, a sea between two continents. To the north lies Europe and to the south Africa, aloof and mysterious to me, even its name giving a foretaste of a possible adventure. We trail a green wake through blue waters, smoothing a path between billows. Storm petrels play, some fifty or more, over the waters with a buoyant flight like butterflies. The sea is never the same, every hour there comes over it some subtle change, like a shift of key in music or the nuance of mood in a poem. Observing it quietly and attentively is to become aware of a continual symphony rich in harmonies, an interplay between two main motifs derived respectively from sea and sky. In the evening, the sun, glancing low over the surface, strikes through the waves' crests, colouring them a brilliant bottle green, above which little showers of spray form transitory rainbows. At sunset, each wave carries its own shadow over which the water curls, enclosing it and finally engulfing it, only to let it rise again as a reborn shade. At such a time, from the topmost decks, there is an almost intense awareness of distance. The eye travels further and again further out over the open sea, finding delight in every hollow until, rising above the thin edge of the world, gazing into unfathomable space, I follow the sun down.

Yesterday we began to do a little work which helped to remove the wet-rag headache the rising temperatures and enforced lassitude had brought upon me. I was Orderly Officer of the Day. The job entails accompanying various senior officers about the ship, inspecting the troopdecks, the men's cafeteria, recreation rooms and lavatories. On this great ship of extraordinary complexity the experience was often bewildering. Luckily, in the motherly way of the army, I was supplied with an Orderly Sergeant who knew both the ship and the worries of newly-fledged subalterns very well. He was cooperative and friendly and let me into the troop's opinions of the vessel.

Apparently they liked it and I supposed it was certainly more fun than the drab barracks of most depots in England. A number of older sergeants told me that, compared with other troopers, the *Fowey* was a floating palace. Yet to me the troopdecks seemed woefully crowded. Tiers of narrow bunks, three to a tier, stood in rows along the length of each troopdeck. About two yards separated the rows and there were larger passages at each end forming a central gangway. The lavatories and washrooms were spotlessly clean and rigorously inspected yet, in spite of open ports and a powerful ventilation system, the smell of sweat, made nauseating by the heat, was considerable. The troopdecks lay mostly deep in the body of the ship and often the ports had to be closed because of the seas. At night only the blowers saved the men from considerable discomfort due to smell and heat.

At 11.30 hours I went with my sergeant to visit the cells as part of the Orderly Officer's official round. We descended several flights of steep steps and emerged among the entrails of the ship, well below the water line and infrequently lit by electric lamps. A sergeant major welcomed me with a not very smart salute, while the rest of the guardroom stood to attention. He handed me a ledger to sign but I decided to look around, rather than let him get away with a signature for nothing.

"Right," I said, "I want to see the prisoners."

"Yessir!" he said, perceptively more alert.

In the space of twelve hours, I came to realise that most of these floating visits by officers, to make some sort of an inspection, are a matter of staged effects. A reasonable presentation is made by the NCO with lots of "Yessir, Nosir, three bags full, Sir." The officer signs and drifts away back to the upper reaches. Most of the sergeants and NCOs, although usually much older than the National Service officer, are simple folk who appreciated the joke of strong-handedness, especially if a touch of the film star is added to heighten the occasion. I found that so long as I presented a clear, decisive appearance all went well and people shot about the place but, should I have let the slightest note of indecision creep into my bearing or voice, then, at once, everything began to sag into slackness. I could feel it going!

The Guard Commander flung open the cells with a tremendous clatter and called the men inside up to attention. Squaring my shoulders I strode in. I went to each cell in turn.

"Any troubles? You? You? You?"

They really looked quite cheerful and of course there were no troubles, not a word. So, "Right, Sergeant Major!"

And that gentleman responded, "Stand at ease there, SHUN, stand at eeeaase! Lock 'em up Joe."

I signed the book to the accompaniment of clanging steel doors and twisting keys. Feeling like some medieval sheriff followed by his jailer, I climbed back to daylight.

The 'criminals' had almost all been absentees from muster parades either at Southampton or at Algiers. Every cell was occupied, so the story of the unfortunate subaltern, newly-commissioned and given forty men to take to Germany, who arrived with only eighteen may well have been true!

During the evening rounds I came upon a large party of men, under a ferocious corporal, cleaning out the recreation rooms. I was not at all sure who they were and, in any case, it was time for them to be below decks. I spotted a stocky, rather grandiose sergeant, dressed a little out of the ordinary. He came to a magnificent attention, saluted courteously and asked if he could help.

"These men? Oh they're defaulters, Sir. They work till I'm satisfied with them, that is to say, you and me, Sir... which won't be till about midnight, Sir!"

I looked at my watch. It was about ten thirty and time to close the sergeants' bar. I said so to the sergeant, who was now accompanying me. I discovered he was a special species of sergeant – a provo-sergeant, an intelligence that left me none the wiser. It was only after five minutes of agonised ransacking of my memory of military terms that I realised, of course, he was in charge of Military Police duties, and hence the defaulters. The sergeant consulted his watch too.

"I make it two minutes to go, Sir," he said, politely but persuasively. I was amused and followed him into the bar. Somehow the door slammed and all heads turned my way.

"Last drinks gentlemen!"

At least five huge tankards followed one another through the open hatchway and the Provo-sergeant, who appeared to want an audience, stood me a drink.

"Whisky, Sir?"

"Light ale, thanks very much, Sergeant!"

"Right, Sir," with resignation.

He told me he had been in the Special Air Service during the war, an especially daring variety of commando, the parachutists and glider men, and had been drafted into the Royal Scots from a cushy job, driving and conducting VIPs about the place. Yes, he liked the ship; it was the best of the four trips he had already made to the Far East; the men were well-fed and housed; but – the discipline – Sir – was poor. That was where he came in, he and the RSM. Mind you, it was not for lack of material, good stuff these boys, even the National Service men and that was a concession.

I mentioned that by the time he reached Korea life there could well be more peaceful. He regretted the thought. The regiment was highly trained. "If we have the luck to get a scrap the lads can show their mettle." I supposed a trained and experienced regular soldier must yearn for some action, for some genuine context in which to test and prove himself. Several of the infantry subalterns with the Royal Scots had voiced the same sentiment for they too were volunteers, keyed to the ordeal they had accepted and looked for, confident and determined young men. Yet they were capable of a longer view and I suspected that, in spite of the upper lip, their disappointment was blended with relief. A man can never be so much of a man as he may at first appear.

There were a number of other things the Provo-sergeant said but some of them, especially on the matter of women on board, had better not be elaborated upon. He would have liked to see them completely segregated and not "flitting about" all over the vessel distracting the men. Life on board a trooper was frustrating and the heat and motion stimulating enough without that. We closed the bar and bade each other good night. He saluted smartly and marched off to keep the defaulters moving. "The blighters never do a thing unless you keep chivvying 'em, Sir!"

*

The Canal

The *Empire Fowey* stopped offshore in the huge harbour of Port Said, awaiting our turn to enter the narrow waterway of the Suez Canal. The Royal Scots battalion had their pipe band aboard and it played merrily on deck, as a number of officers from the Canal Zone force came aboard to greet us and wish us well.

Hoards of little green bum-boats began swarming alongside us like water beetles. They were filled with excited Egyptians, all trying to attract attention. Trade was poor, since orders had gone out prohibiting it, but, even so, a number of ropes dangled between ship and bum-boat and the little baskets containing goods for purchase came and went busily. Bargaining was brisk and prices absurdly high. Altercations were frequent and one especially rowdy one broke out, when a tommy's beret fell overboard and was promptly donned by an Egyptian, who would not part with it without a reward. Words began flying and it was clear that the Egyptian's knowledge of British Army adjectives was as good as the Scotsmen's. The latter were not to be outdone however, and, amid loud booing, someone turned a fire hose on the boat concerned and a score of bright white balloons were flung over the side, to bounce insultingly on the wavelets between the boats. This impromptu adaptation of the Algiers issue of 'French letters' caused riotous mirth on the troopdecks and the Egyptians lost their composure and flew into little tempers. Three of them clambered up the anchor chain on to the fo'c'sle and, armed with knives, started prancing about there. A burly Scot lumbered up on to the platform and moved towards them in a crouch. For a minute they laughed and jeered at him but his advance was unhesitating and, suddenly, they bolted to the anchor chains and fled back down them, to the accompaniment of jeers and more white balloons.

Chris and I returned to our cabin and found a bum-boat a few feet below our port, with a jolly little man swaying to and fro, urging us to buy something. He particularly mentioned Turkish Delight so, after a brief hesitation, we had him throw us a rope with a basket, passed him down the money and examined our purchase. It was a nice little box wrapped up in cellophane with "Turkish Delight" written in large letters on the cover. We opened it in joyous anticipation but, alas, all we found within were a few rotten dates. We rushed to the porthole but, of course, he had gone. We cast the box overboard with suitable vocalisation and gestures.

The passage of the canal was impressive. At intervals cheering sunbathing troops lined the banks shouting "Get yer knees brown!" and other comments to which appropriate replies were given. Jeeps were everywhere, tearing along the road that ran parallel to the waterway, while the landscape braised and shimmered under the sun. A sudden sandstorm took us by surprise, fine dust infiltrated everywhere, even filling the books we were reading with dirt. A suffocating heat filled the ship, half stifling us and we sat about sweaty and dirty waiting for it to pass.

At dawn the following morning, I was on deck watching the sun glinting on the roofs of Suez and marvelling at the delicate beauty of a white minaret etched sharply against the brown hills and the clear sky. By breakfast time we were heading south towards the Red Sea with the temperature rising horribly. We prepared for the biggest heatwave any of us, new from England, had ever known.

*

Off Socotra, June 9th 1953

Today for the first time we have met the monsoon in earnest. All through the Red Sea, at Aden and on past Cape Gardafui, we had hot, sweaty weather, during which we could do little except drink gallons of lemon squash and search the decks vainly for a breeze. Away to starboard now looms a range of great, grey cliffs, often shrouded from our sight by a haze of flying spray. The wind whines in the rigging, roars about the masts and lifeboats and howls around the bridge and deckhouses. It is a ferocious sound, merciless, and full of power. Crested seas run at us lifting our prow, rolling us to port and then buffeting us with clouds of spun spray as the ship rights itself again. The sea is awash with white rollers combing along, with deep troughs of dark blue water between them. The spray whips over the lower decks, to the delight of many of the men who sense the exhilaration of the scene. The sun beams down and little rainbows ring us about, coming and going as the spray flies through the light.

All morning we have been advancing down the coast of Socotra. This is indeed a barren island, the hills end in tall cliffs or run down in valleys to meet the sea in high sand hills. There is little vegetation. Soon after lunch, we shall move beyond the shelter of these empty shores and face the full monsoon coming north across the open ocean. To the south there will be no land before Antarctica.

Yesterday, off Aden, it was calm, a slight swell and the sea as blue as a clean sky. I saw turtles, each about eighteen inches long, swim by the ship, miles from land, and shoals of large flying fish whipped up into the light breeze before our bows. They were magnificent creatures; the largest about ten inches long, blue green on top and snow-white below. The smaller species, which we had seen in the Red Sea, seemed to flutter their "wings" in flight, but these went gliding along on outstretched planes, flicking the water with the long, ventral lobe of the tail every now and then and giving a little flutter to gain height for a further glide.

We were all very glad, I think, to reach Aden. The passage of the Red Sea had been trying and the shores impressed us only by their aridity. Blithe BBC talk about desert islands is all very well in England but, on the first sight of a real one, the grim inhospitality of the lonely shores conjures up pictures of a desperate and, maybe, unavailing search for water and shade, the horror of a castaway's life, for which even a gramophone cabinet of Beethoven could do little to alleviate. We sailed close to the coast of Arabia, passing between the narrow headlands and cliffs of Bab-el-Mendab, and then along sandy shores with brown and yellow cliffs, sometimes streaked a shining white with veins of quartz. Finally, we rounded a headland of unsurpassed ferocity; huge dunes and cliffs ran down into the sea and narrow valleys inland, filled with sand, stretched up towards a range of slopes strewn with rocks, above which jagged peaks rose severe and dark against the sky. In the more open valleys, the wind caught at the sand and whirled it into the air; streams of yellow dust blew like mists across the land and often for a little way out to sea. As we rounded the point a group of mountains faced us across a wide and sparkling bay. At their foot cuddled a number of large, white and shining buildings and, nearer the shore, many others, smaller. We could pick out green trees and shrubs around them but nowhere else, neither on hill nor shore, could we see any vegetation at all; everywhere only dry earth, bare, hard, blackish rocks or sands in shades of brown, grey or khaki. In the harbour lay a host of ships, several of the Blue Funnel Line and many foreign merchantmen, two or three Arab dhows and a tug, rather remarkably, flying a Danish flag.

Aden, being British, posed many more problems than Algiers before we were able to get ashore; there were forms to fill in and passes to obtain. When all was done, we sallied forth. The place is divided roughly into two parts, the town around the port and the 'Crater' which lies over the hill. Troops from the ship are not supposed to visit the Crater nor to go further inland and we had to obey this restricting regulation. There is a smart European quarter near the port and an Arab shantytown next to it. Three of us were in need of cummerbunds to go with our tropical dining kit. A little tailor, deliciously named Kut Kut, assured us he knew exactly what we wanted; of course he knew the correct colour for the Royal Artillery. Two hours later, we returned, to receive three resplendent scarlet cummerbunds and it was only on returning to the ship that we learned the RA colours to be electric blue!

We visited the Officers' Club, very horsey and the drinks disgusting, but a swim in the swimming pool and the discovery of a little air-breathing hermit crab in a small seashell made the visit worthwhile.

The people in the streets intrigued me, Ethiopian and African faces mingled with Arab and Jew, an ethnological paradise. There were, of course, hordes of rapacious vendors. On a doorstep sat a little Arab.

"Sirs! You see this naize pack of cards, fifty-two all different. Come, have see!"

Several of the lads were inspecting them, so I went to have a look. Sure enough, there were fifty two, all different nudes. Popular items! Last evening, in the smoking room, I noticed at least one party playing a discrete game with them.

Another Arab boy of about thirteen came up to me flashing his devilish eyes.

"Give me a shilling for my supper!" he demanded and then, as if amused by my expression of amazement for he looked remarkably healthy, or perhaps realising the impression made was a hopeless one, he burst out in a peal of laughter. All three of us and the boy ended up gurgling with amusement.

I could not imagine what the Arabs do with their women! In Algiers they were so shrouded the most one could see was half an eye. In Aden it was difficult enough to see even a single woman. Most mysterious – for I hardly thought the busy and rather ostentatiously healthy people suggested an absence of ladies. But wait – I remembered now. There was one dusky creature swinging her hips in a doorway. Some of the younger subalterns were straight from school and hardly dry. On seeing such sights they feigned blindness or else they really were unaware of the unmistakable signs of the lively port life we had been seeing all the way. Needless to say, the men were by no means blind and not at all reticent. For some of them the voyage was a progression from bed in one port to another in the next. If beds were not available, the nearest park or group of bushes was good enough for most of them. The tommies were not a vicious crowd and, animal delight apart, it was the spirit of adventure that sent them roaming, in their little groups of concentrated Glasgow, Edinburgh, Birmingham or Liverpool, through the ports of the wide world.

*

Assistant Troopdeck Commander

Soon after leaving Algiers I had been appointed an Assistant Troopdeck Commander, thus becoming responsible for the occupation and well-being of some thirty men, a mixed bag of signallers, drivers, sappers and gunners. At first, if not exactly an ordeal, it was at least something of a strain. I had to give lectures in the morning or organise quizzes and military knowledge competitions. Before breakfast, I had to take PT classes for a quarter of an hour and, in addition, there were visits to the somewhat unsavoury troopdeck, pay parades and currency exchange to be effected on visiting a port.

I endeavoured to be as informal as possible with the men and I thought this had been reasonably successful and without detriment to my insecure position as a fresher subaltern. They responded quickly to any question about how they liked Algiers or what they did in Aden. One or two were bright lads and most of those had at least one stripe on their arms. So far everyone had shown himself to be friendly and revealed an appropriate, if unmerited, respect for me. Occasionally I cursed somebody who forgot his hat or who arrived on deck too untidily dressed to be passed over. Faults, once corrected, had not appeared again. Sometimes the man in question had disappeared and upon enquiry I found that he was in 'jankers'; apparently a vigilant NCO policing system rapidly collected new recruits for the defaulters' squads by noting the names of those corrected on parades. My sergeant was a stolid engineer and for weapon training I usually got an infantry sergeant to talk about the bren, sten or rifle.

In spite of the months of conditioning at Mons, when I first found myself operating within the army system, I found it outrageous. Who was I to order people about? It seemed a gross presumption. Although I was myself a beneficiary, I objected strongly to the great difference in the conditions under which the officers and the men travelled. Once I heard one man muttering to another something to the effect that "T' bloody officers do nothing except drink whisky on t' top deck," a judgement by no means correct but containing the germ of a valid criticism. At every turn I found I tended to identify my own lot, my own sympathies and opinions with those of the men. This was not a genuine identification, but rather an instinctive siding with the weaker side in what seemed to be inter-class warfare. Furthermore, a National Service subaltern was clearly a member of an outgroup, when the majority of officers happened to be regulars. A National Service sense of isolation was justified more easily by feeling oneself to be one of the men rather than as one among an officer class to which one could not, and to which, in any case, one had little wish to belong.

After some time I began to see the military organisation in a clearer perspective. I realised that the respect I received was not at all to myself but to the role I was supposed to be fulfilling. The respect was for my peaked cap and the authority that a peaked cap could use when required. I occupied a position in a hierarchy and had to fit myself into the role prescribed by that position. The men, in turn, occupied their own positions. They were the effector units in the scheme. While I directed or taught, they put such direction into practice. I, in my turn, was no more than an effector unit in a plan drawn up at levels above me. The immensity of the military machine became apparent. The Provo-sergeant and his policemen dealt with recalcitrants and failures; a system within the first. Feedback controls limited the errors made and kept the whole in a steady state of "efficiency". Efficiency is indeed the keyword in all military affairs. To be efficient is to rule one's milieu and to avoid the suspicious glances of colonels. It seemed a reasonable sort of ant colony.

Yet, I asked myself, where in this great organisation did the individual personality have a role to play? At first it seemed to be of little account. I considered the individuals in my section. Not one bore the remotest resemblance to his neighbour in looks, alertness, bearing, response to questioning or in his attitude towards his companions. All, however, had a quality in common, not merely the mutual bond uniting people of a similar rank under a common regime, but also a collective psychological quality. They were all so obviously the workers of this world, derived from families of stokers, roundsmen, behind-the-counter men, clerks or, rising a little, small shop owners or tradesmen. These were the folk who, in whatever walk of life they found themselves, would put into practice plans formed by others and carry out actions originating from a higher source. The inequality of human material in class categories as well as individual ones became clearer to me.

I tried to compare the army with the civilian society from which it is drawn. Discipline brings with it a tidiness and compactness lacking in society at large. There are no trades' unions in the army and 'justice' is administered directly and without argument by authority. Yet I doubt whether the expression of the personalities of individual men is any more restricted in the military than in civil life. Restrictions on individual expression from group or gang consciousness, Union loyalties or Hollywood conditioning are probably as significant, although not so obvious, as the effect of a military discipline supported by a military law which is at great pains to be scrupulously fair. Military ideals of personal smartness in dress, bearing, honesty and loyalty to barrack-room friends are genuine and of real value in the development of a late adolescent. There is also continuous advice on health and morality, of a simple common-sense kind, given at intervals by the Medical Officer and the Padre. Such ideas provide at least some reliable criteria for personal conduct and principles that are often absent in the wilder streets of our cities.

I am sure that sensible men, amenable to discipline but lacking any great powers of intelligence, dominance or native curiosity, are improved by the army life. Certainly, latent traits of leadership, companionableness and tolerance may well be brought to the fore. The National Service soldier, far from being restricted by army life was often improved by it and returned to his home environment a better citizen, more tolerant and understanding of his fellow men and the possessor of an established self-discipline and personal pride in appearance. In face of these conclusions I asked myself why it was that my first impressions were of class conflict, exploitation of lesser mortals by opinionated people of better schooling and the idea that life on the troopdeck was degrading to humanist principles.

The answer lies, I think, in understanding the opposition between real and ideal existence. Ideally, an individual should be free to mind his own business and be responsible for his own conduct and dealings with his neighbours. Organisations reduce freedom by the imposition of rules. The family or the tribe are natural organisations whereas complex military or civil structures, within which family life plays only a minor role, are not natural in the same sense. The happiest state of man is presumably that in which biological, psychological and religious needs are satisfied and in which opportunities are available for the practice and improvement of skills and interests. I sometimes picture the happy man, content with wife and family, in a home of their own devising, without luxuries but with friends and security in the immediate neighbourhood, freedom of opinion and reading matter, ability to read all that is within their capacity, to learn as much as they are able or desire and to understand these matters not only for the improvement of the conduct of life but also for the culture of mind and spirit. Beauty of landscape and means to travel are also essential for happiness that comes from broader development. Obviously, life within this great termite-like military structure falls far short of such an ideal.

It was, I feel, an awareness of this difference that brought me a certain feeling of revulsion. Indeed to some extent the termites are revolting, not as individuals but as a collective, pullulating all over the ship, giving and obeying orders, with a kind of mental trophallaxis motivated by fear of punishment. Yet this is a real world not an ideal one; we generally presume that the termites exist in order that ideals elsewhere may survive.

More emotionally than rationally, it seemed to me that this condition of humanity, this condemnation to suffering for the maintenance and realisation of the ideals of others, was an infinitely pathetic one. Sometimes, from one of the higher decks, I looked down on the men sprawled about on the lower decks like caged animals. I could see the fragile humanity of their bodies, the structure of limb and chest, some appearing strong and others weak and poorly formed. There, too, was the incipient patchy hair on their bodies, symbolic of physical pride and anticipatory of desire. The sight filled me with a wearying sadness, the feeling that all the grand intentions of man, the lesser intentions of individuals, the many separate and personally valid motivations towards the "good" were in the end cut off short by some other characteristic of the human condition; that man's noblest ideals were in the end frustrated by the realities of each individual's life.

Perhaps this sensation of pathos in life sees further than the strictly rational mood, penetrating into the mysteries of universal existence rather than dealing with immediate problems. The army, it seems, is an essential reality and within its falling short of the ideal there is none the less much that is good for the individual soldier, and especially perhaps for the national serviceman. It is a true saying that there is no such thing as a bad soldier, only a bad officer. Bad officering leads to poor discipline with discontented men leading an unnatural life without family roots and this, of course, is destructive to citizenship. Such destruction must always be the care and duty of the officer to avoid.

I know so little of officers and officering that it seems presumptuous to criticise or invent theories, especially from my unexalted rank of subaltern. Yet, since soldiering is for me a temporary duty to my country rather than a profession, any observations I make, doubtless lacking value from the professional's viewpoint, may nevertheless have the value of an opinion unbiased by close membership of the system. I am in the army for only a short time and it is inevitable that I shall record my impressions. I am like that.

So, what then of the officers? There are plenty on board ranging from the Lieutenant Colonel downwards. Most of them are bound for Korea with the Royal Scots and one or two have already done a spell there. One infantry lieutenant has been mentioned in despatches. Although there are several naval officers on board and one RAF type, the majority are military. Among the regulars and apart from the four gunner subalterns from my Pass Out at Mons, there is a fair sprinkling of national service subalterns. The majority of captains and majors conform to type pretty well. They are strongly-built, hearty men, friendly enough but liable to be opinionated or even a little pompous. The 'authoritarian personality' is common enough in the less distinguished officer ranks of the army. Their principle aim in life appears to be the endeavour to make oneself as comfortable and as genial as possible. Most are well-read men of considerable perception but they lack any great flexibility of mind. Almost all have a characteristic manner of speaking and a professional bias that insinuates itself into all aspects of life.

The chief evening activities in the smoke room are poker dice, canasta, bridge or other card games with matches as counters and a copious flow of drinks from lemon squash to double whiskies. Conversation, if not on military matters, appears superficial, although not without interest and conducted with animation. There are of course cliques for the occupation of the few young ladies' favours and other cliques dominated by the more matriarchal officers' wives. The senior officers keep themselves largely to themselves and restrict their talking to their own small circle. Any conversation with us is limited and one-sided, since they like to remain on their official pedestals. As national service officers, I suspect we are objects of a friendly scorn yet, at the same time, of a veiled envy. We do our best but can never quite achieve the military aplomb of the regulars and most of our interests, music, poetry, philosophy and such-like, which loom up, snatchily, in our conversations, seem to mystify them. On one occasion I heard it remarked without malice, "Ha, these young chaps – you never quite know where you are with them!" It is simply a measure of our occupational difference, I suppose.

As a class, the regular subalterns ape the fashions and ideals given them at Sandhurst. Heartiness, athletics, machine-like efficiency and the aim to be a 'bloke among blokes' seem the most important of these. They are certainly first-rate at all of these and we mere novices cannot shine beside them. One of them regrets the absence of a university education but, for the most part, they are content with an enjoyable, healthy life, with a prospect of excitement. The magnificent uniforms lend themselves almost slyly to that air of affectation and overt lifemanship that is never quite absent from a gathering of officers. No army officer I have met so far has, at first sight, been a bore; to say this of so marked an occupational type is certainly a compliment.

Chris and I find ourselves together on this troopdeck lark. Naturally there are other senior officers around to help us. Our immediate senior is a regular lieutenant, a healthy, good-living lad, brusque and quick in authority, friendly with the men and always a confident master of a situation. Chris and I have had cause many times to be grateful for his quick-thinking good humour. Our troop commander is a jovial type who sets up a programme on Sunday night and does precious little else for the rest of the week, leaving us three to cope. He is always available if needed, however. The following Monday, he relapses back into total idleness, when we get a new troopdeck commander in the shape of an infantry major.

The Royal Scots padre is a charming man, short in stature but rich in human virtues, generating friendship, yet shrewd in dealing with men and officers alike. The other evening, sitting together with a Royal Scots subaltern and a national service doctor, the padre initiated a long discussion on the relation between biology and religion. I reviewed in simple terms the theories of natural selection in classical Darwinism. The padre amazed me with his completely anthropocentric vision of the relation between the Universe and God and I felt great doubt regarding the value of theological training in our time. Another evening, we sat together waiting for one of the gramophone concerts, arranged periodically for the officers and their wives. After a day of military jargon, these were pleasant little events. We were about to hear a piece by Ravel, when the padre turned to me and said, "The officer likes to feel he is listening to something good, something classical, but he likes it to the accompaniment of clinking glasses and merry chatter!"

On Sunday evenings, he organised a hymn-singing hour for the men. It took place on the port deck, with the men lolling on the decking or propping themselves against the rescue rafts. Beyond the ship's rails the sea lay silent under a moon and we rose and fell in steady motion, the sound of the water revealing our forward speed. He had a good attendance, and after one such event was over he remarked that it was a good thing no officers had come, since white shirts and cummerbunds might have put the men out of tune. I agreed. We went strolling together on the top deck under the stars, the Southern Cross lying on the horizon to starboard.

*

The Indian Ocean

In spite of the heavy swell the Indian Ocean is wonderful. Now that we have settled down to a steady routine, life aboard is not difficult and much of our time is free. We sunbathe on the top deck, play deck quoits and other games and do a great deal of reading. I am mastering Plato's *Republic* and digesting a book about Hong Kong. Sometimes I join Chris at the piano, where he plays to us with characteristic off-hand brilliance. We while away the evening in drink and discussion. Chris is teaching me to play chess and we are into our thirteenth game. I have not come near to beating him yet. One day he took four of us on at once and beat us all, the scoundrel! Another time he took on the entire room, moving around from table to table without losing a single game.

Have I told you about our two Lascar waiters at table? One, a small, wizened monkey of a man, was all smiles the whole way from Southampton to Aden. The other, a fuzzy head, dark and sinister, looked as if he would knife us all quite happily at the first opportunity. As soon as we entered the Indian Ocean and began to roll, the smiling one turned glum looking murderous and irritable, while the other blossomed into a toothy smile and even cracked a joke or two.

"Wot, no more today, Sir? O zat is a very bad thing. And you, Sir. Curry? Entrée perhaps? Very good Sir. Very good indeed!"

At the very stern of the ship, live a number of Lascar hands. They spread their mats on the open deck of an evening and proceed to smoke their long and curly hookahs. They come from obscure villages in the north-west of India and show a great interest in the sternpost musketry. Squads of soldiers visit the stern and shoot live at balloons thrown into the water. It is tricky shooting and excellent practice. The ship's Second Officer remarked to me the other day that the Lascars were itching to get their hands on some rifles to compete with the soldiery and that, in all probability, they would beat our lads into a cocked hat into the bargain.

Tonight we shall have a film on the rear deck and will sit there under the stars. Afterwards, I shall walk on the top deck studying them and listening to the sea, experiencing it dividing as we sweep through it and washing turbulently together again into the distance astern. Up there is silence and I can be alone. Afterwards, I shall turn in. We are as bronzed as Greeks and sleep like dogs.

*

Colombo

It was a delight to watch the tree-lined shores of Ceylon heave themselves over the horizon. To see greenery again was magical. The long oceanic swells went roaring up the sandy beaches in lines of mountainous surf. Behind the sands, there were calm lagoons and clusters of steeply-roofed native huts gripping the ground. To the north of Colombo, the jungle ran right down to the shore and a dense wall of vegetation waved and shimmered there, the tall trunks of thousands of coconut palm trees each letting their leaves stream like a girl's hair in the wind. As the ship closed on the land, the colours became more intense, the palms darker and silhouetted against the sky.

"We shall have to be tourists," said Chris.

"I am afraid so and it'll have to be in a taxi too!"

We went ashore in a giant landing craft because the ship was moored some way out in the harbour. The first excitement was, of course, the people, rushing everywhere, with a hooting of frantically driven cars, the steady tread of overladen ox wagons and the cries of innumerable rickshaw men. The ox wagons were intriguing. A rickety platform on two wheels was surmounted by a high, wickerwork cover. A heavy shaft and cross-piece was attached to the patient beast of docile appearance and odd humps. They were quiet little animals, not much larger than donkeys but they could move at a respectable speed pulling tremendous loads.

Rich smells scented the air, food, flowers and the sweet sweat of vegetation in the parks. At Aden, life had seemed a bare, tenuous thing, here it gallivanted before the eyes, warm, damp and luxuriant. How different the people seemed from Europeans, a fact not at all hidden by the many modern buildings. The pullulation in the streets had a quite novel feeling to it and the cries and brightly-coloured clothes were all confused, in a turmoil of fleeting figures, dodging between the latest car and the oldest wagon. There were very few white men about and, far from finding this at all disquieting, I welcomed it. The slight, brown people impressed me at once with their friendliness, their smiles and their obvious pride in their new-found freedom, their houses of parliament and their premier and also in their membership of the Commonwealth. The film *A Queen is Crowned* was being shown at one of the cinemas and, as we drove by in the heat of the mid-afternoon, I could see an immense queue waiting to go in.

We had an evening meal in the YMCA and the waiter told us that he had been in England when the King died. He brought out his identity card to show us his lodgings' address in London. All the time I felt immensely glad that this beautiful place really belonged to its inhabitants. It seemed so natural and right that this should be so. Our driver, a jolly, twinkly-eyed and rather wizened little man told us of his likes and dislikes. The Americans were not in his favour. We passed the American Embassy and he remarked, "Amelican Emblassy-nasty," which entranced us. We could not get him to be explicit, yet when we saw a number of Yankee sailors from some destroyers in the harbour, in port on their way home from Korea, their loud demanding voices seemed harsh and carried far over the traffic. The Ceylonese had perfect manners; they were quiet, self-possessed, even reserved; except, of course, when they were trying to sell something. The remarks in our little army guide to Eastern places and people seem very true; the Oriental admires self-possession and a quiet, authoritative bearing. Loud-mouthed people and irresponsible appearance do not impress and that was where the Americans failed, I think.

We visited two temples. The first set some way down a side street not far from the docks, was Hindu and therefore Tamil. The driver, evidently a Ceylonese Buddhist, was not keen to stop there but the architecture looked so remarkable that I insisted. The driver told us it was very old and it certainly appeared so. A stone pyramid without a top rose above a metal, studded door. It was a sugar cake of a structure, with innumerable alcoves carved upon it in intricate detail. Two gaudily-painted statues stood on either side of the door with ferocious faces, like something out of a Hieronymous Bosch painting or the Mexican Art Exhibition. Above them were hosts of fearsome creatures, dragons, fanged serpents, dogs with bared teeth, the raw materials of nightmares. High walls beset with narrow, barred windows extended from the doorway. Within, I could see a bell tower, again covered with intricate carving. A robed figure, no doubt scenting money, appeared and bade us climb up on some railings to look in. In the dim light, beyond the iron bars, I could make out a pillared hall along one side of which stood two ornate altars bearing two intricate metal figures. Two rather odd bundles on the floor were recumbent men. One looked up at me and glared, while the other lay curled up, a ragged mass of skin and clothing, below the altar. The driver informed us that services to Siva the Destroyer were held within and often services for the "evil one" too. While we were looking around, he kept well away, clearly disapproving of the place.

Driving out of town, we were delighted by the residences of the government officials; elaborate little bungalows with extensive loggias and airy, half-shuttered windows. They were in all colours, browns, greens, blues, greys and each set in a very English style garden. Everywhere, we enjoyed the huge trees, luxuriant foliage and intensely-coloured flowers. The most common was the jacaranda, a large tree like an acacia, bushy with a cloud of delicate yellow flowers all over its crown. At nearly every corner and in the glorious parks, we saw the flame of the forest trees, fantastic under the weight of their scarlet flowers and delicate air-floating leaves. We admired a great banyan tree, with its myriad supporting trunks running from branch to earth. A small boy ran up and threw a handful of blossoms into the car. They resembled the heads of arum lilies but grow on trees and emit a perfume rich and tantalising – passion flowers.

Under the banyan, we found a snake charmer, who showed us two rather dopey-looking cobras that swayed from their boxes to the tune of his flute. They had had their fangs drawn and, although he did his stuff well, I did not think he was a master of his craft. He did some cunning little tricks with woollen balls that vanished and appeared again with a disconcerting rapidity. A small crowd of boys and young policemen gathered around us and we all sat and joked, watching the tricks for a quarter of an hour or more. The charges were not excessive.

We drove on along some magnificent avenues of flowering trees to the great Buddhist temple well outside the city. We parked in a courtyard surrounded by tall trees, and walked across soft sand to the temple. It was a white, polygonal building, with the main structure towering above numerous side chapels. An arcaded ambulatory led around the outside, with little sanctuaries commemorating various incidents in the life of the Buddha, a peaceful and holy spot. Beyond the arches of the ambulatory stood a great bo tree, bowing under the weight of its foliage, its thick trunk warped with age. Somewhere within its depths a bell-like bird call sounded, a strange cry, like a piping upon a flute begun and then left hanging upon a stillness. We left our shoes in the porchway and, led by a bare-footed temple guide, padded over gaily coloured tiles and through a tall archway to the sanctuary. An immense statue of the Buddha, seated in his curious, cross-legged posture upon a lotus, rose above a flower-strewn altar. He was twenty-three feet high and painted in the most vivid colours, yellows, whites, black and gold. The benign but inscrutable face looked down upon us from high up in a dome, painted all over with intricate patterns. On either side of the main figure stood others representing his disciples while, upon the surface of the vault, gods and goddesses were ranged representing abstract virtues. Two huge and hideous Hindu gods stood on guard beside the doorway. The whole scheme of decoration was amazing, yet entirely without meaning for me. I could detect no spirituality there, it was all too brazen. I felt, however, that visiting it in the way we did gave us little time to pause, wonder or understand. Being tourists, as tourists we reaped.

The Colombo zoo is set within a garden paradise. Little hills and miniature valleys abound and delicious lawns are cool under the trees, jacaranda, bougainvillea and hibiscus abound together with cannon ball blossoms and temple blooms. Here, too, the bell-voiced bird sounds from the shade and, on the top of one tree, stood a secretary bird, pensive and aloof. The elephant dance in a small amphitheatre was about to begin and we joined a small crowd of graceful Ceylonese, two Yankee sailors and a very old Englishman. To the music of a flute, the elephants danced and gyrated and one of them played the mouth organ held to its lips by its trunk. In one trick, the biggest elephant lay down upon its trainer and followed this by walking over him, resting a foot meditatively on his back for a second.

The Ceylonese people took their pleasure quietly in the garden, almost without chatter. Again, I felt a pleasure that here, perhaps, the past predacity of white imperialists were being forgotten as the people began to manage their own affairs. There have been civilisations older and wiser than ours and probably our only superiority lies in technology and, in Britain at least, some gift for stable democratic government. Perhaps it is dangerous to take first impressions at face value, but I have seen enough to want to return.

Only the money mania in the streets begins to pall after a few hours. Things are pressed upon one everywhere and beggars are numerous. Sometimes it was as painful to refuse as to give. In the evening, a local lad took us through a maze of shops in search of a snake charmer's flute. Loudspeakers shook the narrow streets with exciting music from Radio Ceylon and we stepped carefully around sleepers on the pavement and avoided the occasional beggar, bowing away at us from the dark shadows between the shacks. The shadows of the ox carts and rickshaw runners went weaving over the rubbish-strewn pavements, while small flames from little cans of oil guttered on table tops and boxes where foodstuffs were on sale. The air was pungent and, among the decaying fragments under our feet, we saw a sinister arthropodal creature go scuttling for shelter.

Two men rowed us back to the ship. They stood in the boat facing the bow in the manner of the country, the lights of the vessels glistening on their finely-muscled backs. We passed under anchor chains, along the sides of tramp steamers, freighters and liners, while an American sailor, who came along with us, told us about his life aboard a small destroyer. As we came alongside it, he said, "But gee – I guess I'm tired of the sea. You should just feel this old tin can in a roll!" We sympathised and, climbing the gangway of our big ship, went straight to our bunks.

*

The Straits of Malacca, June 29th 1953

We are steaming steadily between narrow shoals, pale green water between patches of a deeper brownish blue. The coast of Malaya lies in the distance to port; flat, tree-lined with a rocky promontory visible astern. We have seen much of the coast of Sumatra, mountainous and jungly but with many cultivated plantations. Birds are few but sooty terns circle us from time to time. This morning a *Mosquito* (aircraft) zoomed low over us, our first welcome to Singapore. The mention of mosquitoes reminds me that we have to start taking Paludrine prophylactic tablets against malaria today, since these insects can reach us from the shore.

The character of our voyage is changing. Last night we had a very happy ship's concert, some fine singers and one or two excellent comedians. The night before had been the fancy dress ball. I designed a futuristic evening dress, which ended up looking like something out of Aladdin. The prize went to a group of Iroquois Indians, who came on in bikinis and war paint, as fancily undressed as anyone could imagine. The dance was fun but could have been better organised; it took the MC until ten thirty to decide on a Paul Jones.* Generally, it was more of a spontaneous riot from start to finish than a dance. When the party ended, the ship's colonel made a short speech bidding goodbye to the ladies, who were to leave us at Singapore. He went on in a sombre note:

"This party concludes a period in our voyage, one that I think all of us have enjoyed very much, a pleasure cruise halfway around the world! At Singapore, the commanding officer of the Royal Scots will fly on to Korea to prepare for the take-over at the front. We know that the battalion will take over from the Black Watch on the Hook and it has been an honour to travel with them into action. When we leave Singapore we shall be in radio silence, entering the war zone."

There seems no doubt that within a month these men, whom I have come to know quite well, will be fighting on one of the most vital positions of the Korean battle front. We have all read about the heroic stand of the Black Watch on this shattered mound of a hill called the Hook. There is something very stirring, yet infinitely pathetic, in the determination with which the young infantry subalterns face the possibility of their ordeal. The smooth passage of the ship now seems fatalistic, driving us on to a confrontation which, although I shall not have to face it, nevertheless becomes almost mine, as I listen to the quiet, self-possessed, cold-blooded yet human deliberations of those preparing for action. The men, plucked out of their Edinburgh lives,

---

* A dance in which partners frequently change: a good way to engender conviviality, "breaking the ice" in the rather formal dance occasions of the period.

will be thrown, innocent of any offence, barring those inherent in all of us, into a battle from which, it is inevitable, some will not come home again. I feel conscious of an evil working its way to a culminating death orgy among desolate hills.

I have not found in anyone a hatred of the enemy; only a determination to uphold freedom and democracy, even at the expense of life. A few, the hardened campaigners, show a genuine pleasurable anticipation. I was too young to experience the last war but now I understand what it costs to look ahead to battle. Sometimes I feel I am no more than a playboy soldier, that I ought to have some part in what these men will know, that, in an act of sharing, I should know what now I only observe. Yet service has led me to a safer place and it is no cowardice to admit that I am thankful for it.

Last night, playing Socrates, I questioned the Royal Scots padre concerning religion among the officers and men. He seemed saddened by the puzzled agnosticism shown by many officers. Their education was sufficient to breed doubt, he told me, but their occupation was unlikely to allow them time, nor the literary and cultural means to test or renew their childhood belief. Of course this was not true of all, he added. The men, he found, were more sentimental at heart than religious, but being closer to the earth, they were easier to talk to. Soon he will be doing his job behind the lines – he made me think of Woodbine Willie.

*

China Sea, June 30th 1953

Some twenty hours out of Singapore, Chris and I were lying on our bunks, blowing through our 'flutes' from Colombo, when the wind began whistling in through the porthole. It had been overcast all morning but now we saw a huge sheet of grey cloud, stretching from sea to sky, sweeping towards us. A wall of flying rain, streaking over the waves so powerfully as to flatten them and whip off their crests in a continuous stream of flying spray, hurled itself on us hitting us with a great blow – force eight at least. In a moment, water was pouring out of the scuppers, running half an inch deep over the decks, flooding in through the deck doors, making runnels along the passageways and washing into several cabins. It poured in through any open ports and went leaping and jumping like water from a hose, off the lifeboats, sunshade tarpaulins, derricks and masts. The ship heeled over in the full broadside, water pouring off decks and roofs down into the sea. Visibility fell to nothing, lightening flashes lit us with a momentary brilliant light, thunder rolled, and our great foghorn boomed out a warning that we were sailing blind. Then, almost as quickly, the gale died away. The white pillar of rain disappeared into the distance, the ship righted herself and we stopped our demented hooting. A naval officer remarked that you never knew what the weather might do in these waters.

Conversations come back to me, word ripples, leaf murmurs, children's voices. The officers talk platoon attacks, relief at the line, medical treatment, the padre's role. Snatches emerge in my memory.

"What would you say to a dying man, Padre?"

"Is the Church blessing sufficient for a man who has never understood Christianity? Would you be able to comfort him according to his belief and needs? Suppose you had a dying communist, what would you say to him?"

And other matters, other questions.

"Hallo, National Service?"

"Yes."

"And afterwards?"

"Oxford – history."

"And then?"

"Oh, I don't know, business I expect."

Later he told me:

"So many of us infantry subalterns know so little about war. I'm lucky, too young for the front at the moment. They have given me three months in Honkers first and maybe by then a truce will have been signed. It is obvious the Chinese are as fed up with it as we are. All this is a last minute bust up. They can afford to lose lives for they value life much less than we do. Each individual means so much more to us, not only in terms of manpower but also from an ethical perspective. You see, it would be terrible for our parents if, just now, at the end of the fight – well – it's so easy to expose oneself to danger when one knows so little about it. And again it's such a bloody, silly, pointless war now. Oh yes. Two years ago it was terribly important – but hardly now. Both sides are changing plans – back to the cold war I suppose. All we are heading for is an aftermath of an outmoded history."

In the first-class lounge someone said,

"Let's go to the music room."

"Fool! There isn't one!"

"I know there isn't. I mean let's go to the piano."

"You know Brahms' Fourth in E?"

"Yes."

"I call that subjective music, a spiritual aspiration, a searching for a kind of transcendence, trying to reach another world."

"But what of Mozart, isn't he subjective too?"

"True, his music flows and eddies in the sunlight, an affirmation of joy in life and in music, forgetfulness of reality. But the mood of his absorption is different."

"Well – Bach?"

"Ah, Bach!"

One of the lads in my squad was taken ill this morning and I had him carried to the MI room. Bilious upset and feeling sick, the results of shore leave probably. Later I went down to the troopdeck to visit him and found that several others were ill in the same way. They said they had had some bad meat for lunch the previous day. I had a chat with one of them, a pleasant northern country lad. How they seemed to appreciate informality! Sometimes it makes me strangely sad to visit the troopdeck without my hat on. You hear little scraps of personal ambition and difficulties. The lad said, "Thank you, Sir!" when I left him to return from the ill-ventilated deck to the spacious, cool lounges of the first class. How I appreciated the privacy and rest that these rooms afford but, equally, how unfair these gross differences in comfort seem and I often feel guilt within me. I did not deserve his thanks. I felt myself a triviality in a trivial world; only the sick men in their stuffy bunks had any significance.

After inspection parade I asked him,

"How do you like the trip, Signalman?"

"Oh, s'awright, Sir, not so bad, I suppose."

"The Army certainly sends you places, doesn't it?"

"Does that, Sir – but I'd rather be back in Blighty any day. Korea is such a bloody way off. Better'd be at home with the gal."

And he gave me the resigned grin of the soldier. The ways of the authorities who rule our fates are indeed like those of the gods.

The Gods very subtly fashion
Madness upon sadness upon Earth
Nor knowing in any wise compassion
Nor holding pity of any worth.

Swinburne

I sometimes imagined myself heading north across China in a train bound for Korea; another subaltern in a different uniform. What would we be saying, I and my changed companions? I felt we would be saying very much the same things and our companionship would have much the same quality.

If evil lies in neither party from where does it come? Where does hate come from? Do I underestimate our enemy?

In my squad we have both an Abbot and a Costello! Pay parades are apt to be amusing.

"Abbot!"

"SIR!" – crash to attention.

"Costello!"

"SIR!" – crash to attention.

Sniggers all round.

We also have an extraordinary humorist by the name of Engledew. One day, after an instruction period, I asked him to explain how to find north by the Pole Star. He pursed his lips, got slowly to his feet, and everyone noticed his daringly shabby attire and the neckerchief hanging soddenly around his neck. There was a dramatic pause.

"Well, Sir, as Oi sees it – it's like this." Long pause and some anticipatory chuckles.

"You see this 'ere 'at?" He took off his beret and held it crown forward facing his audience.

"This 'ere 'at represents the 'eavens and screwed into it, as a manna o speaking, are several stars. Now, there's two of them shiners wots called the pointers – thats 'ere say. Now, 'ere there's another woppa wots called the Northern or Pole Star cos 'e stands up proppa dolly-like above the North Pole. Nah, imagine this 'ere 'eaven a revolving round." His cap spins in his fingers. "Now, the only one wot's still is that there Pole Star wot I was telling yer abaht, the fella wot stands up straight like above the..."

"That's enough, Engledew, thank you, a most demonstrative answer!"

"Yussah, very good Sah!" Crash to attention, crash to ease. Engledew subsides to the deck leaving the squad bursting with half-suppressed mirth.

"Cor, 'e's a card 'e is, a regular comijin!" said someone.

At pay parade much of the usually strict formality is relaxed. We do it on the troopdecks and the lads come up just as they are to take their money; not so Engledew, however. At other times, the idlest and scruffiest of individuals, at pay parade he proves himself a regular bullshitter. The paying officer shouts his name.

"Engledew!"

"Saah!" – an enormous bellow.

"Pay and book correct – Sah!" Crash, crash, vast, spotless boots upon the floor, everyone else in plimsolls, and, finally, an immaculate Guardsman's salute. Even Sergeant Major Brittain at Mons could not have complained.

"Cor, 'e's a card 'e is, regular nutter!"

Then there's Sergeant Slaptock, the sergeant in charge of Chris's squad, a lean, sour-looking man, who shows the greatest disinclination to do anything. At parade times, my section is usually more or less all present due to the strenuous efforts of my sergeant. But not so section C; in their training area, a small space between a derrick and two lifeboats, I usually see firstly Chris looking harassed; secondly Sergeant Slaptock spitting over the side; and thirdly five men biting their nails or playing cards.

One day Chris said, "Sergeant Slaptock at 11.30 hours tomorrow you *will* take a period of rifle instruction. Quite easy, I expect no more than bolt action practice." The sergeant mumbled something about being an engineer and not ruddy PBI. Anyway, half an hour later, he decided he was in the army after all and went up to Chris with a grand crashing of boots and saluted.

"Oh, yes, Sergeant?"

"Sah, I will take that period, Sah!"

"Oh will you, Sergeant? I'm so glad. Thank you so much. That will be all I think!"

Eventually we discovered the sergeant's soft spot and the probable cause of his lassitude. It was as if the pages of the Man Management notes we had taken at Mons, and spent much time giggling over, had come to life. Obeying the usual rules for friendly approaches to sergeants, we asked him, casually, one day, how his family was.

"Well, Sir, there's the youngest, sickening for the German measles she is, the eldest had it last week but the wife's all right, bless her." Out came the inevitable wallet and we were treated to a private viewing of his wife and two jolly little girls. He was all smiles, filled with a renewed zest for life. He expanded his theme. He was living for the day when his family could join him in Japan. I asked him how he had enjoyed the stop at Singapore. "Very good, Sir, thank you. I got some nice presents for the wife." Chris told me he had taken a considerable sum ashore. We laughed no more at those notes.

One morning no sergeant arrived to take the PT parade at 7 a.m. It was Sgt. Slaptock's turn. Later Chris asked him, "What happened at PT this morning, Sergeant?"

"I was there, Sir."

"Where?" Chris asked, flabbergasted.

"Chasing them up from below, Sir!"

The dear man did not know that, contrary to our usual practice, Chris had himself gone down to the troopdeck that morning and chased the men up. Never mind, it was not worth doing anything about it.

Hong Kong on Thursday!

Chapter Two
Arrival in Hong Kong

First encounters, July 3rd 1953

It was a stupid hour to arrive anywhere. In spite of our resolution to be awake bright and early, we overslept. Struggling to the porthole some time after first light, we saw golden green shores, steeply sloping mountains and occasional clusters of junks and sampans passing close on the port side. So this was Honkers. There was the frightening thought of disembarkation, interviews with senior officers, heel clicking and salutes. Indeed the voyage was over.

After a hasty breakfast we were on deck. The ship rested in a huge harbour, tugboats manoeuvring us alongside a quay. Across the harbour lay the mountainous length of Hong Kong island and the city of Victoria crawling along the shore, with the great white shapes of the Bank of China and its chief competitor, the Hong Kong and Shanghai Bank, standing out like cathedrals. The rooms of the tenements were set so far back behind arcades and balconies that, from a distance, the buildings had a derelict appearance, as if the facades had been blown out of them. The sun was brilliant, the waters sparkled, great liners and cargo boats moved about the harbour like kings and queens in a forest of rocking pawn-like junks and bobbing sampans.

Hosts of little sampans clustered alongside. They seemed to be crewed entirely by women and small children, dressed in shiny, black pyjamas made from a Macintosh-like material. They were lifting large nets on the ends of poles up to the open portholes, where many of the soldiers were dropping odd coins and other things into them. We went down to our cabin and fed a stream of unwanted articles down to a grinning, old crone below, several packets of Lux, various half-consumed bars of P & O soap, some party hats, a pair of ladies' shoes that had been in our cabin throughout the voyage and other odds and ends. Two small children jumped up and down with excitement in the prow of their small craft, as they stowed the objects in a little cupboard or under the decking. Some young men and boys began diving from the sampans after coins thrown into the water, thick with sewage, welling up from the sluices under the ship.

The morning was hectic. A young RA subaltern, bursting with keenness and welcoming good spirits, rushed us through a series of important visits: clothes from the Officers' Shop, uniforms of olive Hong Kong green, long khaki socks, monkey jackets and other items, thence to arrange an account with the Hong Kong and Shanghai Bank, referred to by our guide as "Honkers and Shaggers", and, finally, a visit to the CRA of Hong Kong. He was out, so a colonel interviewed us.

"Ah, Crook – had a good voyage, eh?"

"Yes, Sir, very good, thank you."

"Ah, jolly good. Well, I see you're posted to the island. Better than the territories, nearer the bright lights and all that, ha. And what are your interests? Games – play ruggah?"

"Yes, I have played quite a bit – on the wing, Sir."

"That's something then. Good climate for it here. Much too hot, of course, but it keeps you slim and fit like nothing else, ha."

"I am interested in scrambling in the hills and watching birds."

"What? Ha – bird-watcher, eh? Good, but mind the hills, most of 'em a bit crumbly around here."

We discussed various features of the colony and he took me around it on a huge wall map.

"Well, I guess that's all, Crook. Enjoy yourself and watch your money. The ruddy Chinks will fleece you if they can. Good bargainer, eh?"

"Not so bad, Sir."

"Well, s'about all – ah – take a tip. S'long as you go split-arse over everything, you'll be OK in the Army. Specially out here. Good luck to you!"

I walked out a little dazed and we all drove off in a Land Rover, over the main range of the island hills, to the headquarters of the 27th Heavy Anti-Aircraft Regiment, Royal Artillery, at the end of a long promontory projecting out into the China Sea, Stanley Fort.

Our arrival at the regimental mess was like entering a madhouse. Two enormous majors, with northern accents, conversed in loud, table-shaking voices over tea, slapping each other on the back and pounding the tablecloth. A story was going on about a comic strip officer who was in trouble with the 'Old Man' for losing a tyre and half the military transport stores. The humour was rollicking through the room, the ceiling split with their laughter and the subalterns joined in with lighter pitched cackles of mirth.

We were hustled down from the mess, a large building, magnificently situated on a hilltop, commanding a stupendous view of the sea in one direction and the large military cantonment on the other, for an interview with our Commanding Officer.

Outside his office, a strongly built lieutenant with a pugnacious jaw and a highly seasoned hat, curved like a crescent over his head, paced theatrically before us, evidently in the throes of anxiety and gasping in and out of a Benson and Hedges cigarette.

"Hallo, you two new here? For God's sake keep out of this dump. They chase you from pillar to post. Got on the wrong side of the old man. Twenty pounds out on the MT accounts, lost a Matador tyre somewhere in the hills, must have fallen off or something! Spent all last week hunting for the bloody thing!"

Gasp in – smoke out via nostrils.

"National Service – what me? Good Lord – no. Not likely. I'm a regular but I have just resigned my commission and I'm off to Kenya tomorrow to farm, born and brought up there – God's own country. I've told the CO that, when I went to Sandhurst, I had no intention of being in the army for more than a few years. Coo – he wasn't impressed!"

The office door opened, "Mr Crawley, please."

Three gasps on the B and H, he stamped it on the ground. "See ya latah, I hope!"

During the day we discovered the nature of our regiment. This Heavy Anti-Aircraft regiment is divided into three batteries, each of which is divided into two or more troops, each manning four large anti-aircraft guns, with their attendant radars, trackers, predictors and other electronic apparatus intended to place an explosive shell near enough to an intruding aircraft to bring it down. Each troop was placed on a hilltop or outstanding site with an all-round field of fire. The regiment ringed both the island and the city of Kowloon across the harbour and was supposed to prevent an aerial attack, presumably from China. The system had been a good one during the last war but was beginning to date, as we were to find out. Newly-arrived subalterns were sent to one or other of these hilltop gun sites.

"There's not much to choose between them," we were told. "Avoid Brickhill if you can, it's in the bleakest position, no proper officer accommodation – converted ammunition bunkers, sanitation poor and it's pretty well cut off on a mountain at the end of a cape. Look – you can see it over there, the last headland before the horizon."

A tall mountain ended in a narrow ridge before plunging, as a blunt cape, into the sea. I could just make out a line of low buildings perched on the end of the ridge.

Next morning the Adjutant decided on our fate. "Morning, Crook," he said. "I am sending you to Brickhill." Chris was sent to another site on a mountain crest, overhanging the city of Kowloon.

*

Brickhill

A three-tonner came to take myself and my luggage to my new abode. We drove along the southern coast of the island, past two scintillating little bays of shining sand, set between long capes and backed by jungle-clad mountains. Some way short of the Chinese fishing village of Aberdeen, we turned left off the main road and began winding our way up a tortuous road, along the side of Brickhill, and so towards the ridge I had seen the night before. My driver, an intelligent man, was surprisingly enthusiastic.

"It's not a bad place at all, you know, Sir. Bit rough and ready but nicely out of the way of the CO. We are not bothered very much by RHQ. In fact, we're pretty much an independent unit. We've just started playing cricket on the Police School grounds in the valley below us. Are you a cricketer?"

I told him I could bowl a bit and he waxed enthusiastic, being evidently the only competent batsman on site. We were twisting up a series of hairpin bends on a road carved from the living rock. Sometimes we dived into little cuttings, emerged again and coiled along the flank of a hill with steep grassy slopes, beset with small fir trees falling away to the sea below. Above us, the grey cliffs of a mountain frowned down at us, tufts of tall, pampas-style grasses and gnarled pines gripping the ledges throwing sharp silhouettes against the sky. We swung around the inner face of a little valley, set deep into the hill, and I glimpsed a patchwork of paddy fields and a Chinese hut opening on to a tiny cove several hundred feet below us. We groaned up a final slope into a cutting, across the end of which stood a pair of stolid, black, iron gates with a guardroom behind it. A gunner emerged and let us in, giving me a smart salute. We drove on into the camp up a steep slope and stopped halfway up.

"Your quarters, Sir!" said the driver with a grin. "Shall I unload your trunks?"

At the side of the road, set back a little below the roadway, two doors and windows looked out from a concrete bunker set into the rock of the hill, with fir trees growing from the soil directly above the windows. There were two little concrete caves carved from the hill as cellars. One of these was mine. I took a look inside. Damp whitewash gave forth a musty odour and an enormous electric fan hummed and clattered like a traction engine. There were two ancient chests of drawers, a wardrobe with warped doors, a small writing desk and a bed, upon which lay a straw palliasse, which I surmised dated from the Crimean War. My batman-to-be introduced himself and showed me around. Some twenty yards away, on the opposite side of the road, on a ledge above an almost vertical hillside, perched the wash hut. The latrines, set into the side of the hill next to the bunkers, contained huge buckets with rough wooden seats and were known locally as thunderboxes. The batman was not the most cheerful of men.

"The worst things, Sir, are them big centipedes. Quite six inches long they are, with their legs sticking out all along 'em. Sometimes they crawls on you at night and if you brushes 'em off the wrong way, they just digs their little legs into you and that's that. You 'ave to pick 'em off, Sir, and every leg has a sting. One of the chaps in our billet was sent to hospital the other day, his chest covered with stings. There's snakes too but they dursn't come inside much. Yet, in one thing, Sir, we're lucky. No mosquitoes here, we're too high up and the air is fresh from the sea."

There was the sound of footsteps on the road and a strongly built subaltern appeared, a tough young man with a projecting jaw. He welcomed me warmly and I took to him at once. Roger Thompson was also doing his National Service, before going on to St John's College at Oxford to read history. I saw at once a determined, perhaps stubborn, character who would make a reliable companion. He took me in hand and introduced me to the Troop Commander, a regular captain, of a friendly, if rather harassed, appearance, who showed me the camp.

At its widest, the camp was spread some seventy yards over the narrow ridge of the promontory and, in length, it ran for about one hundred and fifty yards from the base of the steep upper slopes of Brickhill to the four hundred foot cliffs at the end of the cape. A loop of road encircled our cliff top and, on the outer side of this, the hillside dropped sheer in narrow valleys that ran down to the sea on either side of the camp. A whirled line of barbed wire marked our perimeter, which, at night, was illuminated from powerful lamps set on stakes.

Within the loop of road, the humpback of the ridge was carved into four rock-protected gun emplacements, each reached by a cutting in the stone. The men's quarters consisted of further bunkers set in the rock, while the office and control rooms were deeply dug in stone with strong iron shutters on doors and windows. There were three Nissen huts, one a billet for the radar operators, another for the sergeants' mess and the third, the officers' mess, set a little apart, in a higher position commanding a view over the whole camp and the sea and islands beyond. Below the main camp, there were a few more buildings where a number of Chinese employees lived. Two radar sets stood high on the site and in the control room were placed the machines of the gunnery prediction apparatus. The site was manned by approximately seventy men, the number varying with national service intake and release. Four or five sergeants supported the Troop Commander and his three subalterns. Our troop was one of two belonging to a battery, the headquarters of which were on Stonecutters Island in the harbour but our very isolated position gave us a virtually autonomous role. Orders from outside came by telephone and one soon learnt the military skills of misleading intrusive senior officers over a wire. For the most part, we evidently ran our own show with quite an independent spirit.

It seemed to me that, in spite of the rough accommodation, I had come to a very pleasing little place. Although smartness was not the most obvious feature of the men moving about the camp, there was a good cheer and easy friendliness that indicated high morale. Clearly this was not a camp for bullshitting parades; rather equipment drills and gunnery practice, live or imagined, were to occupy most of our time. For the rest of the time, the men amused themselves freely and without tension between ranks.

In the evening, with the rush of settling in completed, I sat outside the mess and gazed out over the superb view beyond our shacks, radar sets, the guns covered for the night and the squat tower of the tracker position decorated with the aerials of the signallers. The entire length of the western coast of Hong Kong lay before me. To the north, green mountains sloped steeply to red and grey rocks and beaches of clean, yellow sand. The sea, so calm as to leave hardly a cream of foam along the tide line, lay blue and shining in the evening light, sometimes corrugated and glistening, with intricate wind and current patterns, and always alive with a subtle shimmering movement. Chains of golden green islands, steep and unapproachable, humped themselves from the waters. Beyond Lama Island, only three miles away, there were others and again, beyond a further stretch of white sea below the falling sun, yet more and again more, vague shapes beyond the horizon, delicate in a haze of blue gold hue. Dense little fleets of fishing junks dotted the waters with their lateen sails rising in a host of shapes as if cities with towers, spires, turrets and masts were sprouting from the sea.

Opposite, across a small channel, the island of Apleichau, the Duck Bill Island, guarded the entrance to the harbour of Aberdeen, from which the fishing fleet was setting sail for the night, moving slowly down the channel under our guns and heading for the fishing grounds near the Chinese communist islands of Lema. To the south of us, near the end of the channel, lay Aberdeen itself, a miniature city, with an immense Chinese cemetery of shining hillside graves perched immediately above it; in the still air the murmur of distant people sometimes reached us. Above Aberdeen, the forested slopes of The Peak climbed to a high summit crowned with the beautiful, white buildings of the most select residential district of the colony. As light began to fail, whisps of cloud appeared to twine around them, until all were enveloped in mist.

After dinner Roger and I, together with Dennis, our senior regular lieutenant, drank a toast to my arrival, sipping whisky and swapping yarns for hours. I went to bed content, filled with a pleasurable anticipation for the morrow.

*

Settling in, July 8th 1953

My cave-like home fits snugly into the mountain. The two little rooms are no hotel, more like an air-raid shelter in fact, but they are becoming more habitable day by day. My collection of books decorates the small writing desk, like Vesuvius over Naples, and my first Chinese prints and maps begin to relieve the monotony of bare, slightly damp whitewash. The routine shaking out of beds and shoes to disclose lurking centipedes or arachnids is becoming a habit.

Our garrison is, indeed, a compact little unit, isolated from everyone else, no doctor, no padre, no flowing water sanitation, post only three times a week and only one way in and out, down the narrow cuttings in the hillside. The contact between the officers and men is very direct and 'Man Management', as it used to be called at Mons, has to be of a high order. Morale in a small unit fluctuates just as the temperature rises or falls more quickly in a teacup than it does in a water tank. Not only do we have to keep the unit fit and trained and the equipment operational, but also we must devise games and exercises to keep the men happy and occupied. With so little space on our hilltop and with a drill square with a precipice along one side, this is not so easy. But we have our blessings. The most important is an outstanding Army Catering Corps cook, whose productions do more than anything to keep the lads content.

"I like to make 'em jellies and trifles at the weekend, just as their mothers would, Sir, you know."

It is a strange feeling to sit in our little mess of an evening and to reflect that we hold sole responsibility for the security of our equipment and the behaviour of our troop. The Troop Commander leaves the site every evening for he lives with his wife in a hotel in Kowloon. In the night air sounds travel far; nearby, we hear voices in the NAAFI, the cookhouse or from the men's billets along the hill; down on the water below us junks and sampans trail the laburnum petals of their lamps on the rippling surface of the sea and, on a still evening, the croaking of frogs rises from the paddy fields.

Sometimes, from within a silence, a great insect chorus begins, swelling slowly until chirrups, in a thousand different keys, on a thousand different frequencies, mingle with other strange squeaks, rustlings, scrapings and puffings everywhere in the night air. A moment's pause in our conversation permits a subtle infiltration of sound, a reminder that, beyond our narrow circle of light, outside among the trees and grasses, is another world of moonlit desire in cold insect shells. From the mess ceiling a great fan turns and turns stupidly, in an effort to cool the air.

Last night Roger came precipitately into the mess, looking behind him into the darkness beyond the pool of light around the door. He swore something had rustled in the grasses by the entrance. Our minds run on snakes for one or two species here are lethal strikers and one very dangerous one had been found recently, hiding under a refrigerator. This time I could reassure him for I had seen a large toad outside, earlier in the evening, and it had probably jumped out of the way at his approach.

Once a slight tapping at the window revealed a creature scrabbling against the glass. It was a huge praying mantis, some five inches long, propped up on its hind legs and peering in. It seemed excited by the light, goggling its head about and tapping the glass with the hard spike on its predatory front legs, as if seeking an entrance. In the morning it had gone but, in its stead, was a long, thin twig. On looking closer, I saw insect legs propping it up and realised it was a stick insect, another entomological treat. All day, large, gaudy butterflies parade in powerful flight up and down the roads and around our buildings. Last night, I found an enormous brilliant green long horned grasshopper sitting on the ceiling. All these insect experiences have stimulated me to write. Here goes my latest attempt.

Beetle

Blundering beetle burbles into my room
bloop – blurp – blop – careering curves and plunges
– whoosh and zoom against the bed back, wall,
tin box – ping and window – clunk
and round the lamp in delirious circles
weaving madness in concentric dance.

Beetle! You blithering blurp –
bumble more bravely that soon
with stunning plop you fall
and downside-up with legs awry and waving
like a helpless cotted child
you'll plead my pardon.

You funny thing! I stroke your carapace
and fold your wings.
You were not made or this –
there into the darkness thrown
go find your beetle mate
and play with better things than grinning lamps.

My companions are both very pleasant, quiet types, unlike the raucous fellows at RHQ. They do not have much to say but we are good friends. There is a lot of routine gunnery to learn and much administrative detail to attend to. The Troop Commander is a radar expert and a Korean War veteran. At first sight he seems a delightful man, appreciative and very keen to make the place excellent, from an equipment and human point of view.

I am Messing Officer and in charge of hygiene and health, as well as the radars. I command some twenty men, the radar people, drivers, cooks and guard-dog handlers. Since we have no doctor on site, a gunner, who has taken a fancy to playing with medicines and plasters, has been given the task of Medical Orderly. He has a room full of drugs and instruments and treats cases of mild indisposition. Once or twice a week, we have a visit from the regimental medical officer, who is available more quickly in an emergency. Gunner Drabble and I work together and, while he congratulates himself on the absence of lice, we are instituting a bedding check, the incidence of bedbugs being rather high. At midnight, two Chinese come and clean out the thunderboxes and we have to check their work, Drabble liberally distributing Jeyes fluid and DDT in the urinals and wash places. The result is an absence of fleas and a sweet smell of disinfectant.

We are well looked after in our mess. The small Nissen hut is subdivided into our dining room, lounge, writing room and general dump on one side and the cook's kitchen, living room and general dump on the other. The cook is a Chinaman, who speaks a bizarre cross between a pidgin English of his imagination and a coolie English full of unintended riddles. Concentration is needed on both sides of the compartment before a menu is settled.

"You eata da kippla dinnla, today?"

"No, Cook, kipper for breakfast, tomorrow."

"I keepa da kippla tomlows blekfast – eh?"

"That's right!"

"Tanu Sah – kippla tomlows blekfast."

And brilliantly cooked too.

Him is the mess waiter. Of ghoulish expression, laboured English and shambolic appearance, Him is certainly a little vague (kerosene in the pineapple pie the other day), yet his perpetual grin is a tonic for everyone. When I showed him the praying mantis he began praying too, so I supposed the Chinese name for this insect must be similar to ours.

Our clothes are washed by the dhobie amah who comes up every day to the camp. She is the cook's wife, a charming and retiring little lady. The previous one was quite notorious. At that time there were fifteen Chinese in their quarters and the dhobie slept in the same hut. Now she is pregnant in hospital and Him, the young scoundrel, is the suspected father. Him is often very sad for he wants to marry a girl in China and is contemplating a visit to Communist territory in the near future. We doubt the wisdom of this because he has lived many years in Hong Kong and works for the army.

Every evening, the duty officer of the day mounts the guard. The Guard Commander parades his men on our little square for inspection. The officer arrives and inspects, moving elegantly along the rows with the sergeant trotting behind. My first occasion was a near disaster. "Guard ready and correct, Sir," said the sergeant, with a smart salute. "Thank you, Sergeant," I warbled – and promptly strolled to the wrong end of the line of men. Halfway along, I realised my mistake. It was essential to carry on regardless, even though the men looked as if they were suffering from extreme suppression of mirth. Back at the mess, Roger, who had been looking on, was pissing himself with gurgles of joy and, of course, I was not allowed to forget it in the weeks ahead!

Once in Brickhill, it is difficult to get out. Although we are on Hong Kong Island itself, the city lies on the far side of a great mountain and it is not easy to get transport over it. There are buses but these entail long walks and several waits. On certain days, a recreation truck takes officers and men alike into town.

*

Work and Play, about July 15th 1953

One of my first jobs here has been to sort out an impossible muddle. We have three generators supplying power for the electrical installations of our equipment and also for lights, fans and fridges. A record has to be kept of the hours for which they are run and the oil consumption. There are a series of work tickets and forms to be maintained day by day and week by week. When I arrived, the system was in chaos, with all our records differing from those at Battery headquarters. The only way to get them to match has been the usual military solution to such problems. You begin with the correct figures of the last entry, falsify the intermediate running hours, and so obtain a correct present reading. This task is now completed and nobody is surprised by the methods used, methods which I was more or less authorised to use. I am actually a bit peeved that the first thing I do here is to put someone else's cock-up straight and correct a whole set of bewildering figures. I am starting afresh with a system of my own, which I hope will work. One of the generators is overdue for servicing and the other two have either oil or water leaks. To complicate matters, one of the engine attendants tells me he has lent some oil to some engineers, cannot remember how much and doesn't know how much he has had back!

So far, my two radar sets are out of action but the bombadier in charge tells me he hopes they will be okay soon. It amuses me that the predictor, the machine that calculates where a shell has to be placed to meet a moving target, is extremely ancient and the drills for its use are different from those I learnt in England. It has many primitive features that bewilder me. The system I was taught uses one radar to survey the sky and locate targets, while the other tracks a chosen target and sends data about height, speed and direction to the predictors. The system here uses the two sets simultaneously in target acquisition, in a manner known as box and cox. Most of the modern apparatus has not reached here yet and I understand that we cannot lock on to aircraft doing more than 400 miles per hour. Since the Chinese now have *Migs* we would have little chance of an effective shot at one!

The radar and predictor operators are bright lads and pleasant to get on with, efficient with their work. In fact, one or two are a bit too quick-witted and some tact is needed in handling them. By contrast, most of the gunners are as dumb as deaf frogs, lacking all visible signs of intelligence, even though they are good-hearted fellows.

I have been preparing a loose-leaf file, containing details of my chaps' personal record sheets. Some of these make very depressing reading; unhappy marriages, one remand home boy and many adverse comments on character, in general. Personnel selection officers do not mince matters in their reports on the men and I shudder to think what some of the lads would say if they knew what was written about them. Some, of course, have more complimentary comments written about them and may well become NCOs, in due course.

My faith in the gunners is a trifle restored by my batman, a bright-eyed lad, very willing to help and quite intelligent. How he manages to clean shoes so well I don't know but I strongly suspect he pays one of the Chinese to do it. Several of the men employ their own Chinese batmen who, for a small sum, clean kit extremely well. It seems a colossal cheek for the men to have private servants like this – but the latter do get some remuneration for it.

The sergeants here are not impressive, lacking the qualities of initiative and leadership shown by the young infantry sergeants and corporals on board the ship. They are mostly fairly old, a bit gruff and uncooperative and often get odd bees in their bonnets about something or other. One of them has been refusing to swim in the sports this year because, on some past occasion, he and others were paraded in full kit to watch swimming sports. Yet he is a fine swimmer and enjoys it. Roger and I, by dint of much cajoling and invocations of British fair play and 'being a sport' are beginning to win him round, I think.

Some of our officers seem to me to be the utter end! Our Battery Commander comes up to Brickhill from Stonecutters Island once a week and criticises everything he can in a petty 'know-all' manner, which infuriates everyone. He always tries to 'put it over one', in such a way as to make the person concerned feel a fool. So far he has said about ten words to me. His favourite comment is: "You will do

so and so – if it spoils your plans, then its just hard bloody luck."
The main 'bloody luck' about him is his dour personality and total
lack of wit. Even our Troop Commander is apt to get frantically
excited if anything goes wrong, blames someone else and then
discovers it is his own oversight. He seems unable to distinguish
between what is essential in troop management and what is trivial
detail.

One day, when the predictor went wrong, he took out the insides
of the CC10 machine and fiddled about with micro-adjustments, until
he realised he had forgotten to operate an important and very obvious
switch. No one seems to take these little trials calmly, there is always
shouting and swearing, the sending of orders whistling in all directions
and, finally, the hunt for a scapegoat. I suppose that regular officers
can never afford to slip up on anything, in order always to remain in
the good books of their seniors. Thus, you have an excellent captain
eating humble pie before a half-mad major. The whole system lacks
spontaneity and flexibility. Certainly, by comparison with the Royal
Scots, the standard of efficiency in this regiment is, at the moment,
very low.

At Mons, we were told repeatedly that the quality of a unit
depends on the quality of the officers. Here the CO of the regiment,
Colonel Adams, is first class; a big-minded man, firm in decision,
precise in judgement and justly tough on everyone. The battery
commanders, however, are another story; all of them seem odd in one
way or another and their talk is continuously military and very boring.
My main interest concerns the welfare and education of the men, yet
Roger and I now have an increasing set of involvements because our
senior subaltern leaves the troop next week and, when the Troop
Commander goes home of an evening, we will have sole control and
responsibility here.

Deep Water Bay, below Brickhill, is beautiful. High hills
surround calm, azure water, soft, limpid and warm. There is a little
sandy beach, where we take the men for a bathe, and a neat golf
course. Above the shore, the jungle-clad hills rise steeply, revealing,
on level ledges, a gleaming white house or two, like fairy castles.
The roads to these houses are masterpieces of engineering, creeping
around dangerous bends and through vertical cuttings in the rock. The
beach is socially select and only the upper class Chinese and
Europeans bathe there. Sometimes, in the evenings, we have the

place to ourselves. The diving rafts offshore give us a lot of fun although swimming out to them needs care because of the occasional jellyfish, the stings of which can bring up nasty weals on the body.

Talking of bodies – we have to do a weekly medical examination of the whole troop, to check on skin diseases, foot rots and *tinea*. Everyone strips off, and then Roger and I examine them, while our medical orderly takes down the gory details.

On the rocks, near the number one gun site, lives a large rock python, some ten feet long reputedly. One of the lads on guard duty told me that, one night, he was walking near the spot, when it slithered off the rocks above him and dropped on the path glaring at him. The poor boy was scared out of his wits, although I suspect it was the python that had the greater fright.

Chapter Three

Chinatown

Downtown visits, July 19th 1953

The Royal Hong Kong Yacht Club on Kellet Island lies in the sheltered waters of the harbour, connected to the waterfront by a narrow causeway. Offshore, in the busy harbour between Hong Kong Island and Kowloon, numbers of picturesque junks and sampans move their way laboriously among the graceful little racing yachts of the club. Any officer of the regiment is automatically a member of the club and can have his expenses here placed on his messing account. All you have to do is to sign a chit, no cash is needed. It is a spacious building, with large, shady terraces, cool, carefully tended lawns, a dance hall, bars and other rooms more directly concerned with sailing.

It is rare for Roger and I to escape for any length of time from Brickhill, since every three days one of us has to be Orderly Officer and stay in camp. This weekend I got away to meet Chris again and explore the Chinese environment. In the evening, we walked for an hour within the maze of streets between the bank and West Point. Leaving the large buildings of the commercial heart of Victoria behind us, the roads became narrower and lined with cavernous arcades, resplendent with Chinese shop signs. Each shop opens directly on to the arcade like a row of brightly lit caves. The whole area was full of bustling, chattering Chinese, wearing their distinctive pyjamas and, often, great coolie hats.

It grew dark early in these shadowed streets and we turned off into an alleyway and thence up a broad flight of steep steps covered with squatting Chinese eating from little bowls. The crowding around the little food stalls was intimidating. Rice, soup, curries, dried fish – oh the smell – bananas, melons and other fruits, were all on sale as were suits of clothes, underwear, curious Chinese toys and, indeed, almost anything from a watch to a walking stick. All the while, the vendors chanted their wares in toneless, chirping voices. Above us rose the tiers of tenement balconies, each with a set of bamboo poles and lines, for holding washing, suspended over the street from every floor. The Chinese seem to have a mania for washing and such cleanliness must account for their generally healthy and fresh appearance. Such cleanliness is limited to personal concerns, however, for the dowdy streets, with plaster peeling from the walls, are full of waste, rubbish and rubble piled in corners. Rows of camp beds were being put out for the night, lit by thousands of little lanterns flickering against a backcloth of neon signs in Chinese characters. Many of these streets are out of bounds to the military but the signs are difficult to see and we have probably gone beyond the limits already. The Chinese seem peaceable enough and untroubled by children running naked and barefoot in the streets, while families eat their bowls of rice 'chow' in the open air. Mothers carry babies in shawls on their backs and even eight year olds do the same.

On visiting a cinema in the Wanchai District, we went up several floors to find ourselves at a window on the top storey, from which we could look directly into the upper tenements opposite. Each room was lit by candles in lanterns or by dim electric lights and was subdivided into numerous little cubicles, of which we could only see into the outer ones. There were camp beds, hanging matting to mark the divisions of the room, occasional tables, piles of clothes, hungry children being served food in bowls, pots of ferns and other plants and birdcages. Yesterday, I saw two Cantonese coolies walking along with their birds in their cages, presumably giving them an airing.

The street below the cinema was now filled by rows of camp beds placed strategically between the stalls. Although it was a poor quarter, it was ablaze with lamps and candles and the milling people created an ever-changing pattern of reticulated shadows, dramatised by the great Chinese signs hanging in front of the shops and covering every wall space.

Returning along the causeway to the yacht club, we found yet another way of life. The causeway, like the street, was full of people, most of them sitting on the low stone walls above the water and dangling their feet or fishing lines over the edge. Just offshore and against the causeway itself, lay the sampans of the boat people, each loaded with a family, the lady of the craft dishing out suppers to father and kids. The little boats were spotlessly clean, the decking scrubbed and the white or blue bowls of rice shone in the light of the lanterns, above the filth in the water around them.

On this first occasion, the smells, the dirt and the unfamiliar slant-eyed faces rather appalled me. It was an overwhelming first encounter with another culture. Gradually, as I am beginning to see more of it, I accept the environment and I would like to get to know some of these polite and gentle people. Chinese loyalties are clearly to their families and friends. There is little sense of responsibility to a community. They are said to show a social callousness at times, not bothering with other people's lives. An injured man would be left at the roadside in all probability, unless he was one of the family. In my limited experience, the Chinese here are easy to put at ease, a word or smile will make their faces wrinkle up with pleasure into a great grin. Some, however, look taciturn and very self-sufficient.

When I go about these streets, I try, so far as I can, to feel Chinese; to feel what it must be like to live in a sampan community or in a crowded tenement. In a way it horrifies me, this plentiful ants' nest, gyrating about the shores of this green-hilled island. There is so much poverty preventing self-improvement or the exploration of life. Even so, the Chinese of Hong Kong do not seem degraded by poverty. They remain clean, polite and family-conscious. You should see the way they play with their children.

The average Englishman in the Army out here has little interest in the problems of life of the Chinese in Hong Kong, a people split from their motherland by politics and protected by an alien and largely Victorian regime. Colonialism and imperialism are written all over the English higher classes here. We have done much for the Chinese but I am sure it is really China they feel strongly about, not Britain, Queen or Commonwealth. In this, the atmosphere is very different from Colombo, where a sense of loyalty to Commonwealth and the Crown was manifest. Most of the young officers I meet do little else except go to American films, play cricket, visit expensive and palatial European clubs and behave and talk exactly as if they were at home. Their conversation is dominated by the latest happenings at Lords or Wimbledon. I see nothing wrong with that, but it is oh so rarely balanced by anything other than a sort of stupefied bewilderment and condescension, if not arrogance, towards the people who form ninety per cent of the population of this densely-crowded city. I am continually amazed by the lack of understanding and even humanity in the way in which many of our British officers, especially the younger 'sporting' types, treat the Chinese with whom they come in contact. Chris tells me that, in his mess, the Chinese 'boys' are ordered about as if they were slaves, no 'please' or 'thank you', no smiles or tolerance of language problems.

One such officer remarked to me, "Of course, they are so uncultured, an illiterate people. Look how far they are behind us! I cannot see any point in living like that at all, caged together on a small boat like animals – worse than animals because of their diseases, which wild animals avoid. They work all day. How futile, no ability to think or do anything else than squat amongst the filth. They're dirty, just smell them. Ugh, horrid!"

Apart from their utter lack of charity, remarks like these reveal an appalling ignorance of the ancient history of civilisation in China, the enduring culture which has given rise to family systems, customs and religions curious to us, and also a quiet refinement and politeness that is to be much admired. All the paraphernalia which marks the technological advances of the Europeans, should not obscure from us the fact that a civilisation rests not on loud noises, the pops and bangs of ingenious machines, but upon the dignified, tolerant, reasoned and gentlemanly behaviour of its peoples. The Chinese, of some education, often show a cultivated sophistication above that of their British and American equivalents, many of whom, in spite of their university accomplishments, fail to realise that self-centredness is the basis of all misunderstanding.

Yet, I must not write too harshly of these young chaps, since most of them have come out, as I have myself indeed, either through compulsion or simply to see a few exotic sights. Of course, seeing in itself demands rather more than the uncritical use of eyesight. It is insight and understanding which are important. As Chris reminds me, "Just because you want to know Rome as a Roman, it does not follow that you should forget you were originally a Londoner, nor should you expect everyone else to show such enthusiasm as you do for this overpopulated den." Fair enough criticism but I do find it strange that there is so little curiosity or desire among these subalterns to get to know any of the Chinese personally. Naturally, the language difficulties are considerable and, unlike European languages, there are no Latin roots to help, no common linguistic culture or trend of ideas.

On Sunday afternoon, Chris and I went up the tramway to the Peak. The tramcar is hauled by a long cable, which waved to and fro in the air before us, as we climbed a concave slope at an angle of quite forty-five degrees. As we rose, we passed through dense jungle broken by occasional fashionable houses, perched like castles in the air for the Olympian gods. The higher up the Peak – the higher up the Hong Kong social ladder, I am told. Yet, Jove himself, the Governor, who should be perpetually enshrouded in cloud, lives well down in Victoria, near the cathedral. The Peak was indeed beautiful. Wooded slopes fall away into extraordinary, dreamlike views. There is a fine waterfall supplying a reservoir, great houses and miraculous gardens. It is certainly close to a paradise of the gods, even if all too frequently cloud-encompassed and very damp. From above, the Chinatown areas again have that burnt-out look. The gaunt tenement balconies, festooned with forests of poles and washing, have a kind of hollow appearance, enhanced by rotting plaster and a lack of paint.

*

Taxi dancing – not quite

From time to time RHQ holds a regimental party at which ladies are invited to the officers' mess. After one such event Roger, two other subalterns and I went into Kowloon with two young ladies, whose looks and general desirability had been greatly improved by the cocktails. They turned out to be a couple of gold-diggers with a vengeance. Poor Roger has not got over it yet.

They seemed to know their way around and told us of a very good dance hall where, provided one did not drink, one could dance for nothing. After a four dollar taxi ride, we found the place shut and returned to the Imperial Ballroom. Here we had to pay a five dollar fee to gain entrance for the ladies, which made me suspicious. It was, however, an impressive place, with dim lights hidden in pilasters and recesses, changing in colour all the time, so that, at one moment, the room was red with a green ceiling and, the next, yellow with a blue one and so on. The band was sprightly and two Chinese sing-song girls were rendering native songs very nicely and English ones not so well.

We had some coffee and perused the scene. While the ladies were 'out', the elegant Chinese *maître d'hôtel* approached me and spoke softly in my ear.

"Excuse me, Sir, but before the ladies return, there is one little matter. I see two of you are without ladies, would you enjoy the company of two of our dancing hostesses for half an hour at eight dollars each?"

By the time we had begun to consider this question, our own 'ladies' were seating themselves. They expressed great amusement at the idea, until they suddenly realised that two of us were quite prepared to dance with a hostess, going halves for half an hour! At that their amusement turned to horror. But the *maître d'hôtel* was still enthusiastic.

"Sirs, this is an opportunity. I will, myself, choose the prettiest, slim and young, only nineteen years old and a perfect dancer!"

The first dance had begun and I bagged one of our girls and was away into a quickstep before the others could wake up. Sobriety paid, and, although I had been fairly merry over the cocktails, I was now as alert as a judge. Roger was pounced upon – the wily *maître d'hotel* having caught his name.

"Mr Roger, Sir. Just think of it. Only eight dollars for half an hour."

At this the lordly Roger thumped the table.

"Look here, I am the Duke of Beaufort, don't you know? I will not have these sordid women at my table – and, anyway, we have two perfectly eligible popsies as it is!" The Chinaman fled.

These dancing girls are not what they might appear. They are very companionable, talkative and friendly, probably first-class amateur psychologists, but they allow no monkey business and, perhaps with one or two exceptions, are chosen for their good behaviour. Such entertainment is known as taxi dancing and is very popular in the East. I was amused by the fact that one would have to have paid ten per cent government tax for one's pleasure. Out of respect for our ladies we desisted and, anyway, the price was rather high. The gunners dance with reputedly poorer quality girls at fifty cents a go.

The total cost of our evening, what with cover charges, taxis and other extras was a high one. But did our ladies offer to pay a cent? Not a bit of it! So four of Her Majesty's subalterns are rather ruefully poorer this weekend. Roger and I arrived in camp at twenty to three, the guards having hollow chuckles to themselves as we passed our gates.

*

Cathedral

One Sunday morning, Chris and I went to explore the Anglican cathedral. It lies in a little valley full of flowers and vegetation, right in the heart of the city, a sizeable church, opening to the gardens on all sides, cool and airy. During lunch times, many Chinese come and sit quietly in there, relaxing from the city rush.

The bishop preached a sermon, describing the expansion of the Church in Hong Kong. We were invited to a sort of Sunday fellowship meeting where we 'got on to' the dean's wife, who became most excited when she heard my name. Apparently, someone had told them of my impending arrival and they had sent to meet me off the ship. Plans had gone awry for they were told I was not on board. I promptly became a deanery mystery and the dean and friends now gave me a great welcome. We played party games in the large Cathedral hall, a modern gothic building, with a high timbered roof. The whole event was so astonishingly like a church club in England that I had to rub my eyes to believe what I saw; tea and gentle friendliness with a group of Cathedral ladies and keen Christian youngsters – but very few Chinese. I was invited to serve at Holy Communion but this I had to decline. I did, however, express great interest in welfare work amongst the Chinese and, since this is the bishop's pet theme, it may lead on to other invitations. I am not sure how all this Englishness fits into the rest of the world I am seeing here, nor whether this can be the best introduction to it.

*

Aberdeen

Below Brickhill lies a one-time fishing village, now a growing port called Aberdeen. It was once a hamlet called Heung Kong Chai and it is said that, when the British first set foot on the island, they named it

Hong Kong after this comfortable harbour. Aberdeen has flourished, yet it remains almost entirely a harbour for the fishing junks and is influenced little by the British. One evening, Roger and I drove down from Brickhill to have a look around.

A major part of the coastal fishing fleet of Hong Kong finds shelter in this anchorage, protected from the open sea by the island of Apleichau. Together with the other junk harbours on Cheung Chau Island and at Tai O on Lantao island, it forms the main centre for the fishing activities of the colony. The inlet is always crowded with a multitude of craft, hardly ever identical in appearance but differing in outline of hull, housing, sails or rigging in a thousand ways. The bat-veined sails, ribbed like a pterodactyl's wing, may be blue, white, brown or yellow or a merry patchwork quilt of colours. Sometimes they are so holed and tattered that it seems the slightest gust of wind would bring the slats clattering on the deck. Parts of the harbour dry out at low tide and then one can admire the shapely lines of the hulls. This is a species of ship that sailed these coasts centuries before the first caravel headed south from Portugal to find a route around Africa to the East. Fishermen sailed this way many centuries ago and, while in Europe we have forgotten the galleon and the clipper, the Chinese junk, older than either, still sails superbly across these seas, which may suddenly become terrible, sullenly ferocious, in moods less predictable than the windy aggression of the Atlantic upon our shores at home.

Three prettily painted houseboats sit out on the tideway. They are fish restaurants, where one can choose one's prey, alive, from a glass tank or a wicker frame suspended over the side in the water and have it cooked to one's delight. As we stood on the quay, a car load of would-be diners drew up near us. A gang of young women at once rushed, like vultures, upon it and, after peals of merriment, remonstrations and bargaining, one of them was chosen to ferry the party across in her sampan. The army calls them 'Sampan Annies' and no one can approach the quay without being besieged by them. To avoid such an assault, we parked in the main street, down the side of which runs an enormous open and stinking sewer, that soon disgorges itself straight into the sea near the restaurants.

On the streets the busy people were spilling off the pavement and filling the roadway in a throng of blue pyjamas, shiny black tunics and flared trousers, khaki shirts, white shirts or flowing, stiff-collared robes, all selling or buying vociferously, laughingly pricing articles absurdly high and buying them deliciously cheap; cigarettes, medicinal drugs, stamps, lanterns, paper monsters for a feast day, bananas, pineapples and mangoes. Here is somebody mending shoes, another shaving the heads of children and, in an alcove, a letter writer slowly inscribing characters, while a fishwife sits on a stool and dictates. A thousand clogs go clip clap click clat along the arcades and the smells in the fetid air are so hot and sweaty you could smear windows with them. This Hong Kong smell is like nothing else, rich in spices, body perfumes, the peculiar Chinese sweat smell and the odours of rotting foods that lie, slowly crushing to an ooze, underfoot. The sewers add their taint and the blocked drains, ill-ventilated interiors of the houses, car exhausts and the fish in baskets just off the junks, all combine to create a unique, aromatic mixture. Old China hands will comment pensively on the blend of odours, as if tasting teas, and even tell little stories beginning: "Now I remember a little place where the flavours..." leaning all the while on a sewer railing, with a Chinese kitchen opening on the street behind them.

Little boys and girls play barefoot in the roadway, some with sores and skin diseases, others clean and robust, in spite of the overcrowding. Pavement sleepers lie in odd corners of the arcades, covered with a sack or a piece of ragged cloth, and, from time to time, an old woman, horridly malformed and wrinkled, sells a Chinese newspaper to a passer-by, while another crone comes up to us cackling 'Gumsah, Gumsah' and holding out her palm.

The purpose of our visit was to find a cobbler who would mend a pair of sandals. In one alleyway we found just the man. He was sitting on an upturned box, stitching shoes together, with a boy apprentice beside him. We watched them. First the sole was selected and the leather sewn laboriously around it inside out. Then, turning it outside out, the final titivating was done by the boy, who was already adept with the immense cobbler's needle both of them were using.

Roger sat on a box and removed his sandals. A clean piece of paper was set beneath his feet and the cobbler got to work at great speed. A little crowd gathered, all smiling and friendly, jabbering away, as if we were an eclipse of the moon. It was growing dark, so they drew out an electric light bulb on a flex, from a hole in the wall, and dangled the light over the workers. At another street stall next door, a barber was shaving the heads of his clients and, on the other side of the road, an old woman was brewing a kind of stew and selling it to people sitting before her on upturned boxes.

In half an hour the shoes were completed and we were delighted by the excellence of the work. We retrieved the car and drove back up the mountain, feeling we had discovered an excellent artisan and made several friends.

Chapter Four

Men-at-Arms

Officers and Men

This afternoon I am alone in camp, apart from some twelve gunners, the guards, a generator attendant, the Orderly Sergeant and a few men on fatigues. It is Wednesday afternoon and Roger and the Sergeant Major are playing cricket with some of the lads, while the others are away swimming. I have just played two games of badminton on our new court marked out on the road below the camp. Last week, I swam in the troop swimming sports and came last in the back stroke. The Battery Captain came last in the next race, so we had a mutual congratulation.

Most of the time now, Roger and I are the only officers in camp and run it together with our Sergeant Major, a kindly man of about forty years, with a good knowledge of men and officers. Our routine daily work is taken up almost entirely in chasing the men and getting them to do the jobs they are supposed to do.

I am on good terms with my batman, our cook corporal and several others and enjoy hearing their ideas. I was touched the other day, when I was told by one of the cooks that he had ten letters to write. It was his twenty-first birthday and he seemed rather forlorn, so I talked with him awhile and he told me about himself and his family. I can imagine the labour ten letters will be for him. Some of these lads take five minutes to spell out a sentence and the effort they put into writing is agonising to watch. From time to time, one or other of the men uses his section officer as a shoulder to weep upon and I am learning the appropriate 'bedside manner'. I have been hospital visiting several times now and it is often difficult to know what to talk about with a sick gunner, with few interests in life, except

Hank Jansen and any comics he can lay his hands on. Even so, I have not failed entirely and manage to leave the man smiling when I depart.

This whole outfit is not unlike a glorified outdoor school. Man-management is the side of army life I enjoy most. Every new soldier presents a challenge. You have to get him on your side before he will do anything for you. Giving orders to men has no real effect, unless they respect the order and are encouraged in carrying it out.

The sergeants are the hardest nuts to crack. They understand very well that they know far more about army life and are more expert with the equipment than a national service subaltern can be. It is vital that the roles of sergeant and subaltern in interaction are appropriate. The sergeant has the clearly defined duty to work the machines and to see that his team, be it on the guns or in the control room, understands the work properly. The officer supplies the orders controlling the use of the apparatus, and on him rests the responsibility for any action. Many young officers either tend to assume the sergeant's role and tinker about with the machines themselves, while the sergeant stands aside with a know-all look on his face making dark comments to his men; or else they give a few ineffective or ambiguous commands, thus losing control of the sergeant, who interprets the command his way and, thereby, takes over the officer's role. Like other subalterns, I have had to feel my way and to discover how to exert authority based on accurate knowledge. This is especially important if the sergeant is a little truculent, and many old soldiers are.

The men are easier. In many cases an officer can learn their jobs in a few minutes and carry them out if need be – to set an example. There are exceptions however; the REME mechanics and Radar operators have specialised technical knowledge, which they like to keep to themselves as a personal mystique.

Every Tuesday all the officers assemble at RHQ for the Commanding Officer's training day. The CO usually gives a forceful lecture, in which we learn to "get our fingers out", to "start sparking – Gentlemen!" and in which the adjective "bloody" is used as punctuation rather than descriptively. Chris and I squirm with delight at his military clichés but we find him a powerful speaker and a joy to hear. He growls away till some of his audience are almost asleep and then bombards us with the most searching questions. Failure to answer is followed by a freezing silence or a muttered crescendo:

"Every bloody subaltern still in his bloody cradle ought to know that –
so *why don't you?*"

I am in charge of the "Star Classification" system, whereby the
men undertake a series of aptitude tests, in order to improve their
qualifications through attendance at appropriate courses. In this way,
I gain much information about each man. It leads to a certain amount
of welfare work on the men's behalf. Two days ago, I had to write to
one of the lads' elder brother. The family had become worried about
him. I said he was well, had volunteered for Korea but would not be
sent there because of his defective eyesight, for which he had recently
seen a specialist, who had prescribed a new pair of glasses. I hope
somebody's mum is a little happier.

The other evening, the Troop Commander, Roger and I sat down
to write the yearly reports on our soldiers. Each one consists of a
fairly comprehensive account of a man's abilities, aptitudes and likely
progress. It is intended as a guide to potential employers, when a man
has completed National Service and returns to civilian life. There is
no mincing matters in these reports for we are as truthful as our
collective and personal bias can allow. Naturally, a report tries to
bring out the best qualities of a man but sometimes it is difficult to do
so. I am inclined to paint a double picture, expressing the man's bad
points but, then, referring to such good or redeeming qualities he may
have. Instead of damning or praising a man out of hand we try to
achieve a reasonable balance.

We take into consideration: i. personal habits, tidiness etc, ii.
sobriety or otherwise, iii. stability and maturity, iv. ability to do jobs
of stated categories with or without supervision. As the evening wore
on, I was interested to see that, again and again, we were using the
same pairs of adjectives to differentiate an individual's qualities. I
made a list of them and tried to see the connection between them and
what they might say about our troop, as a group of individuals. In my
tabulation, I tried to show what influence these words may have on a
job to which a man is suited and which may be within his abilities.

Adjective and Quality	*Its opposite*	*Relationship to employment*
a Enthusiasm	Nonchalance	Determine effectiveness
Efficiency	Inefficiency	with which a man will
Reliability	Unreliability	carry out a task

b Sobriety	Hooliganism	Determine the functional
Maturity	Adolescence	character of the man, his
Friendliness	Surliness	relationship to authority
Security at home	Social insecurity	and suitability for
		responsible jobs
c Intelligence	Stupidity	Determine the social
Technical knowledge	Muddle-headed	level of occupation; i.e.
Precision of thought		whether manual, clerking
General Education	Ignorance	or technical
d Personal initiative	Idleness	Determine the ability of a
Dominance	Hesitancy	man to lead and hence
Ability to influence	Easily overruled	suitability as NCO,
others	Easily influenced	foreman or authoritative
	by others	executive in any form

If a man in enthusiastic, reliable, sober, cooperative, lives in a happy home with a good wife, has a good education, has done well in some technical course and shows an ability to influence others positively, then he scores top marks and the references he will take to a future employer will be impressive. One of our REME men is just such a case. He maintains the Radar sets in action, through all sorts of trials (including the interference of ignorant and muddle-headed officers!) and to do so he works overtime, often till eleven at night, checking voltages, amperages, connections and valves, all with complex wiring diagrams, tricky numerical tables and small meters. He is always cheerful and sends quite half of his limited pay home to his wife each week. He is a real treasure on the site. The other REME men who look after the predictor, gun controls and other electrical equipment are also not far behind him; even if one of them is under weekly inspection for VD.

At the other extreme we have a gunner who is phlegmatic, inefficient, unreliable, irresponsible, undisciplined, socially insecure, disliked by his mates, stupid, ignorant and always in poor company – probably in a brothel, if he has enough character to enter one, or mooching about by himself. He is constantly in detention and forty pounds in debt. All we could do was to hint that in another job he might do better.

Most, of course, are in between these extremes. One gunner is a strong lad from the north of England, with curly black hair, a bit of a gypsy, who avoids trouble by the skin of his teeth. His enthusiasm depends upon the quality of the leadership given by an officer or NCO. He can be resentful and almost disobedient, if handled badly and, being a dominant personality, can influence others towards insubordination. Given clear orders, however, he will do a job well. Wild at times, often disgruntled, he is nonetheless usually sober and clean living but not very bright. He will do a supervised job well but can be unreliable, if he gets resentful. Promotion to Lance Bombadier might make him more responsible and allow him to use his powerful personality effectively.

Then there is one of my welfare cases. Gunner Jimmy Worrel is, undoubtedly, a pretty boy and a number of ladies in Kowloon know it. He is an honest, kindly lad, who visits Chinese families as a guest of their daughters. Always cheery, bright blue eyes always sparkling, mischievous, he has a wicked grin. His mother has not written to him for months, so I wrote a letter to her this week, hoping to stir some buried maternal instinct. The Troop Commander said my letter was a masterpiece of guile and young Jimmy himself was delighted with it. I doubt if any mother could resist the appeal. Yet, little does she know that Jimmy is far from being the lonely boy I made out; he can make friends at a moment's notice with almost anyone. He is, however, worried about her and I saw puzzled affection in his face as he spoke of her.

I will write anything to get these selfish parents to write to their sons. I know only too well how deserted one can feel, when the hoped-for mail fails to arrive. I am lucky; if there is nothing in one post I am sure there will be something in the next. Jimmy has signed on for three years solely because he says his parents care nothing for him and there was no point in hurrying home. On top of this, some remote uncle writes to him asking for money for his mother. He is already sending seventeen and six a week, so I told him not to send more, until he knows why it is needed.

Our MO considers my Medical Orderly the best in the regiment. He keeps his little medical inspection room spotless, except for a large ginger cat with a kink in his tail, and he treats the men with firmness and confidence. He is a dominant personality who expresses his opinion loudly and aggressively to officers and men alike. He is, therefore, sometimes difficult to manage, especially since, if he were ever to be put on a charge for insubordination, the camp would suffer by his absence. He could easily come out in a resentful revolt and is best either led tactfully or given an order very sharply and suddenly, from as far away as possible. Nonetheless, he is a good judge of character and I doubt whether he would so misjudge the authority of an officer as to go too far. I have heard him come close to swearing at the Sergeant Major but, since he had a lad with a temperature of 104° on his hands that evening, we decided to let it pass.

The story was like this. When the MO was away in Macao for a weekend, one of our gunners took sick. At six thirty Drabble ran in to me, "Sir, come quickly, Jameson has a temperature of 106°!" Certainly the man was lying on his bed smothered in blankets, sweating gallons and very pale and clammy. I rang for an ambulance but then decided to fix up a bed in the three-tonner and take him at once to hospital myself, thus cutting the time by half an hour. We put three mattresses on top of one another, the sick boy on top and trundled out of camp, Drabble and I in the back keeping anxious watch. Drabble, having recovered from his initial panic, was superb, keeping the lad smiling all the way. At hospital, we were commended for our prompt action in driving him to town straight away. Jameson had tonsillitis, but fortunately they did not have to operate and he was soon back with us fit and well.

Drabble ought to be in the RAMC for he is always in and out of the hospitals learning new things. Before coming to Brickhill, he had been a dog handler, a difficult job requiring skill, a strong mind and constant vigilance. The army dogs are often poorly trained and several handlers have been badly mauled by them. Drabble himself was knocked down by a dog in its cage once and it stood over him for two hours before he was rescued.

Our Catering Corps corporal is a fine cook and baker who rules his cookhouse with a rod of iron. My main job as messing officer is to keep him here – since his food is a great factor in maintaining our morale. Away from his job, he is a rather unpredictable man, a fine athlete, a swimmer for the Colony team that beat Singapore recently, a beautiful diver, a fine gymnast and the possessor of a rare physique. When stripped, he looks like an advertisement for Charles Atlas body culture and he knows it. He has thousands of pictures of himself, 'poses' they are called in the body culture world, poised on a rock or posturing in various muscular attitudes on diving boards, parallel bars or ropes. He will talk about himself for hours and is moody, subject to depression. He lives an entirely body-oriented life and often seems surprisingly immature. He is kindly, works hard, often in overtime, and is a good disciplinarian when need be. He was in the merchant navy for some years before he joined the army and has been to many far-away places; South America, Buenos Aires which he calls BA, Chile and Easter Island with its strange monoliths. He speaks good Spanish and some Cantonese and claims to know more about the practical enjoyment of sex than any one else in camp. Last night he played with a homosexual in the public gardens below the Governor's house, and, in the company of another bombadier, enjoyed a 'knee trembler' at the back of the Cheero Club with a prostitute, who possessed, in addition to a pretty face, a document signed by a Hong Kong doctor saying she was free from disease. He tells a good story about the Hong Kong 'queers' club', which is not repeatable here.

There may be many outside the army who find such goings-on shocking, but to most of our lads these events are the accepted thing, part of an evening's pleasure and entirely without shame, embarrassment or vice, simply a 'bit of a cunt', as they say, which ranks about equally with a 'booze-up' or a 'western' film. Our cook admits that he is usually not entirely sober when he lets go like this but, then – "It's so dull being sober all the time." As their officers, we exercise a certain amount of tact and tend to 'look the other way', but, when we ride back to camp in the truck with them, leaving the Cheero Club near midnight, they love to tell of their evening's adventures.

Fortunately, their private and military lives seem to be entirely separate and discipline and respect on site seem better now than when I arrived. The Troop Commander knows little of these concerns, indeed, if he knew as much as I do about his men, he'd have a fit. He knows such things go on but the reality of it all never reaches him. He speaks of the men as if they were somehow from another plane, a sort of decadent species, much less important than his beloved machines. The other day, he said to me in a puzzled voice, as if the thought had just struck him and he doubted whether it was a proper one, "Do you think they are happy?" What could I say? I felt like asking him "Are you?"

I was quite touched the other day. When it became known that a new regular lieutenant would be joining the site, one or two people thought that would mean I would be posted elsewhere. The long faces of the two lads brightened when I told them I was not going anywhere. Such expressions are very reassuring because, although I care little for the army, I identify myself with the men rather than with the officers and try to lead by influence rather than by shouting orders. A section officer on this lonely site has to be authoritative but also a bit of a doctor, an impartial friend to each and all and sometimes, perhaps, a kind of priest. The men are so lovably stupid; they let one down one minute and do wonders the next.

I am trying to understand all this. It is true to say that many of the soldiers here have their horizons severely limited by lack of initiative, poor intelligence, social insecurity and little education. They know of little more than their own bodies, the things they touch, pop music, sex and the cosy dark of a cinema, where their personalities merge with the phantoms on the screen. It is dangerous to think these ineptitudes are inherited; they seem an expression of our social system. A major said to me the other day, "Considering Britain's education system and the sums we spend on projects for the benefit of youth, we really produce very disappointing people. In Malaya, I preferred many of the Malay soldiers to our own. It wasn't like that in the old days."

With greater discriminative ability, a man may do what he wishes rather than what the group wishes. He discriminates between friends and can read character in others. This seems to be the beginning of thought and intellect for the whole structure of literature, art, science and the cultured life is based on fine discrimination between objective qualities which produce corresponding feeling in the subjective self. Only some half dozen of our men could sense such fine differences. Very few possess 'sensibility', yet this is simply an ability to discriminate.

*

Firing Camp

Every so often we fire our guns in earnest. At Firing Camp the CO turns up to watch, a plane flies slowly to and fro over the sea before us, dragging a sleeve several hundred yards behind it and we attempt to shoot it off. Because we face the open sea, other troops come here to fire our guns, which puts pressure on us to keep them and all the gear in order. Normally something goes wrong. Indeed, this equipment is extraordinarily tricky to keep working just right. The CO fumes and blows his top, Battery commanders, majors, lieutenants and we lesser fry whizz about trying to avoid the larger brickbats, while the sergeants struggle to keep the show on the road.

On the last day of firing camp, our troop redeemed itself. The Troop Commander flung himself on the equipment the evening before and, thanks to his undoubted skills, all the early morning checks went through without trouble. At 11.30 hours prompt, the scheduled time, we put up our first round of 'check fire' and found it well within the tolerances allowed. We even had to wait while the target plane came on course. Then away we went, tracker and radar engagements coming one after the other in quick succession. As plotting officer in the control room, it was most exciting to see the little spots on the cathode ray tube of the Electronic Plan Position Indicator chasing along, showing the geographical position of the target, to hear the orders and reports coming through without hitch and, then, a great moment of power, giving the order – *'fire!'* The gun crews did well, one chap banging the firing plate so hard that he enabled our troop to fire off more ammunition than any other during the whole fortnight. We have since given him a stripe, the restitution of one he lost some six months ago. The sky was neatly spotted with straight lines of puffs of smoke and, at the end of the day, the CO pronounced himself almost pleased.

On two days I performed the duties of Gun Safety Officer. This is a tricky and responsible job, intended to ensure that the guns do not fire directly at the aircraft or at ships on the sea. One has to stand right behind the gun, avoiding the bouncing shell cases after discharge, and peer through the smoke to check that the gun is traversing at the right speed and has not crossed the permissible practice arcs, beyond which one might hit a vessel. What with the continuous explosions and the strain of watching the rapidly moving gun, it is nerve racking. Diffident safety officers hold up the show and receive the wrath of the CO for so doing. I decided to obey a simple rule told to me by a senior subaltern – "When the CO looks your way let go – if you hit a junk, he'll be delighted." The CO admitted he was "a bit British" about junks trespassing over the firing range. Once, when we were clearing a misfire at elevation zero and thus aiming at the sea, I really did hesitate because a small steamer had started to enter our range. I appealed to the Chief Safety Officer but the CO intervened. "FIRE!" he yelled. Whoosh – the shell bit the water a hundred yards from the vessel which fairly skidded out of harm's way.

*

Dinner Night

Once a month, there is an extraordinary function at the regimental mess at Stanley Fort. On Dinner Night all the officers of the regiment tog up in their best blues trousers, white dress shirt with bow tie, starched monkey jacket and dress hat. It's a magnificent rig and Roger and I feel most frightfully important, as we drive out of camp to an accompaniment of derisory gunner whistles!

The dinner is a sedate and formal affair full of regimental etiquette, toasts to the Queen, guests and other matters. The meal is often disappointing and our mess cook at Brickhill could do better. At the end round comes the port and the cigar box. The cigars are excellent but only a few of us attempt them. Cigar smoking after dinner is pleasing and I choose one carefully. On one occasion, a junior subaltern committed the unthinkable error of fumbling with the port decanter and spilling a spot on the table. The Mess President, a real warthog, gave him an extra day as orderly officer for that. After the meal, there are social 'games' to be endured. We throw each other about, balance on beer bottles, play a damaging form of leapfrog and sometimes rugger in our mess kits, acclaimed as the height of revelry. The CO reveals, by a simple test, that lactic acid accumulation overcomes his stomach muscles later than those of anyone else. Well, it's not so bad, I suppose. There is usually a row of smirking, older officers looking on, clearly dreading being asked or compelled to join in, while they assume an air of smiling sympathy for those who have succumbed. I feel like an ape performing in a zoo. It is left to the subalterns to supply this sport and, suffering fools badly, I felt two such games were enough last time. Chris and I, feeling like anti-social criminals, crept away with a quantity of beer and played billiards. Next time, Chris is bringing his chess set.

*

Typhoon, August 14th 1953

All yesterday evening, large black clouds meandered across our southern horizon and I went up to sit near the guns and watch the sun set. It was a furnace of glowing gold, deepening to a rich ruby crimson, shooting out purple beams in a magnificent fan across the width of the sky. It was as if the old Japanese flag had come alive. Then, as the purple sky deepened into nightfall, the cloud thickened, rolling in fast from the south east, bringing a night of impenetrable blackness, broken only by our powerful perimeter lights. After nine o'clock, the sky was broken by vivid flashes of sheet lightning, etching the horizon suddenly with the black silhouettes of islands and casting a momentary silver glare upon the sea. Typhoon warning one had been issued and the two green lights on the mast of the Aberdeen police station indicated the possibility of strong winds.

I was orderly officer and, before dark, I checked all gun and radar covers and had the radar paraboloids lowered on the sets. I sat down to read in the mess but, on turning out the guard at midnight, found the signal had changed to red over green. I fetched the typhoon orders and looked up the signal; "Winds increasing – gale force". Outside, however, the night remained calm, so I went to bed giving orders that I should be called if the signal was to change again.

Soon after one thirty, one of the guards rushed into my room.

"Aberdeen flying red over red, Sir!"

I knew the orders for the final precautions to be taken in the face of an oncoming storm, so I was up in a moment and down the hill to the guardroom. The guard was to collect as many men as might be needed and I told the Guard Commander what to do.

"Remove radar paraboloids. Lock and lash down all guns. Remove the tracker from the Command Post. All vehicles to be parked on the lower road, with their canvas covers removed. Typhoon bars to be fixed on windows and doors. All personnel confined to camp for the duration of the warning."

The telephone rang.

"Orderly Officer RHQ speaking."

"Orderly Officer Brickhill here."

"Typhoon warning number seven just issued. Do all you have to do."

"Wilco – that all?"

"Yep – and here's to you!"

The wind had risen considerably and gusts were striking the exposed gun positions with some velocity. The men, as cheerful and as delighted as schoolboys snowballing in a year's first fall, worked with tremendous good will and humour. We had a frantic ten minutes looking for torches to unscrew the radar paraboloids. Several of us had to climb up on top of the sets, the windiest spot on site, and fiddle with nuts and bolts, not knowing when the next ferocious gust would hurl itself out of the night and perhaps fling us all into the valley below. Our nervousness added zest and amusement to the work. One vehicle with a flat tyre had to be manhandled out of the wind but, at last, everything was stowed away or battened down and we prepared to go to sleep. My radar bombadier came up to me.

"Sir, may I apply for a junk licence?"

"A what, Bombadier?"

"A junk licence, Sir. My hut is shaking so much and, with the camp situated as it is, we thought we might end up in the sea in it. We had better put ourselves right with the authorities afore the morning."

"But, yes, of course, Bombadier. I'll refer the matter to the Troop Commander first thing in the morning."

"It'll be too late by then, Sir, but I'll tell the lads. It'll reassure them."

"Well done, Bombadier. Oh and, by the way, take some tarpaulins to bed with you. You may need them as sails."

He replied with a cheery goodnight and was away into the wind and darkness.

In the morning it was blowing hard, with Radio Hong Kong reporting a tropical storm heading up from Pratas Island and due to pass a hundred miles to the south of us. HMS *Birmingham* put to sea together with an American aircraft carrier and destroyers. The harbour can be dangerous in a typhoon, with ships getting badly beached. About ten o'clock, I joined our tracker crew in the Command Post and, with target indicator, binoculars and tracker telescope, we watched a flank of the storm emerge out of the south east and pass across the face of the Lema island, a great white wall of rain, like a curtain hanging from the clouds. A *Vampire*, from Kai Tak airport, flew along the edge of the storm plotting its position. Around midday, a wing of the storm hit us, the pouring rain bouncing off the rocks, creating a great mist of flying vapour. We hid indoors awaiting the worst.

At seven in the evening Roger and I collected Wong, the NAAFI manager, and together we set off around the camp, visiting the men in their billets to see everyone was indoors and well and to sell them some cigarettes and other items. It was then that the full force of the typhoon came roaring upon us with a stinging, horizontal rain shooting out of an impenetrably black night. The velocity of the wind increased and we could hear it roaring and pounding the mountain in ferocious gusts. We crept from billet to billet bent double, our legs braced, clutching at the rocky sides of the camp road and clinging to the rails beside the steps going up to the telephone exchange. As we rounded each corner, we were repeatedly blown flat against the rock face beside the path and had to hold on to prevent ourselves being blown over. Wong, a lightly-built, little man, was nearly sent over the side of the hill by one gust but, luckily, grasped a ledge in time.

The telephone exchange is near the Command Post at the highest point of the camp and it took us quite five minutes to struggle up the steps to it. We were fighting to open the door, when a violent blast hit us, whipped the door open and dragged the operator, who was on the inside holding the handle, violently out into the cold air. Having just got out of bed, he was naked and his sudden apparition sent us into peals of laughter. The poor lad crept back hastily between his sheets and promptly purchased fifty cigarettes. By this time, he told us, we had no telephone communication with the outside world and he assumed the lines were down. The wireless had also broken a valve, so we had no news of the progress of the typhoon either. As we left the exchange, another gust swept me clean off my feet and threw me two yards over the ground against the bank. My companions were blown down the steps and had to cling to the rocks at the side for dear life.

In the end we visited everyone; they were quite happy with bottles of beer, their own good company and stacks of cigarettes. As we were leaving the last billet, two of the guards rushed in, followed by a flurry of rain.

"Cables are down – sparks flying everywhere!"

Out we went into the night and groped our way towards the generators. Suddenly, from a twenty foot pylon some thirty feet in front of us, a stream of sparks went crackling out along the wind and another cable fell wriggling on the path before us, while further sparks showered down from the pylon.

We now had to reach the generators and turn them off before somebody was electrocuted; with water everywhere there was considerable danger. The Signals Bombadier, who was with us, rushed off into the blackness ahead and, grabbing a torch from one of the guards, I crept forward, finally sprinting across the danger area with the two guards at my heels. As we arrived at the generators, Roger appeared, having come by another route, and, together, we got the nearly frantic Chinese operator to switch off. At once the camp was plunged into total darkness. We climbed down from the generator site to the path below and, stepping carefully, sorted out the muddle of fallen cables. I went off to the store to collect hurricane lamps and, on the way, found more cables over the road. An hour or two later saw the loose cables cut down and stowed away; lamps taken to each room and myself blown flat on my face, while making my way up the slope to the officers' mess.

Roger and I had a double brandy apiece, took our dinner and ventured forth towards our rooms. By this time, part of the cookhouse boiler shed had been carried away down the hillside, the Nissen hut of the Radar operators was shaking dangerously, corrugated sheeting from the NAAFI roof had narrowly missed a bombadier's head, two chimney stacks, innumerable tins and a couple of diesel drums were rolling along the road, my room was two inches deep in water and my bedding soaked. I fixed up a mattress on the floor of Roger's room and slept there.

Our Chinese in the mess did not enjoy the typhoon – until afterwards. As the wind howled around the mess and we ate supper in the light of a home-made oil lamp, both cook and the waiter Lau Chi Wing said hardly a word. Next morning, however, with the wind dropped – the usual grins and "Jolly good typhoon – eh!" We had a visitor in the mess throughout the storm. A bulbul, a thrush-sized hill bird, had hit the truck on its last trip up the hill. It was very ill at the height of the storm but, like the barometer, it got better as the winds passed.

The men on guard had done a magnificent job under truly alarming conditions. The sight of two of our guards, in overcoats and tin hats, tripping down the slope to the guardroom in the wind, holding hands, amused me immensely. "Well, Sir, we was abaht blown to Aberdeen just now and we'd rather go together than separately!"

Morale among the lads is at its highest on these occasions and, on that account, I only wish they were more frequent. Under alarming and chaotic conditions the indomitable character of the ordinary Britisher appears with humour, high spirits and good cheer. The boys here are tough and good; I only wish there was something better for them to do.

In the morning, we found that a corrugated iron roof from a fair-sized shed, complete with wooden frame, had been lifted by the storm, carried through the air over the crest of the hill between the officers' mess and the sergeants' quarters and deposited in one piece some way down the hillside. We were thankful the troop had come through without a casualty.

Chapter Five

Social Encounters

Chinese restaurant, September 26th 1953

I had gained an introduction to a Chinese professor at the university, who was willing to take me out to dinner and tell me about China. It was Saturday evening and the Hong Kong waterfront was teeming with people darting about between the overflowing pavements and the long rows of cars, taxis and rickshaws, jostling along the centre of the road. Ma Meng was the son of a well-known Chinese scholar who had a special knowledge of painting and the arts. His own interests were in sociology and anthropology and he had studied at the London School of Economics. I met him at his house below the university and, after some Chinese tea and introductions to his family, we ventured forth and threaded our way through the streets. At his home, I found myself embarrassed by strangely addressing this cultured man in the pidgin English of our mess waiters! He made no comment but I reprimanded myself severely and kept a close watch on my tongue.

Sea-going junks were busy loading and unloading along the quayside and, on some of them, the Festival of the Hungry Ghosts was in such full swing that the boats were almost invisible, beneath the masses of bunting and paper decoration that covered them. Just beyond the pier for the steamer to Macao, Mr Ma told me that we had arrived and, turning abruptly out of the arcading, we climbed a steep flight of narrow stairs at the back of a ground floor shop. As we entered the restaurant, the waiters bowed and smiled and one of them led us through the mass of little tables to one which looked out over the waterfront, the busy junketings and the harbour, stretching away to the shining white buildings and big ships along the Kowloon waterfront. The room was not large and the tables covered with oilcloth.

Several were already occupied and others were being rapidly taken. Near to us, a number had been put together and a party was assembling around them, grandma on the far side, very clearly the matriarch, and several of her sons and daughters and in-laws. The children were intrigued by my European face and gazed open-mouthed in my direction. The slightest sign of a smile set them grinning but their adults at once put them in their places. It was clear that Europeans were not frequent diners in this establishment. Two men, dressed in the loosely-fitting, black clothes of the Cantonese, came in and played to us on two-stringed instruments that emitted a weird and wonderful sequence of sounds. Mr Ma told me it was a set tune of old China but I found it difficult to appreciate.

The room was filled by a deafening sound of Chinese chatter, combined with the twangings of the two-stringers and the rattle of the many Mahjong boards next door, while outside in the growing dusk the lights of the great liners, anchored in the harbour, flickered upon the waves and ferries came and went continuously. Passengers were boarding the little boat for Macao with its gay Union Jacks painted on its bows.

We were to eat a Pekingese meal. In the north of China, rice is not the basic constituent of meals; instead rich savoury batters and pastries of wheat flour are eaten, with portions of meat, fish and vegetables cooked in strongly tasting oils. We began with tea, and then three large dishes were brought in, piled high with shrimps, small pieces of chicken and larger portions of fried river fish. Each had a tantalising aroma and every morsel was a treat to lay upon the tongue. The food was transferred by ladles to small bowls or eaten with chopsticks directly from the plates. I acquitted myself passably with these instruments, the most difficult manoeuvre involving a sizeable piece of fish held with them in one hand, while one nibbled the meat from it to leave a clean bone. Eating with chopsticks is, at first, quite a strain on the muscles of the hand and brings on a kind of writer's cramp.

A plate of thin batter cakes was brought to us, filled with oily vegetables, rich, tasty and aromatic. Spring rolls followed, small toothpaste tubes of pastry filled with a pungent mixture of chopped shrimp, chicken and vegetables. All these delicacies were accompanied by sips from small glasses of Chinese rice 'wine', like a thin sherry, served hot like tea. The final dish was a refreshing soup of cabbage and vermicelli, cleansing the mouth pleasantly after the oiliness of the earlier dishes.

When we had finished, the waiters arrived with two little plates of neatly folded towels, hot and steaming after being wrung dry of water. We mopped our faces, lips and fingers and, selecting a little wooden toothpick, leaned back in our chairs to enjoy a final cup of tea, some tooth picking and a cigarette.

All the time, I was plying Mr Ma with questions to which he responded nobly. He seemed to enjoy our conversation. In the old days, Ma told me, China was a very static country. There were minor upheavals, revolutions and invasions but the country was so vast it absorbed them all, without much effect on its essential way of life. It was a pastoral, agricultural country, ruled by the "Celestial Emperor", who was always the greatest of conservatives. Prime ministers and lesser rulers were selected for office from scholars who had come up through the sieve of an extensive public examination system. A candidate had to be an expert calligrapher, intimate with the Chinese classics and philosophies and his knowledge of characters had to be immense. Such men had memories of an extraordinary capacity. Often whole books would be learned by heart. Yet, while such learning by memory required considerable mental ability, it did not encourage speculative thought or innovation in ideas. Everything hinged on the old books and ancestral law; there was never anything new in the established way. No doubt many of these mandarins were wise and, on the whole, the system worked well. They lived according to a code of gentlemanly behaviour, created by the school of Confucius and based on filial piety, the son respecting and honouring his parents and elders, while daughters kow-towed to their mothers and, especially, their mothers-in-law. The young wife of a parentally-arranged marriage was more or less a servant to the mother-in-law, who was often a vicious and cruel tyrant. Of course, in the end, the young wife became a mother-in-law in her turn, so repeating the cycle.

At the summit of the system, the Celestial Emperor reigned supreme, god, pope, king, all in one, and hidden deep in the Forbidden Palace of Peking. Civil government tended to be effective due to the respect given to elders and old laws and, although these were rigidly enforced, the people were not unduly oppressed. Any progress, in the modern European sense, was, however, well-nigh impossible. There was generally a passive acceptance of a person's social position in the cycles of family life. Criticism was heresy.

The social system was feudal, with peasants working for the lords of estates, yet successful farmers could become rich men. Wealthier men could afford the leisure to cultivate the arts, philosophies and politics. So long as an individual was bound by relative poverty and had to work to keep his family alive, such interests were barely possible. Even so, Ma said, it seems that deep down in the Chinese character there is a love of nature, silences, contemplative philosophising and idleness which those, free from physical privation, soon come to express. Confucius was at one time a minor ruler or minister, who eventually renounced office to become an itinerant teacher with attendant students and disciples. Lao-tzu, the founder of the Taoist school of thought, is also reputed to have been a member of the aristocratic classes.

During the second and third centuries BC there were many schools of philosophy in China and explorations of the meaning of life were subjects of endless discussion. Out of these emerged the Confucian ideals of the perfectly behaved and cultured man and the mystical Taoist thought of Lao. Mencius fused the two into a philosophy of leisure through the contemplation of nature as a way to happiness. These thinkers were not concerned with "God" nor with the sort of sectarianism that appears in Christianity. Laws of behaviour were associated with a love of nature, to encourage a deep feeling of a direct knowledge of the agelessness of the world. Early Taoist thought was preached by monks through riddles and quietism, "keeping oneself low" and "inaction is better than action" being important principles.

"Politics, competition and strife at court led many of the greatest politicians of China to become weary of the intrigue and corruption that went with power and they retired to their farms to philosophise, enjoy music and poetry and to practice various Taoist meditations and yogas. Tao Yuanming was such a one, but we must remember," said Ma, "that, however much he eulogised his land and his fruit trees, it was not he who worked them. Although a relatively poor landowner, he enjoyed his musical evenings." We agreed that every nation owes its culture to those who had the leisure to cultivate it, such as the upper classes in Europe since the Renaissance.

When Portuguese and British ships first appeared in the China Sea, the Celestial Emperor closed all doors in the face of the "barbarian outsider" (Fan Kwai). Europeans were pitied for their lack of enlightened high culture and treated as lesser beings. Their extraordinary success in reaching the Chinese shores at all did not seem to strike the rulers as significant.

The British were allowed to set up warehouses in a reserved cantonment outside Canton and from their so-called 'factories' they could conduct trade. They were allowed no women, either European or Chinese, and the rules for their behaviour were strict. No travelling in China was permitted. The Emperor believed he could contain the influence of the foreigner in this way, not appreciating Professor Toynbee's later point that even the smallest penetration by a powerful culture into another civilisation will lead to changes in the more static way of life.

The behaviour of the British merchants was as vindictive as that of the Chinese was non-cooperative. Opium was grown cheaply in India and shipped to the dens of old China. Soon it was causing great social harm and the Emperor ordered a halt to it. He cut off the 'factories' from Canton city and rebuffed all gestures of goodwill. The Opium War followed but, along the coast of China, the Emperor's ill-equipped forces stood little chance against the advanced seamanship and gunnery of the Royal Navy. Eventually, a treaty was signed giving the British five trading ports, including Shanghai and Canton. Hong Kong was acquired for open trading from its splendid harbour.

From this time on the westernisation of China proceeded apace with Christian missionaries streaming in. There were many interchanges, the Europeans finding Chinese art and culture fascinating and the etiquette and "quaint" customs intriguing; yet they were also convinced of their moral superiority over this heathen people. The Chinese, meanwhile, remained convinced of their own cultural superiority but admitted a limited admiration for western creativity. Old political forms collapsed and the imperial court dissolved. Sun Yat-sen attempted to establish a form of democracy in China and was followed by Chiang Kai-shek, who originally held similar high principles. His regime, faced with economic and political problems on all sides, became repressive and wealthy ministers began to practice intrigue and corruption, much as before. He lost the faith of most of the people. By and large, the Communist victory under Mao Tse-tung was welcomed by the majority of ordinary Chinese as a chance to remove corruption from their lives.

Ma Meng believed that Mao was a shrewd and brilliant man who, through a profound and intimate knowledge of Chinese ways, was introducing a poisoned pill into Chinese life and thought. The sweeping reforms of the first phase of the revolution, the changes in land ownership, the ending of traditions, such as the bound feet of women, and the establishment of women's rights, were all to the good and the imposition of change by force had not been unknown in China's long history. Many people were delighted by the dramatic and refreshing reforms. Indeed, many Chinese, in other parts of Asia, turned their heads hopefully to China. The progressive restriction of personal liberty under an intolerant police state had, however, spread insidiously like a fungus through the arteries of an only partially revived national life. Independence of thought, criticism and creative argument were increasingly replaced by oppression and indoctrination, expressed in simplistic slogans which everyone had to believe. Ma said that never had personal freedom been so restricted as it was now in China and, as in the days of the old empire, China had closed her doors on outside influence.

Ma went on, "We Chinese intellectuals of Hong Kong and Southeast Asia are in a very unhappy position for we are loyal Chinese but to whom? We have little empathy with Mao's communism and even less for the old clique in Taiwan, which represents no political force nowadays."

I asked him about the refusal of the USA to recognise the new China politically. Ma said that this was about the most unrealistic policy that any such powerful nation could maintain. He considered the American way of life a complete failure, lacking even the roots of true culture, concerning itself with such superficial and temporally unimportant things such as personal wealth, success, careerism and McCarthy-style witch-hunting. The US fails in both personal and national diplomacy, he informed me.

Ma Meng's own views were socialist but without adherence to any particular party. He was very critical of the social situation in Hong Kong.

"You know the medical service really only serves the rich. A Chinese coolie, without strings to pull, has no chance of medical treatment until at death's door or beyond. The middle class, shopkeepers, teachers, lecturers, and such like, are badly hit by medical charges. Doctors charge enormous rates. A maternity room in hospital incurs costs for the room, the doctor's visits and the food brought in by an outside company. Penicillin injections may cost twenty dollars [twenty-five shillings]." I was shocked by this information, remembering the fifteen or so penicillin injections I was given at Mons, when my hand was slightly crushed in an accident and the fact that, on a week's patrol, a soldier may consume some thirty-six Paludrine tablets for nothing. We have a large stock in camp. A tin of a thousand could be flogged downtown for a considerable profit.

"The social services are embryonic here and the government is, of course, undemocratic. How could it be otherwise, where the citizens feel a natural loyalty to China – even if they are not sure which one! Representation of the Chinese in government is not possible – at least for the present. Hong Kong is a colony. We understand that and, indeed, benefit from British protection and the rule of law but Chinese needs are inadequately considered. The legislature tends to be drawn from the wealthy and is elected by British citizens who, even if some of them are Chinese, are an extreme minority of the population. Chinese intellectuals have little say, since few of us are British citizens."

Ma told me that before the war it was possible to get very rich quickly in Hong Kong and some of the millionaire Chinese have houses in Europe and America and move around with the seasons. Concubinage remains frequent and, when the legislature was about to declare it illegal, one influential member announced it was bad to interfere with old customs. Privately he had said that, as a solicitor, he would lose most of his clients if he supported the motion.

Ma Meng became upset and so angry, as he told me this, that for a moment he lost the fluency of his English. Au Boon Haw and the other wealthy cranks of Hong Kong would donate a hospital here or there but their whole way of life was false and absurdly luxurious, he said.

"I do not like the rich of Hong Kong. They do not love China. They have no love for Hong Kong. They care only for themselves and their wealth and keep in place old practices that long ago should have been consigned, like themselves, to a dustbin!"

I sympathised with his mood. The great differences between rich and poor here, the grandeur of the Peak mansions and the fantastically expensive cars that cannot go far on a small island, are indeed vulgar, in a way that only the mindless rich can be.

Ma told me of his friends in Hong Kong, their hopes and despair.

"We cannot do anything in our time. War would bring no good to China, only devastation, as in Korea. My generation will never go back. We can only hope that, in the circle of years, peace and freedom for the individual will return again."

He told me that he felt an ever present fear of Communist expansion throughout the world.

"The Communists have one set purpose whereas the West can never speak with one voice. American physical strength may well, in the end, be the only deterrent. Yet we cannot predict the future from day to day or year by year events. It is the larger, often unknown, forces at work behind history that are vital, not the transience of day-to-day incidents. History cannot be read from a chapter of incidents!"

We walked back along the waterfront and stopped to view the brilliantly-lit junks arrayed for the Hungry Ghosts festival. On one of the vessels, a puppet show was in progress, fantastic colours and costumes. On the other, Taoists were officiating over a ceremony. A high priest sat in scarlet robes and crown below a resplendent array of electric lights, flashing in all imaginable colours. One, in particular, flashed on and off within a great, scarlet, plastic heart. What with all the bowing, tinkling of little bells, chanting and clashing of cymbals, I supposed some religious rite was in progress but I experienced it more as a Whit Monday fair in England.

I was grateful to Mr Ma for a richly informative evening, a wonderful tutorial, as it were, on the history of China and the situation in Hong Kong. I felt moved by his impassioned sense of social justice and saddened by his plight and that of his friends, isolated from the great culture they loved so well and saw so threatened by a soulless creed.

*

The Sino-British Club, October 10th 1953

For the most part the Chinese and the British in Hong Kong go their own ways in their characteristic communities. The culture vultures, however, do make some attempt to bring the races together and to foster mutual understanding for those interested in such things. The Sino-British Club has this as its aim and, one evening, Roger and I went to one of its festive parties. The club was meeting at the palatial residence of Mrs Violet Chan, a wealthy hostess, who has created quite a 'salon' for intellectuals and artists. Her house, well up on Hong Kong mountain, was a magnificent Georgian structure, with terrace and lawn below a balustrade opening on an immense view of the harbour and Kowloon.

The rooms appeared somewhat Edwardian in style but more spacious and set with monumental Chinese furniture and cabinets full of delightful little ornaments and many fat Buddhas, sitting, reclining and laughing uproariously. Some of the many pictures and hanging scrolls were remarkable. We gathered in one of the main rooms to hear a musical recital put together by the Maestro Civaldi, an extravagant-looking Italian, with flowing hair and wild eyes, who is professor of the Hong Kong music school. A tenor and two sopranos sang for us. One of the girls, a film star from Shanghai, besides singing with charm and ability, was strikingly beautiful. Beauty in Chinese women is a very particular sort; some faces are too oriental for me but some, rather Spanish in style, surpass any English girl I have so far known. Physically they appear slim and more finely-built than our native girls, an appearance the gunners call "streamlining", seemingly athletic and wiry rather than hothouse plants.

Their usual clothes are long, tight-fitting dresses of a fine material, with a high, starched collar and a slit up the side, cunningly revealing a leg which is, without question, attractive.

The recital enabled me to compare European songs, Italian and English, with the Chinese. The European songs seemed concerned with the subject of the song and his love, springing from internal emotion and romance. The Chinese songs, by contrast, whether concerned with love or not, had a quality of space about them, as if the singer, besides being conscious of herself and her love, was aware of the immensity of mountains, the silence of the hills and the lone cry of the wind; a backcloth of disinterested mystery and impersonal beauty. The evening closed with Hong Kong's prima ballerina giving us a delightful piece of ballet, for which there was much applause. I was a bit overcome by it all, not being used to occasions such as this.

We met Mr Ma again at the recital and had a conversation about the Hong Kong University where he taught. Only the rich can afford to send their children there and the education is primarily in English. Entry is by examination and not at all easy; many are disappointed. Mr Ma argued that these features prevented many excellent young people from having higher education. He would like to see a Chinese language university in Hong Kong, run by Chinese professors in their own way, yet embodying principles of democracy promoted by such great modernisers as Sun Yat-sen. He believed that students from such a Chinese university, which does not exist anywhere in Asia at present, would do much to spread peace and critical thought among Asian peoples. Such a university would not be modelled on the American type for these were already common in the East and did not truly reflect the history and culture of China.

At present, many able young Chinese seek higher education in Canton where they find excellent technical teaching in agriculture and engineering but little cultural or historical learning, since everything is taught from the perspective of Marxism. Furthermore, once they go to Canton, they have difficulty in returning.

Mr Ma deplored the decline in the knowledge of Chinese thought, history and art due to communism within China and the lack of job opportunities in the Arts and Humanities in Hong Kong.

*

The Moon Festival

The Chinese love festivals and public holidays and there are a lot of them in Hong Kong. Roger and I went into town for the Moon Festival. The typhoon had gone on its way and, for a week, a great moon had swung across the sky, shedding a charmed light over the mountains, streams and valleys. Silvery paths shimmered endlessly on the ripples of a calm sea.

Down in the city the streets were rivalling the moon in brilliance. The crowds spread all over the roads and pavements, cheery, laughing Chinese people, many carrying little paper lanterns in which candles glimmered joyfully. The decorated shops beamed into the arcades, their doors bright with the electrically flashing eyes of dragons, huge lion heads and other faces peering down into the roadway. In places, the arcades were so densely packed with overhead lanterns that the whole air seemed full of dazzling lights. These lanterns were made from coloured paper or cloth, built up on a frame of fine cane to which long tassels were added. Within some of these lights revolved painted scenes, powered by the heat of a candle or light bulb. Some were made in the shapes of fish, aeroplanes, caramcora fruits, spiniferous prawns or lobsters and other creatures. Jolly, fluffy-headed Chinese children filled the streets, each carrying one of these paper creations illuminated from within. One of the chief characters of the festival is the little paper Moon Rabbit, a fluffy and usually rather unleporid-like creature, with which the kiddies love to play. The Hare gave its life for the Buddha, so one story says, and so it was deified and lives on the Moon. In all directions, fire crackers were exploding dramatically, like bursts of rifle fire. To the delight of the onlookers, one set of crackers exploded on the top of a tram.

The festival is a mixture of a harvest rejoicing and a feast of women, who play the major role in the simple ceremonies in their homes, dedicating a meal and clothing to the Lady of the Moon, whom the Taoists, particularly, venerate on this day. Tables under moonlight were set out in the streets, with various offerings set out upon them, as if waiting for an important guest. There were bowls and chopsticks, cups of tea, bowls of festival fruits, paracines and caramcoras, a large plate on which lay a set of clothes and a pile of moon cakes, one for each of the months of the Chinese year.

The Chinese know a lot about the moon, our mess cook had told us, because one of the ancient emperors went there. Unlike normal mortals, emperors had the good fortune to mix with magicians, Taoist priests and yogis. One day, the emperor was strolling under the moonlight and remarked to his favourite magician how wonderful the moon was. "Would you like to visit it?" asked the magician. Of course the emperor was intrigued with the idea so, when the magician threw his girdle in the air and it extended itself into a bridge reaching right up to the moon, the two of them set off. They visited the Palace of Jade where Chang O, the Lady of the Moon, lives with her fairies and there they found the great cassia tree, below which the Moon Rabbit sat pounding pills of immortality in a mortar, using a three-legged toad as a pestle. The emperor was very happy and wanted to stay but just then a white tiger, sacred animal of autumn, appeared and the magician advised that it was time to depart. Back in his palace, the emperor still heard the music of the Jade Palace running in his mind, so he wrote it down. The flute music the emperor composed is said to be that from which the traditions of the Chinese opera are descended. Even today, therefore, we may hear the music of the Jade Palace in the moon.

I was so intrigued by these stories that I wanted to know more of them. I soon discovered that Chinese folk tales are a veritable jungle of overlapping and entwining themes. Tales from the mythologies of many of the different peoples that make up China have fused and mutated in interaction, to produce an often bewilderingly complex story. Taoist stories and Buddhist stories are often mixed, so that their origins have become obscured. A Chinese film called *The Lady of the Moon* was showing at the Queens Theatre, so I was able to find out more about the central plot of the festival.

Once upon a time, a very long time ago indeed, a time so ancient that peace and tranquillity reigned, the beautiful lady Chang O lived in a mountainous valley. One day, she was visiting the market, when she met an old prophet known to all as The Old Man of the Moon. He told her that one day she would become Queen. This appears to have troubled her widowed father who, not wanting to lose her perhaps, began to argue with him and was about to attack him when the great archer Hou Yih, who was passing by, heard the quarrel and shot two arrows through the father's long sleeves, thus pinning him to a tree. The old prophet in gratitude gave Hou Yih a red thread, assuring him that it would find him a beautiful wife. Hou Yih, with both gallantry and prescience, handed it, at once, to Chang O.

Some time later, Chang O was seated on her terrace, gazing at the moon, when the Old Man again appeared to her. "You must know that once upon a time you lived up there," he told her. "You were banished to Earth for a misdemeanour. If you accomplish a noble deed perhaps you will be allowed to return!"

There was a famine in the neighbouring lands and the merchants of the valley became inordinately rich by exporting grain at exorbitant prices. Soon, there was little left for their own people, who grew poorer even as the merchants became richer. Everywhere their practices impoverished the people and affected their moral life, so that crime and vice appeared where none had been before. Prisons had to be built for the first time and new laws made. Heaven became angry and sent an onslaught of storms and drought.

The storms were so terrible that they blew down the divine "Tree of Foo San". Below the roots of this tree were imprisoned nine golden crows, who now escaped into the sky to revolve there as nine flaming hot suns. The land became a desert and the people desperate. The ruler prayed to heaven and offered to give his throne to anyone who could rid the sky of the nine suns.

Hou Yih, the great archer, undertook the task. One version of the story says that the sun-crows used to fly back to their tree every evening and that, normally, taking it in turns, it was only one of them that went around the sky each day. The storms had set them all going at once. Hou Yih shot eight, as they were coming back in the evening. The remaining one has done duty as the sun ever since.

Hou Yih thus saved the situation and became king; not apparently a very wise one, however. He fell under the influence of the bad merchants and, only after he had almost banished Chang O into a snake pit for singing songs critical of his policies in the palace, did he relent and set up reforms. The merchants complained that they would cost too much and that the king had better attack a neighbouring state to get the wealth to support it. Chang O was never informed and became most distressed when the neighbouring ruler died in the battle, cursing Hou Yih with imminent death.

Hou Yih, naturally enough, was worried and began searching for the pills of immortality. He set up alchemical laboratories in the palace and was close to discovering the secret. The Old Man of the Moon again appeared to Chang O. "Hou Yih will have endless power if he discovers the secret of these pills," he told her. "If he succeeds it will mean endless suffering for the people. Only you can save them."

In desperation, Chang O forced a way into the laboratory and found the pills in a great safe. At that moment, Hou Yih came upon her and, as she was cornered, she ate the pills herself. Suddenly she was airborne and, like a bird, went rising high into the sky. Hou Yih shot arrow after arrow after her but still she flew onwards and upwards. Crowds heard the news and, in great anger, stormed the palace and destroyed the laboratories. Hou Yih died in a flaming tower. Chang O flew on till she reached the Moon and lived there ever after in her palace of jade.

The cassia tree has long been known for its medicinal properties. If a leaf from the one on the moon falls to earth on Moon Festival night, the woman who finds it will become pregnant. The Moon Rabbit symbolises the moon itself because, like the moon, it never blinks and is therefore always awake at night. The hare-rabbit is also said to give birth by spitting its young out of its mouth. This, again, is like the moon, which is eaten every month by the dark toad, who later spits it out of its mouth again. Rabbit and Toad represent the eternal cycle of life. The Moon Rabbit sits below the cassia tree pounding out the pills of immortality, using the toad as his tool.

In a curiously uncomfortable story ending, one version of the tale has it that Chang O was chased so hard that, when she reached the moon, she had a fit of coughing and disgorged the pills which, at once, assumed the form of the Moon Rabbit, while she herself was changed into the toad. The rabbit thus pounds the fruits of the tree with her to create these famous pills anew.

The origin of these legends is shrouded in the mists of time and, as the variants show, probably have converged from several starting points. An ancient medical work states that a mixture of cassia bark, bamboo juice and the crushed brains of a frog will cause one to "walk upon the waters after seven years". These connections with an elixir of life are specifically Taoist.

The Old Man of the Moon is a keeper of the book of marriages. He determines who marries who and he enjoys sitting in a cave playing chess with the God of Longevity. There are many stories about marriages that seem unlikely but nonetheless come to pass because of the Old Man's decree. At the Moon Festival women make wishes and many of these concern love and marriage. They wonder what he is writing in his big book.

These stories seem to resemble rich dreams and could perhaps be interpreted in similar ways. In particular, their moral and social content reveals a depth of insight that tells us much about the character of the Chinese.

*

The Jesuit monastery and an expelled bishop

The other evening I walked down from Brickhill towards Aberdeen and climbed another small promontory to visit the Jesuit monastery and school in its magnificent Chinese-style buildings, airy and well shaded, set among tall long-needled pine trees. Pacing slowly along the path towards me came a white-robed priest wearing black Chinese slippers and deeply engrossed in a little book of meditations. As he approached, he looked up and smiled. I told him that the Roman Catholic padre who comes to Brickhill had suggested I visited the place and, since we were neighbours, make myself known. The priest became very friendly and, in a broad Irish accent, introduced himself as Father Collins. We entered the building and strolled along a tiled corridor into a cool and airy room containing a small dining table. We had a lime juice each and he showed me around. Although the students were on vacation, a number of them were still on site as they had no homes in Hong Kong to go to. Circling the buildings, in the manner of peripatetic philosophers, he told me the story of St Ignatius Loyola and the beginnings of the Jesuit order. All along the paths stood the fabulous trees and through their branches, I could catch glimpses of Apleichau Island and hear the sounds of oarsmen working sampans across the bay to Aberdeen. The distant babble of the boat people came up to us.

We met the Father Director, a tall man with long white robes and large searching eyes like those in portraits of saints. His face seemed straight out of a painting and I felt I would like to know more about him. Benediction was to be sung at six forty-five and I was invited to kneel at the back and listen to the chanting in the wide, windowed hall where slowly revolving fans hung from the high ceiling. The Chinese students, in their long white robes, sang the Latin verses beautifully while a harmonium accompanied them, a robed conductor leading the singing with expansive sweeps of his arms like a big bird flying. At intervals, little tinkling bells sounded and incense permeated the room.

I was moved to see that the service was conducted by an aged American bishop, Monseigneur Philip Cote, who had arrived at the China border that very day from Suchow in Kiangsu, escorted by two guards and expelled after twenty months in jail. He appeared old and weary and wore a small pointed beard in the Chinese manner. He was only fifty-eight and came from Lawrence in Massachusetts, having been ordained in 1927 and having become the Bishop of Suchow in 1935. In 1951, the communists had taken him from church during Mass and, although handcuffed, he had been allowed to kneel and bless the congregation before he was led away. Being a member of the Legion of Mary accused of anti-revolutionary activities, the communist Chinese could not tolerate his continuing presence. A number of other priests had been sent out with him.

I walked back to Brickhill in a thoughtful mood, impressed by the serious demeanour of these fathers and saddened by the religious intolerance now rife in China.

Plate 1. Father and Mother waving goodbye, Southampton Docks, 1953.

Plate 2. Suez Canal.

Plate 3. Brickhill from the hill behind the site, 1953.

Plate 4. Islands and pine trees above Brickhill.

Plate 5. *(above left)* Officer's quarters, Brickhill.

Plate 6. *(above right)* One of the guns on Brickhill.

Plate 7. Officer's Mess, Brickhill.

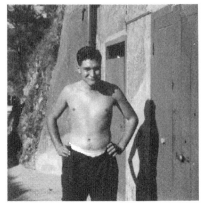

Plate 8. *(above left)* Capt Robin Chandler, Troop Commander. Brickhill, 1953.

Plate 9. *(above right)* Second Lieutenant Roger Thompson RA. Brickhill, 1953.

Plate 10. *(above left)* Chris Gardiner in Mufti.

Plate 11. *(above right)* Chinese labour, Brickhill.

Plate 12. *(above left)* Sergeant and men, Brickhill.

Plate 13. *(above right)* Brickhill: some of the lads.

Plate 14. *(above left)* Outside the control room.

Plate 15. *(above right)* Corporal Riggs *(right)* and cook.

Plate 16. Sergeants trying out bubble pipe.

Plate 17. Preparing lunch, Brickhill.

Plate 18. Hong Kong street scene.

Plate 19. Small taoist temple.

Plate 20. *(above left)* Ploughing with a buffalo, 1953.

Plate 21. *(above right)* Planting rice, Lantao, 1953.

Plate 22. *(above left)* Rowing ashore on first visit to Lantao.

Plate 23. *(above right)* Village scene in Saikung peninsula , December 1953.

Chapter Six

A Night in Macao

October 26th 1953

Just south of Hong Kong the estuary of the Pearl River creates an immense inlet in the coast, a sea lane reaching inland to the city of Canton. On the southern side, lies the tiny Portuguese colony of Macao, much older than Hong Kong but, likewise, also a port, where trading was permitted by the Celestial Empire. It is no more than a small town and its main fame today is as a pleasure ground for those in Hong Kong looking for a weekend of gambling or other more fleshly delights. It is an attractive little place, very Portuguese, with fine southern European buildings, a Catholic cathedral, churches and promenades and, behind its old-world charm and Sunday morning peacefulness, hide numerous dens of vice.

The ferry from Hong Kong sails out past the green mass of Lantao Island and, then, across the estuary. The far coast is hidden in haze; the water changes colour from a deep blue to a muddy shade of green, the sea being full of silt coming down from deep within China, and the numerous distant islands all belong to the Communists.

The passengers on board were as merry and bright as the islands shining in the sun. We five subalterns sat over the propellers, reclining in wickerwork chairs. Nearby, three Englishmen played poker and drank whisky with all the grace of reprobates off for a randy weekend. A beautiful Chinese girl in a scarlet and white European skirt and jumper posed on the rails to be photographed. Rich taipans, with seemingly redundant wives, sipped 'cha' in the first-class lounge. A young American asked for a glass of water and took pills for a sore throat, while his Chinese girl in a black, silky Chinese dress lay in a deck chair charming him. He was "just staying around these parts for a while" before moving on around the world.

An English schoolmaster sat reading a novel, with the assurance of one who believes he will soon win back his fare at the fan tan tables. A group of young Hong Kong teenagers, both European and Chinese, chattered gaily to each other, showing off their mammoth model aeroplanes, while their leader arranged deck chairs, drinks and sandwiches for them. Below deck, a circle of coolies sat on their haunches, gathered round a great dish of rice and titbits, shovelling it out into little bowls and tucking in with their chopsticks.

From the sea, Macao first appears as a long peninsula, ridged along the middle and crowned by an attractive church. The waterfront or "Praya" stretches along the shore lined with verdant trees, behind which the gay green or blue sloping roofs of the houses give a Mediterranean appearance to the place. Rounding the promontory a row of warehouses, quays and jetties comes into view, with flat-roofed tenements and arcades backing them. The steel grey mass of the Grand Hotel dominates the front, overshadowing other buildings. The evening sun glistened upon its windows and lent a richer tinge of colour to the thronging people in the streets, the junks along the quays and a broad flat stretch of paddy fields, lining the shore of a small island opposite the harbour.

Our ship, the *Tai Loy*, trailing a wake, dark brown with disturbed mud, moved slowly up the side of the waterfront and closed on the quay below the Grand. The five subalterns awaited the landing with eagerness: Tom, broad and Germanic with a whisky-coloured moustache, Roger, dark and wiry, thickset, with an aggressive chin and friendly eyes, Arthur, dark with smoothly wavy hair, whose bleak eyes above an aristocratic roman nose would suddenly gleam with animation and Conrad, from regimental headquarters and, thus, the most senior among us, tall and lean, intellectual, with the mind of a journalist and the face of a boy, always a trifle bemused and – myself. On the quay, a string of coolies, ragged men and cowled women, danced a grim fandango across the planks as they hauled in our cables. We made our way down the gangway, where several Catholic priests were greeting a fellow from Hong Kong – one by one they knelt and kissed his hand.

We were spotted from the shore by a tubby little Portuguese, dressed in a grey uniform with an enormous coloured badge over the left breast, who came and introduced himself as a member of the Macao Tourist Agency. He advised us to book rooms quickly, either at the palatial Bella Vista overlooking the Pearl river from a magnificent cliff, the busy Central Hotel rattling with the sound of mahjong play or the Grand, so tall as to provide peace and quiet above the roofs of the tenements. We chose the latter and found the rooms pleasantly airy, each having a bathroom and lavatory attached. The beds were capacious and the views out over the roofs of the tenements attractive. The setting sun sent slanting bars of light through the latticed sun blinds. We had decided to do most of our exploration by ourselves, trusting to our own noses, so the tubby man who had come "with absolutely no obligation, Sirs", left in the same state and we set about getting a meal.

The Chinese restaurant of the hotel was partitioned into little cubicles with swing-to doors. We found ourselves peering over the edge of a little balcony into another restaurant below, where Roger and Tom, having opted for an English meal, were regaling themselves. Our "chow" was inordinately long in coming, so we set to with a bottle of "vino tinto", very cheap but almost as harsh as vinegar. We chatted and sang songs, merrily flicking toothpicks into the whirling fan and sending them spinning into the room below. The white wine that followed was better than the red, a bit rough but enjoyable. But still no food, so we had a third bottle and were halfway through when the food arrived, two piled plates of chicken and noodles for Conrad and myself and a fried rice dish, 'Yeung Chow Chou Fan', for the others. We ate and drank happily until the other two joined us. We all rolled out into the street a trifle bleary.

Within ten minutes of fixing our rooms a hotel "boy" had poked his head around the doors – "Nice girls – very good!" Before dinner we felt this suggestion somewhat excessive and Roger had driven him off with epithets. Out in the street the pace was hotter, however. Several Chinamen stopped us; "You want look see?" and "See special film?" were the main suggestions. We chose the most absurd-looking cove, with a comical grin and dark hair standing up vertically in a great tuft. He told us his name was George and he took pride in showing us a letter of recommendation from a captain in the French navy.

"It's a French letter!" said Conrad.

George was an excellent guide, the captain told us; he would take us anywhere and show us anything we wanted. George's toothless grin widened as we accepted his services.

"I show you nice exhibeesh!" he announced.

"What kind?" asked Conrad.

"Boy and girl," he told us.

"That's no good," announced Conrad. "It's girl and donkey I want to see."

"But Señor, Sir, no donkeys trained plopaly in Macao!"

The main streets of Macao were ablaze with lights, bank upon bank of flaming neons, yellow, green, blue and violet; street signs in all colours, in Chinese, Portuguese, and English. The streets were narrower and the tenements less tall than in Hong Kong, so that they seemed even more animated and full of colour. In the back streets, the lights decreased in number, the shops, dim and shadowy, opening widely to the pavement where much of the merchandise was displayed. Over the cobbles the clip-clop of Chinese wooden shoes echoed flatly from wall to wall. Alleyways twisted up a hillside in a maze of forked turnings, while darkened windows gazed on the passing throng, small groups of people gathering and dispersing in the patches of yellow light pooled upon the cobblestones. Foul drains gurgled and a light litter of paper shavings and vegetable waste lay around in the corners, whence dark passages and stairways led off from the road.

George led us swiftly between the rather sinister houses. The Chinese looked impassively upon us as we passed and one or two old crones and children ran a few paces after us, holding out begging bowls and crying pitifully "Gumsah Gumsah!" Coolies under wide bamboo hats passed us, swinging along in a springy trot, carrying heavy loads on the ends of bamboo poles slung athwart their shoulders. Some were bearing broad pans, on which a most extraordinary mixture of objects were spread out, tins, old locks, nails, keys and rusted metal scrap of all sorts. Each of such men carried a little tin plate and advertised his presence by banging it vigorously with a spanner wherever he went. Bicycle rickshaws bumped precipitately down the steeper stretches, amid a violent clamour of bells, while people jumped aside to avoid them. When the cyclist attempted to go uphill, a group of children would gather behind the sweating man and help push him up to the top.

The miasma in front of my eyes was clearing quickly and I began to appreciate the strangeness of our situation. I doubt if any one of us alone would have dared follow a Chinaman into these streets. Around their murky, ill-lit corners anything could happen to an unwary European. Indeed, only a few weeks before, an American visitor had been found beaten up on the Praya one morning, with all his money and most of his clothes stolen. As it was, we kept close together as we hurried along. At last, George stopped in front of a vegetable shop, where baskets and ropes hanging from the roof cast vivid shadows upon piles of boxes, wicker baskets and vegetables laid out before the entrance. The shopkeeper was squatting upon a little stool talking with some friends. I have rarely seen a more shifty-eyed, lecherous-looking devil, short and broad, whose eyes never steadied on one's face for an instant, sensual mouth, flabby cheeks and receding forehead. He waved his hands dramatically at our guide "Nothing less than ten dollars!" We stood firm at seven apiece. No, ten was the limit. We shrugged our shoulders and walked off. The guide followed us; he thought eight would do. We stopped while he ran back again. Yes – eight would do it. We stuck at seven until at last the shopkeeper agreed and led us even deeper into the dim streets until descending a cobbled hill, we came to a sign on the wall, "Hotela Chau". In the foyer, he made a few brief arrangements and hurried us conspiratorially down a passage, so narrow it would have been necessary to squeeze past had anyone been coming the other way. On either side opened little rooms with curtains instead of doors, somehow highly suggestive of every sort of irregularity. Everywhere the lamps were of low wattage and the whole place shadowed in dim light.

We descended some steps into a larger room; the door was locked behind us to ensure privacy and we were told to keep quiet lest we attracted police. It was a sparsely furnished bedroom, on one side of which stood a vast bed with a matting mattress, with no bedclothes but with several bamboo leaf fans spread about on it. The shopkeeper set up a little 35mm projector and, motioning me to turn out the light, began to project a film on the grimy wall.

He showed us two films and during the running of each reel went outside to keep watch. The first reel began with a medley of this and that, presumably to obscure the true nature of the film. Soon a youth and a girl appeared strolling along a sea beach with the waves seething in the sand. Undressing piece by piece, they eventually sprinted into the sea, playing among the surging waves. They came to grips, struggled, clasped again and the lens closed in to reveal the tantalised boy's organ and the joyful writhing of the girl, as the film followed in intimate detail every movement of their bodies. It had a naturist clarity and freshness about it that had us all aroused. The second reel was less good. It was a bedroom scene with two women and a man lusting together. There were close-ups of the man's penis, while the man gave electric shocks to the women, whose faces writhed in an agony of desire. It was plain pornography and none of us enjoyed its vulgarity.

The "exhibeesh" was to follow. We were once more led along the grubby passage and past sordid lavatories to a room in the innermost recesses of the establishment. George told us to wait, which we did rather apprehensively. He returned with a young girl. We were surprised by her youth and poise but it was evident she did not relish the prospect before her. Even so, she did all she had to do without losing a quality of dignity, maintaining a passionless reserve throughout the operation. I was moved greatly that so pretty a girl, with those large pathetic eyes, should have been so degraded as to have come to this. The need for money must have been very great.

A man entered and, with the same disdainful lack of passion, copulated with her. Lying naked on the bed, they went through a variety of positions, while I found all emotion stifled within me by the almost medical demonstration. Intriguing it certainly was; the rhythmic motion of the thighs, the slight sucking sound as the penis slid in and out of the vagina, the girl's fingers replacing it when it had slipped to one side. They showed us five different postures, before they separated and the man washed himself in the basin to one side of the room. The girl dressed, smiled at us at last and went out.

We filed out silently, chilled and without desire. In the foyer we were offered a girl apiece. Conrad and I felt it would be worth looking at them for the interest's sake. Five girls were brought into the room. The first two looked pale and diseased; the other three were nicely dressed and smiling, just like any Chinese girl one could see anywhere in fact. George informed us that the first two were "second class" and the rest "first class". They sat a trifle ill at ease around the room, as we thanked them and withdrew. Not good enough – we told George.

We had satisfied our curiosity and I felt we had been brutal. In displaying themselves and in being found wanting, even a whore may feel some shame. By withdrawing so, had we not insulted them, I wondered. Surprised by my own dispassionate interest, I felt like some newspaper reporter doing anything for a scoop. The world seemed cold and reptilian as we emerged again into the dingy, cobbled street.

Several hundred yards up the main street from the Grand stands the Central Hotel where the fan tan tables are. We shot up several stories in a lift and entered a wide hall containing four gambling tables surrounded by people, standing or sitting on little stools, with score cards in their hands. The tables were marked out in large, green squares, subdivided into numerous numbered rectangles. Stakes were placed upon the numbers while a bell rang to indicate that stakes might be laid. The majority of the gamblers were Chinese, putting a dollar or two here or there. A well-dressed businessman sat at a side table and crossed to the fan tan tables at intervals to place a hundred dollar bill or two. When the bell stopped, a croupier seated near the centre of each table spun the dice in a glass container covered with a black cloth. Calling out for attention he uncovered the container and shouted out the score. It was a simple matter of odds or evens and losses and gains were, as a result, fairly balanced. We met the English schoolmaster from the boat winning back his fare and, while we watched, the businessman won several hundreds. Arthur put down a few singles and came away without loss.

We retired to a restaurant on a lower floor and had some drinks. After a strong coffee to clear my head fully we went upstairs again to the dance hall. Illuminated dice were changing colour and number at regular intervals above the band at the end of the room, apparently a method of screening results from the tables downstairs to gamblers on the dance floor. As we entered the hall, I suddenly felt giddy and nearly had a blackout but, once recovered, I found myself as sober as any judge in a night-club can be.

Conrad and Roger did not want to dance, so they returned to the Grand while the rest of us remained. Finding the dancing girls somewhat expensive, we looked around for unemployed talent. At the next table to ours sat an attractive Eurasian girl with her Chinese girlfriend. When they got up we found they could dance most attractively. Arthur said he wanted to dance with the Eurasian so, when she sat alone for a moment, he asked her. She thanked him in very good English and said she was frightened to do so in the hotel because she was not employed there. Arthur was crestfallen and after a while we decided to return to the Grand. As we left the building we found the two girls just ahead of us. Arthur intercepted them, just as two Chinese men were trying to engage their attention. In a trice, we were all trundling along together towards the Grand in a trio of bicycle rickshaws.

Back in the Grand, we went up several floors and emerged into the soft lights and sweet music of the hotel night-club, a small floor surrounded by alcoves. People were mostly in pairs with one or two parties scattered about. We sat down ordering "cha", while Arthur and the Eurasian flashed amorous looks at one another and the little Chinese kept Tom amused by pinching his nose with her elegant fingers. Although not especially pretty, there was a naughty jollity about her that was very pleasing. The Eurasian was certainly quite beautiful, black hair, oval face and wide, attractive eyes. She kept apologising to me, saying she wished she could find one of her friends for me. I told her not to worry and, indeed, I was quite happy watching the dancing, leaning back in my chair and puffing on my pipe.

Our sedate ballroom dancing was rather slow for them and once or twice, when the band struck up in a lively jive, they excused themselves and danced together with a delightfully wild abandon, swinging each other around and cross stepping in the liveliest manner. I liked the idea that they cared more for the rhythm of the dance than the necessity of a man to dance with. Their friendship seemed important to them, more so than whatever engagement they might have with us. It felt right somehow that they should career gaily across the floor in so careless a rapture.

For a while Tom and I shared dances with the Chinese girl, until Tom said he had a headache and must be off for a massage and bed. Arthur was making it very clear that he and Julie were going to spend the night together. As Tom departed, Arthur told me I would have to cope with the situation however I pleased. The opportunity was not to be ignored and I decided that I should sleep the night with the Chinese girl but avoid any dangerous intercourse. Arthur too had said he would not "go too far" but I doubted the strength of his resolve.

After Tom had left us, the little Chinese and I began to notice one another for the first time, each knowing instinctively, I supposed, what was now inevitable and that we were to give as much physical joy to one another as we could. She could speak hardly a word of

English but, by smile, touch and glance, mutual understanding was not difficult. Her name appeared to be "Mees" and as we talked she fed me little nuts held delicately between her exquisite fingers. By a mere gesture of one finger a Chinese can express so much, almost like an extra tongue. The long-painted nails on an English girl would have seemed excessive but on Mees they merely accentuated the grace of her hands.

As our dancing became more intimate, we made fewer mistakes, taking pains to follow each other closely, she my feet and I her every change of mood and movement. How lightly she danced; with what naughtiness she laughed in my face. She told me she liked me very much. Desire was growing within me, the slow sweet surge of affection and the longing to caress, and I did not care. All was as it should be. We fed each other on the little nuts and gazed smilingly into each other's eyes. There was nothing affected about Mees, no pretentiousness of dress, no trying to be other than herself. I supposed she was a prostitute but sexual laxity was so prevalent in Macao that it had become difficult to define that term. I thought that all my education and upbringing, my "decent" conditioning ought to have made me despise both her and my own intentions but this was not so. She was so ingenuous, indeed obviously happy in my company and the gaiety in her eyes so fresh and pure that there was nothing sordid or vulgar in our actions. We were both young and vigorous and nothing seemed more natural than that we should enjoy the pleasures and beauty of our bodies together. It seemed a fulfilment of our mischievous delight in living and the logical completion of having met.

It was approaching three when the four of us left the dance floor and stood waiting for a lift, Julie and Arthur clinging together in a passionately physical embrace and Mees and I more quietly close by. We were carried quickly to our rooms and I knocked on my door. From inside came a rhythmic slapping and thumping sound and, as we entered, we saw Roger and Tom lying on their beds all but naked, while two Chinese girls slapped and pommelled their muscles in an energetic massage, while two others, with more dubious intent, hovered nearby. Tom was nonchalantly smoking a cigarette. Mees looked most embarrassed and I too found it, to say the least – awkward. Tom told me to go next door where Conrad was lying in a darkened room. He opened his eyes as we entered, looked surprised, muttered a grinning "Oh God" and turned over. Mees pointed to him with amazement and laughed. "Not here!" she said. I told Conrad to go to sleep with his head to the wall for an hour or two. Placing two chairs between the beds and covering them with shirts and trousers, I showed Mees the screen. She frowned and then, smilingly, put her arms around me.

We fondled one another playing in one another's arms at the foot of the bed. She zipped open her dress and for the first time I looked upon her breasts. How smooth and firm they were, how sleek her slender body beneath my exploring hands. She removed her dress and I took off my shirt. We embraced again and, as her hand slid down to my groin, we rolled over, cuddling one another in the throes of passion. Time passed unheeded, as we lay passionately together, naked, apart from the tiny silken garment I forbade her to remove from around her waist. Her fingers teased me until the tension within me became almost insupportable and we came together heaving and thrusting with violence.

We talked and she told me the names of the parts of the body in Cantonese and Portuguese while I supplied the English. When we reached a certain part of the male anatomy I said "Ah ha!" She laughed, delighted with what she took to be the name. "Ah ha!" she said "Ah ha." I was so amused I forgot to give her the correct appellation and to this day I suppose...

Mees was writing Chinese characters upon my arm with brave little sweeps of her long fingernails; "I like you!" she said. "Do you like me?" I told her yes and we embraced again. Her pneumatic flesh was smooth and wonderful to caress. I had never experienced anything like it. Pretending to be swimming in the sea, we lay beside one another experiencing something of the uplift of surging waves. She knelt beside me on the bed and gave me a massage, her gentle hands pummelling my muscles. Pausing, she looked at me, letting her fingers glide over my legs, between them, easily over my belly and firmly around my chest. We kissed while she sat athwart my legs with my organ between her breasts, writhing in ecstasy together, our hands running wildly over each other's bodies. As I wriggled beneath her touch she giggled and kissed me tenderly. At last we lay exhausted and dozed lovingly in each others arms.

At five thirty she was up saying she had to go. After a wash, she dressed and I gave her some money and, although she implored me to go with her, I said I must remain behind and sleep. She asked me for my Hong Kong address and I was about to write it down when Conrad turned over.

"For Christ's sake, John," he said, "don't be such a bloody fool. You'll be in an awful mess if she turns up at RHQ one day and asks for you. Give her a false name or something."

Bowing to his worldly seniority and impeccable logic, I wrote down an assumed name and gave the address as Army Headquarters, HK. Immediately I felt terrible. It seemed a betrayal of our intimacy. I reflected that soldiers were always moving on and that she would understand that. In any case she would not be lonely for long at HQ. But all that was beside the point.

My main regret was that I had not felt able to give her as much pleasure as she had given me. I could not risk too much for fear of venereal disease, rife, of course, in the brothels of both Macao and Hong Kong. She seemed wary too for she did not try to persuade me and, when she had relieved me, took great pains to wipe her hands. She seemed surprised at the result of her manipulations, so much so that I suspected she was not a practised whore but much more of a novice. Indeed my precautions may have given her the idea that it was I who was protecting her from disease. Being puritans and fools none of us had thought of obtaining "precautions" from the MO before leaving. Sheer folly.

At times during the night, her tenderness for me had been very real and when I had gazed into her darkened eyes trying to understand this little person lying in my arms, to pierce our inevitable separateness, she would avert her face as if bewildered or ashamed. Once she said she liked my nose, another time that my hands were beautiful but, when I responded in kind, she would deny it all. Once or twice, she had turned her back on me, pretending to sleep and I had wondered what she was really feeling.

When she left me I thanked her with emotion but she would have none of it signing goodbye with a wave of the hand. She had not even asked for money for, when Julie had discussed the price earlier in the night, Mees had told me secretly that she wanted nothing. She had with her a little coloured handkerchief containing a few dollar bills, mostly what I had given her, and I had the impression she had not much else in the world.

When I awoke, the sun was slanting through the blinds in parallel rays of gold. I lay half awake for a long time, regretting the day, regretting her absence, wondering where she had gone, regretting the pettiness of my reporter's instincts the evening before. Was she a prostitute? Was she poor and in desperate circumstances? I was not sure of anything in this strange, cruel, loveable world I did not understand. I thought of some of the other girls we had seen; the "second class" ones, frail, ill, enmeshed in the trade and bandied about by pimps. Several of them had shown the same desperate pride of the girl in the 'exhibeesh'. I marvelled at it, at the residual strength of human goodness. It seemed to me that Western and Eastern vice had a quality of difference, the whores of Macao and Hong Kong had not lost their humanity.

We got up slowly. Arthur had indeed "gone the whole hog" and his account of the night was lurid. He claimed to have learnt every possible trick in the business. Julie was evidently a lady of masterly attainment in the arts but Arthur was also apprehensive about his future. Roger and Tom had found their masseuses unwilling and a train of girls had pestered them into the early hours when, as they said, it was much too late anyway.

All these comings and goings had been witnessed by a little man seated, as a kind of guard, at a window near the stairway. Arthur had asked him for some change at three in the morning. "How much she want?" he had asked. "Mind your own business," snapped Arthur.

After lunch we went for a rickshaw tour of the town. With its picturesque streets, little parks and the grotto overlooking the sea, where the Portuguese poet Camoens used to write, it is a beautiful little place. The ruined building of St Peter's Church dominates the town, its baroque façade standing high and serene above the streets facing the sea.

As we were leaving a small amusement park, a little girl of about six started running beside the rickshaw. "Gumsah Gumsah," she cried, as the coolie trotted on. "Gumsah Gumsah," the piping little voice wailed beside us. Along street after street she persisted in following us. "We can't give to everyone," said Conrad, who was sitting beside me, "There are so many, just not possible."

"Gumsah Gumsah," shrilled the child more plaintively. The sound was a pain that broke the mind. Suddenly she fell beside a wall at the edge of the road weeping terribly, sobbing and choking. Next minute the rickshaw was around a corner and bustling amongst the traffic of a busy thoroughfare.

Never have I forgotten the terrible moment of not having given, the despairing scream of the child as she fell, the paralysis of my mind at that moment and the agony of awakening to the meaning of the event. I felt that never could I forgive myself for having been so cold-hearted.

Long afterwards, when talking of Far Eastern conditions with an American friend, he said, "It never does to come too close to these things, to see the tragedies of so many people's lives close up. You can do nothing and it is so much easier to give a dollar a week to charity and forget all about it till the next appeal."

The Tai Loy sailed late in the afternoon. The sun shone on the yellow wavelets while mountains lined the distant horizon. We sat on deck idly talking. Halfway across the estuary the ship's bells began ringing and we made a wide circle to port. Some passengers showed signs of consternation because sometimes a communist gunboat stops the ferry to remove some wanted individual. Looking around, however, we could see no other craft near us. We slowed down until our movement was barely perceptible and some of the passengers began pointing and chattering. It was then that we saw it. Not far away a corpse was floating, rising and falling slackly upon the yellow flood. We dropped the lifeboat, amid a chaotic ringing of bells, winching and tugging on ropes. The passengers were quiet now so that a silence fell over the unmoving ship, a light wind sounding in the mast heads. The boat pulled away, the little waves slapping loudly against her sides. It was difficult pulling the body on board. It had been in the water for a long time, probably having floated several hundred miles down the great river and it was heavy. It had been a man, perhaps a fisherman. The lifeboat returned and the passengers leaned over the rails to see the stiff, half-clothed body, with a swollen, expressionless face, carried aboard and hidden from view. After a short delay we sailed on. The hills of Hong Kong rose before us.

Chapter Seven

The Builders' Rendezvous

Police and Triads, November 4th 1953

Two nights ago the Brickhill subalternary visited the nearest thing to a country pub in Hong Kong. This establishment, called The Builders' Rendezvous, lies on the main road to Aberdeen and possesses a fine outdoor dance floor especially designed for moonlit occasions. The interior has been decorated by the various building firms of Hong Kong and reveals a variety of styles. It combines the functions of pub, dance hall, restaurant and roadhouse with that of an advertising concern.

Hardly had we settled down over some sherry than we were hailed with a rumbustious greeting from the far side of the room. Inspector Guyatt, the chief drill instructor of the HK Police School, had previously been the RSM of the Royal Norfolk Regiment and must have been a holy terror. Often, as we drove past the school, we had seen him drilling his recruits with a ferocity and vigour second only to that of RSM Britain at Mons.

There he sat, an immense gorilla of a man, half-ape, half-toad, his little eyes darting furtive glances around the room and a thin grin below his waxed moustache. He was reputed to have tattoos in more places than most would dare and a total collection of one hundred and twenty-seven designs. A thick leather belt hung loosely from his trousers, holding enough bullets to kill an army, while at his side dangled a black revolver. He invited us over to his table and, to entertain us, proceeded to smoke ten cigarettes in each hand claiming he could detect the presence of an American one in a fist full of British.

The other day we had seen him on parade at the Police School. A small recruit had been so misguided as to appear on parade carrying a personal baton instead of the heavy riot stick that was required. Guyatt had spotted him a hundred yards away.

"What the hell's that there?" he yelled in fluent Cantonese. "Hades, I've got a cock twice the size of that!"

The Chinese apparently love him for it. The more he roars and swears the more amused they are and the better they drill. The methods are often as rough as in any military training today and it is true that no detachment from any of the regiments stationed in HK could approach the excellence of these Chinese in a drill competition. They could challenge the Guards in precision drilling. Guyatt is the sort of preposterous individual all soldiers love. Ferocious yet kindly, shrewd and humorous, he is vulgar, in the delicious way only a product of years in a sergeants' mess can be.

Suddenly there was an uproar outside and in poured a mixed collection of young men, British, Chinese, Portuguese and Eurasian, all of them special constables staying at the school for their yearly week's training camp. They greeted Guyatt with peals of merriment and heavy-handed back-slapping.

I found myself seated between a Chinese businessman, who clearly regarded the whole affair as a remarkable lark, and a young, sensitive-looking Chinese, with an unusually long face, large expressive eyes and a manner of talking that was fast and fluent like a freshman at a university who knows more than is good for him. His name was Chan and soon we were in the midst of a discussion of police ways and a swapping of police stories.

I had heard a little of the notorious Kowloon triad societies but, until then, had met no one who could tell me about them. Triad societies are illegal in Hong Kong because all societies must be registered. This would be embarrassing for an association of pickpockets and other criminals. These criminal associations take their name from the fact that one of the earliest of them utilised a three finger salute whereby members could recognise one another. The salute became known as the triad and the word became the name designating all similar associations which are essentially criminal co-operatives. Should a member of one triad be beaten up by a member of another triad, an inter-triad feud easily develops leading to street battles and the like. Fortunately, the headmen of the triads usually settle such quarrels among themselves by arbitration. There are triads for shoplifters, pick-pockets, burglars, vice racketeers, vendors of obscene literature and pornographic photographs, the pimping of prostitution and other kinds of relatively petty crime. At the end of a specified period, each headman receives the spoils and divides it up equally among the members. He may keep the haul in his possession for a day or two, in case he receives a complaint from the police when he has the wherewithal to respond.

Chan told me:

"Most headmen are well known to the police and there are CID men whose special duty is to maintain friendly relations with them. For example, should a wealthy American of some influence have his pockets picked in Nathan Road and lose his passport, it would most probably fall into the hands of a local headman, who would store it away for a few days. If the American contacted the police, they would have a shrewd idea of where the passport might be. Out would go the CID man and call on the headman. 'Ah, yes to be sure, this passport came in yesterday. So sorry to have caused an inconvenience. Please return it with our kindest regards!' And so, next day, the American would get his passport back and marvel at the efficiency of the police. A complaint to the police has a good chance of achieving a complete return of property but, if no complaint is made or the loss trivial, nothing can be done. The triads flourish as a running sore."

I wondered, of course, why the police did not clamp down entirely upon such goings on.

"The fact is that given a population of three million it is not easy for a police force of five thousand to keep watch on everyone," said Chan. "Furthermore, the population is never stable, there are continuous movements to and fro over the frontier although, with the frontier now more rigorously guarded, it is more difficult to enter the colony than it was a few years ago. Generally speaking, it is considered madness to want to travel the other way, although some do. Registration of persons is incomplete and whole populations of boat people live afloat on their junks and sampans with no address. Were the police to attempt to clamp down on triad activities, the societies would simply disappear underground and no one, least of all the population, whom the police endeavour to assist, would benefit in any way."

In cases of a really serious crime, Chan told me, the police may obtain direct assistance from the triad leaders. Chan remarked,

"It is almost impossible to believe but the police and triads almost exist to benefit one another. Triads flourished especially in Shanghai where the son of Chiang Kai-shek had himself been sent to clear them out. He arrested a few ringleaders, only to find that the whole economy was threatened and he had no alternative but to let his captives go."

Chan told me that only the Communists had been able to defeat the triads. The police state had so ruthlessly wormed its informers into society that the conditions necessary for the secret functioning of the associations no longer existed. Convictions for offences were swift; there was a majority decision and then it was either the firing squad or release.

There was a difference between Hong Kong and Macao in the administration of justice, Chan told me:

"In Hong Kong any charge against a man has to be heard in a magistrate's court. The crime is thus aired publicly as in Britain. Cases are reported in the press and members of the public may attend the deliberations of the courts. By contrast, in Macao, petty crimes are mostly dealt with in the police stations without public knowledge and only major cases reach the courts. The resulting corruption can be imagined."

The difficulty in Hong Kong was the scale of the problem. The sheer bulk of petty crime to be tried in court was fantastic. Many offenders might be placed in the box together, as the cases were often lumped together to speed up proceedings. Corruption of course was not absent in Hong Kong but it was not out of hand. Squeeze was commonplace and the citizens of the colony experts in its application.

When we left the Rendezvous, Guyatt's bear-like figure led the way up the road under the moonlight. We left him at the Police School and climbed our hill to bed.

*

The Walled City and the Japanese occupation

The very next evening, Roger and I were standing forlornly beside the road at Aberdeen, praying for a taxi when who should emerge from one of the fish restaurants but a special constable we had seen the night before. He spotted us and came up to chat. 'Rummy', to his friends, was a Hong Kong businessman, a rotund and jolly young Cantonese gentleman. With him was Mike da Silva, a bronzed Portuguese, who had lived all his life out East. At once they said they would drive us home. They were amazed by our tortuous road leading up beyond the Police School and had no idea it led to our little mountain kingdom. In spite of the lateness of the hour, we persuaded them into the mess and, while Rummy took an orange juice, Mike swallowed a whisky and the conversation turned again to the oddities of Hong Kong life.

"You know," said Rummy, "one of the oddest places in Hong Kong was the old Walled City."

"Where was that?" we asked him encouragingly.

"Well, it was a district that used to exist towards the far end of Kowloon near the Kai Tak airport. Sadly, nowadays, it has almost disappeared among all the other streets of the area but, at one time, it was quite distinctive with walls around it. It was a little Chinese enclave within the territories ceded to the British and, as a result, the British colonial police had no jurisdiction there. It became a great sporting ground for all the activities which the British prohibited elsewhere. Opium dens smoked, gambling dens flourished, criminals fled there for safety and the brothels steamed with trade. In a way, it's sad it has disappeared because a lot of people could let off steam there!"

"What happened to it?" we asked.

"When the Communists took over in China, some of their enthusiastic fellows started a printing concern there spreading literature in the colony that the authorities considered subversive. The Government began to take the place seriously and, one day, the police assembled all five of their armoured cars and invaded it. The raid was a complete success and the walls were gradually broken down."

"You know," he continued, "one of the jollier sports was the art of dancing in the nude, with a bed provided for afters in the brothel upstairs. There were three such establishments flourishing very nicely until the owner of one of them refused entry to some journalists. They published such a rousing story that public disgust, following on the heels of public delight, caused such a shindy that the police had to make another raid. I met a special constable the other evening who told me how sorry he was about it all. It was most inopportune, said he, for he had intended to book a table for the following night!"

Often in Hong Kong we met people who had been in the colony when it fell to the Japanese and afterwards suffered as their prisoners. The Japs made themselves loathed by both Chinese and Westerners alike. They came as conquerors and pillaged, looted, killed and raped for several days. When at last, some sort of law was established it was barbarous and cruel to an extreme. The worst offenders were, apparently, Koreans in the Japanese army, who were exceptionally callous and sadistic. For all their grins, suavity and double-dealing the passive Cantonese had a very hard time of it. One of our mess waiters told me that he was once stopped by a Japanese guard in Aberdeen. He had omitted to kow-tow to the conqueror, so he was knocked to the ground and beaten and then forced to stand in a guard room until someone else made the same mistake some hours later. He was then released and the next unfortunate took his place. The Japs were fond of bayonet practice in dark alleyways and Chinese, captured for minor offences, such as being late after curfew, were at very grave personal risk.

Mike da Silva had a lot to say about the Japs. Apparently the defence of Hong Kong had been hopelessly and badly organised, with little or no co-ordination between different military and civilian services. In those days Mike had been an acting police adjutant and, when the surrender was announced, he was working in makeshift Police Headquarters in the Gloucester Building in Victoria. The police destroyed all their arms and ammunition and then sat dejectedly around a table playing poker until the enemy arrived.

Suddenly the door was struck open, kicked in by the first Jap boot they were to see. In swaggered a corporal carrying a tremendous sword. They were all lined up against a wall and fleeced. Anything of value was stolen and, when some other Japs came in and found nothing to steal, they simply laid into them, slapping, kicking and punching. Da Silva and his colleagues were taken to Stanley Fort. On the way, they saw the wreckage and bodies remaining from the last desperate stand of the volunteers and a battalion of the Royal Scots. They had fought to a standstill on the Wong nei Chong gap road and on the Stanley Peninsula itself.

"The Japs created a prison at Stanley and I found most of the Europeans of the colony there, an extraordinary mixture of administrators, technicians, businessmen, intellectuals and civil servants. After a few days, I managed to escape and, since I speak fluent Cantonese, I grew a Chinese beard, wore a Chinese hat and lived with a woman of the boat people on a junk. I began to organise resistance but, and I am sad to say it, I was betrayed by some of my Chinese friends, taken back to prison and tortured."

Mike had been beaten with a great, rusty iron bar, with the metal frayed into spikes at the end. He opened his shirt to show us terrible scars all over his powerful chest. He did not tell us the end of his story but he was apparently kept in prison until the end of the war, subjected to most of the indignities the Japs could force upon him.

On the whole Mike considered himself lucky. In Stanley and other prisons there had been terrible affairs. One of these had been the water torture.

"A towel is put over the face of a prisoner and a hose pipe rammed into his mouth. The tap is turned on and the prisoner made to drink and drink. The body becomes swollen and the stomach distended, water oozes from the eyes, ears, nose and every aperture. Finally, a small Jap jumps up and down on the prisoner's stomach. Very nice."

Another trick was the staged execution. A prisoner was condemned to death and, on the morning of the execution, instead of the usual handful of rice, he was given a splendid breakfast including rice wine and a cigarette. Of course the wretched prisoner rarely ate it and his guards enjoyed a second meal. Taken to the execution chamber, the prisoner found the Japs to be especially friendly, treating the affair as a kind of party, at which the prisoner was the honoured guest. The executioner then made him kneel with his head over a trough and went through a series of practice runs with an immense sword. At the last moment, someone would enter and lead the man away talking about a reprieve. The whole performance was a farce. Day after day it was repeated until the man was a gibbering wreck. He was then either shot or returned whimpering to the compounds. Sometimes a tough-minded character would walk brazenly into the chamber defying all. His head was removed at once.

Those who lived through those days soon reveal it. They all have a stock of vivid yarns, very similar, a few days of glory, bravery and terror and then years of prison. The Japanese ruined the colony, cutting down the forests, disorganising everything and the women suffered especially badly. As soldiers the Japanese were admired, as men they were despised.

*

A letter home, November 15th-17th 1953

I'm fed up. At least I was some twenty minutes ago, but now, sitting with my glass of beer, some nuts, a toothpick and a packet of State Express 555 beside me, I cannot write with quite the fury I had planned.

The day-to-day routine, the monotonous repetition of daily orders, the impossibility of getting out of camp frequently enough to get to know interesting people well, the inexplicable vagaries and moods of some of our senior officers, all make this army life a very worthless thing – or so it seems. It is often maddening to live in such a fascinating place and to see so very little of it. The army is such an unbelievably stupid organisation; where else could people be detailed for blood donations on Christmas Day? The amount of bumf is extraordinary, forms and returns of stores, equipment, men's necessities and so on, always to be made out in triplicate, quadruplicate or even quintuplicate. The officers tend to become façades, playing roles rather than manifesting personalities, the majors interfere with the captains and the captains put the subalterns in a muddle. Nobody seems to be able to get on with his own job without some senior coming butting in with his own unwelcome modifications. There are preparatory inspections for the Battery Commander's inspection, more for the CO and soon a welter of fuss for the Commandant Royal Artillery (CRA), who appears so much of an automaton that one might as well forget his name. He is THE Brigadier, much as a sausage machine is a sausage machine; to think of him as Mr X or Mr Y is as absurd as calling the kitchen stove Jimmy. Some officers identify themselves so much with their office that they lose whatever humanitarian feelings they may have once possessed. Only a great man rises above the pettiness of office to see the reality and humour of it.

Day after day we do the same routine, examination of equipment, tests, adjustments and co-ordination. As a final delight, we may do an aiming point check and, once a week, an aged aeroplane circles round our mountain, while we practise radar and tracker engagements. At its best, as in a recent exercise when planes from an Australian aircraft carrier out at sea made sorties against the colony, it can be very interesting; at its worst and at its most monotonous, the 'ennui' is terrible. Sometimes I am so bored I do not know what to do. Often, in fact, there is nothing to do except to see that no one else does anything wrong. It's all so negative.

The main trouble, of course, is that sitting on our backsides in a static gun site encourages static-mindedness. I am not surprised some of the lads go after drink and women; they have insufficient outlet in their work and insufficient education to employ themselves otherwise. I confess I find it difficult myself. I know so few people whose houses here I can simply walk into, indeed no one, and the cinemas, although often very good here, become a bit tedious as one's only relaxation. Hong Kong is poor in theatres but there are two splendid night-clubs; so far my pocket has prohibited my going. Roger made a wise remark the other day: "When one's morale is low, one begins to turn to the women."

A few weeks ago, I found our wonderful view growing flat and dull without expression, like a face one has known too well and for too long. When I first arrived here, every glance drew my eyes out through a succession of unfolding distances and succeeding horizons of shores, hill, mountains, sea, sky and the clouds beyond the clouds. Now my eyes have become used to focusing on the great distances and no longer do I find the physical immensity of the scene so compelling. The tedious common round draws the view within its grasp, devaluing its spacious serenity and lending it something of the futile business of day to day.

Yet the view remains quite wonderful. The peace of this great seascape is more like a lakeland paradise than any view of the sea we have in England. Now that the typhoons are past, it is always calm, twinkling in the sun, corrugated by passing breezes or lying flat and smooth at the whim of a current. The air is clear and the quiet of the distant islands shares the tranquillity of the mountains. There are no grey and urgent swelling seas; no hostile rain-filled clouds dropping curtains of mist as they hurry in from the ocean; there is no resemblance at all to the Atlantic we know so well at home. The distances, too, seem greater because, beyond every island, on another and clearer day, another cluster of island hills comes rising from the sea. The view stretches so far that on the clearest days the horizon merges with the sky, and then the clouds and final mountains look so alike there is no sure way of telling them apart.

The view was losing its savour for me. The white light of summer flattened it, three dimensions reduced themselves to two and the physical trick of focusing the eyes on receding distances no longer occurred. I felt that, unless I could recapture that trick, the wonder of the view would go. Its primary and almost religious significance lay in that travelling back of the eyes.

One evening after tea, as I walked down the steep ramp from the mess, I saw a thin, grey spiral of smoke rising from our showers' boiler house. It rose above the hillside, among the clustered mountain pines and twisted away towards the sky. Beyond it, across the Aberdeen valley, the Peak reared its green, wooded slopes and along its ridge, silhouetted against a creamy blue sky, the white houses of the rich shimmered in the evening sun. For the first time I realised that Autumn had really come. The colours of the sky and land were different, suffused with pastel shades from a fine mist. It was as warm as English mid-summer but the air and feeling of the place was changed. At once the wonder began to creep back, the smoke twist became a writhing force and the far hills stood back from it, poignant now with a renewed meaning.

Every evening since that day, I have watched the mists come creeping up the valley and the black silhouettes of the islands etched against a horizon flaming with golden, scarlet and ruby cloud-dragons. Sometimes the sky itself glows like a furnace and a ridge of clouds, ranged across the horizon, is etched black against the brilliance, like a mirage of mountains in another world.

One evening, I scrambled down the steep hillside below the camp and sat on a ledge of the cliff some forty feet above the sea. It rose and fell so gently that not a fleck of foam was fanned against the rocks. A steady procession of sampans was passing, heading out from Aberdeen for a night's fishing in Deep Water Bay and often draped with nets and poles for the work ahead. These were the 'bright-light' fishermen, whose brilliant lamps suspended over the stern of the vessel attract fish into their nets. In the well of one of the boats, a little fire was burning on a metal tray heating the evening chow. Inside a wicker basket hanging perilously over the stern, a duck was quacking. Two or three of the men and women were rowing standing up, using the long, single blades which, with the swing of their bodies and the twist of their hands, screwed the boat through the water. Sometimes one of them sat in the bow and rowed in the usual

European manner with large sweeps. Further out, a small junk was heading home for Aberdeen under a large lateen sail, while its four rowers stood amid ships propelling it with great oars, black silhouettes against the setting sun.

Sometimes a sampan came by close under the cliff with a little coracle strapped across it or towed behind, with a young boy or girl rowing it. Sometimes they rowed beside the parent boat. Two adventurous boys were dodging their coracle as close to the rocks as they dared and, on scraping the base of the cliff, their merry laughter rose in the still air. Each sampan had several children aboard; the little, round-faced boys, cuddly like teddy bears, with their great shocks of black hair standing out all round like gollywogs and little girls, more demure, with their beautifully-tied pigtails hanging down their backs. Often they would spot me sitting on my rock and draw their elders' attention. Through my glasses I could see them smiling and passing some remark to one another. Sometimes they would row on without looking, afraid perhaps of an evil eye. Several sampans were decorated with paper charms stuck on the bow or stern and one of them had a complete eruption of paper on the bow, doubtless an offering to a sea god.

There was something quite beautiful about this evening migration of the boat people, each sampan with its little family, the kiddies, the poultry, the evening fire and the warmth on their faces, as they worked with a will at the oars and talked among themselves. It was a procession of water-borne homes complete with old and sage, young and boisterous, tiny tots and mischievous boys. I wished I could join them, understand their talk and find, like them, their obvious pleasure in the lively movement of their buoyant craft.

Boat People Fishing at Night

Out, far out, in the darkness
beyond the lights of the camp's perimeter
a frail quivering thing hangs
like a star below the cliff.

A slight ghost's eye?
A lost soul wandering the waste
of swelling waters without end?
Finality of loneliness?

Fire above water
a solitary flame
with only space and dark
dark time to comfort.

The sampan bobs on the current
as happy fisher boys
haul in
their long full nets.

*

Mr Ma again

I have been able to meet Ma Meng again. On Saturday evening I took the bus to the university and found his house near the college. It opens on to the street with a fine portico. He welcomed me himself at the gate and took me through the ground floor, which appeared to be a document store, and up a dark flight of steps into a bright and friendly living room opening on to a small balcony overlooking the blue expanse of Hong Kong harbour. He sat me down on a sofa, offered me a cigarette and called for a lemon squash. The tastefully decorated room was equipped with little tables and chairs of a rather Victorian appearance and finely carved. Two long scrolls hung on the walls, one depicting a branch of delicious, fulvous fruit and the other bearing a subtle line drawing of a Chinese magpie. Columns of Chinese characters were written down each side of the scrolls and on two further scrolls I saw more beautiful calligraphy. One of these was a poem penned by the present Minister for Education in the Chinese communist government.

Mr Ma had been a student at a university in Peking where he had first studied sociology. "It has been truly said that until one has seen Peking, one does not know China!" he remarked.

We were joined by two of his great friends named, if I remember correctly, Mr Wong and Mr Chang. They too had been students at Peking, one a political scientist and the other a biologist, but they had given up studies in 1944 and were now in business. We talked books. Ma felt that Lin Yutang was a good writer, especially for introducing Westerners to China but he wrote for money and was not a true artist. He had lived so long outside China that not all of his presentation was reliable.

Ma knew Han Suyin personally and, since a reading of *A Many Splendoured Thing* had been the cause of my selecting Hong Kong as my national service destination, I was most interested. Her well-known name is evidently a *nom de plume* and before her present marriage she had been Elizabeth Tang, the wife of a Kuomintang general killed by the Japanese. Ma said Han Suyin was an exceptionally talented and beautiful person who, besides Mandarin, could speak Cantonese and her native dialect in addition to English, French and a little German. He recalled his surprise when having ordered Chinese food in an impeccable manner at one meal they had together, at another she ordered bacon and eggs!

Han Suyin's love affair with Ian Morrison of *The Times*, killed with Christopher Buckley in Korea when their Jeep ran over a land mine, was the key theme of *A Many Splendoured Thing* and I reflected that many British people had thought her to have behaved in an improper manner in publishing so personal an account when Morrison had a wife at home. In addition, she had, in any case, married another Englishman soon after and went to live in Johore. Ma looked inscrutably Chinese as I said this but he agreed that the book was hardly discrete. I said how much I had enjoyed the book with its many metaphors and passages which no English person could have written. Ma agreed but he remarked that much of her writing, especially about love, was rather "young". It would become more balanced as she matured. He felt she was a complex person hanging, as it were, in a cultural space between the tensions of East and West.

Mr Ma's little daughter, about seven years old, her black hair swept to each side and tied with little bows, her brown eggshell complexion and big wondering eyes, was dressed in a European frock and served us the lemon squash. She had perfect manners, serving us biscuits very seriously. Her more bumptious brothers came bouncing in and soon began piping up with simple English words. I departed to a chorus of 'bye byes' from them all.

On another occasion, I went with Mr Ma to the British Council Library to hear Brother Cassian, a Jesuit member of the Sino-British Club, lecture on "Hamlet – the Taoist". Ma had with him a Chinese businessman by the name of Lai, a round-faced southerner with a pleasant smile and twinkling eyes. He told me he was a part-time writer who wished he could write more.

Lai was most witty, perhaps especially as Mr Ma had clearly brought him along as an uncultured philistine who needed some intellectual lumination. Old Lai, however, was out to enjoy himself in his own way – spotting the absurdity of intellectuals. He took great pleasure in informing me that a repulsively obese man of decayed visage was the president of the Hong Kong nudist club. "Lately, he hasn't been attracting many members," he chuckled.

"Whatever can this lecture be about?" I asked him. "I cannot see much connection between Hamlet and Taoism."

"No more can I," chortled Lai. "You know, I once heard a professor lecture on 'Confucius – the Englishman'!"

Later, Mr Ma was encouraging him to come to the university to hear Edmund Blunden, the newly-appointed Professor of English, speak.

"Hm, well maybe," said Lai. "It will depend on the subject. I fancy an hour on 'The libraries of Oxford' might not appeal to me very much!"

Brother Cassian fulfilled Lai's negative expectations to the full. It was a learned talk loaded with quotations in English, Latin, Italian, Cantonese and Mandarin – ("Excuse my Italian, gentlemen, I speak the pronunciation we have to use in the Roman Faith.") – but swamped in adiposity. Listening carefully, I found I could not agree with even his main points but knew I would have to read not only Hamlet again but also a lot more Taoism if I was to criticise his talk effectively. He seemed to assume that Hamlet's indecisions were a sign of Taoist-like quietism and I very much doubted the sense of that. Hot air on Hamlet, was our agreed judgement as we parted from his learned company.

Chapter Eight
Fisherfolk, Mountains and Monasteries

Upon this path of inclined stones
the pallid moon our hurrying shadows throws
the broken-headed mountain bows its head in night-plume mists
and grass and gossamer go grey with dews.

The moon has chased the golden crow to bed
a black arch spans the hillside path ahead,
beyond this point the eastern mountain lies
where smoke the unquenched candles of a quietened world.

Now wait and watch and you may see
one petal of the precious lily
move.

Lantao Island and fishing village, August 30th 1953

Roger and I had planned to visit the island of Lantao, staying the night high on the mountain in a Buddhist monastery. Unfortunately, the torrential rain made us decide to postpone this expedition and we stayed the night at the Yacht Club sleeping without cost on newspapers spread on canvas campbeds in the large changing room overlooking the sampan harbour. At four a.m. I was awoken by a great volume of sound, thousands of cockerels crowing in unison! I suddenly remembered that, at the stern of nearly all the sampans, there was a little cage containing some chickens. The cocks therein awoke before dawn to produce a sensational alarm clock for the boat people.

It looked brighter on the Sunday morning, so we decided on a trip to the coast of Lantao Island. We rushed to the ferry and scrambled aboard without bothering to breakfast. We were bound for Tai O situated at the southerly tip of the island, the most characteristically Chinese of all the fishing villages.

As we sailed along, we came across many signs of the fishing activities of the coastal people. The big junks trawl with big heavy nets which are often to be seen hung from the mast tops to dry. Smaller craft carry out bright light fishing at night with seine nets. They work in pairs. One boat has the lamp burning over the water, attracting fish, while the other moves out and around in a circle, so entrapping them. Both trawling and bright light fishing are carried out at night – the latter mainly in the summer season and the former beyond British waters in the winter.

As the ferry moved out of Hong Kong harbour, the colour of the water changed noticeably, becoming muddier, and we saw shoals of enormous white jellyfish floating past, trailing yards of stinging tentacles from their foot-broad disks. The silty water showed we were within the floodstream of the enormous Pearl River, coming down from the interior beyond Canton. It washes past only the southern shores of the colony beyond which the jellyfish are less common.

As we passed the inshore end of Lantao Island, a white wall of rain approached us blotting out the hills, the islands and the sea itself. Soon it hit the ship and the air was filled with the roar of tumultuous rain, elephants and donkeys falling from the sky, thick with the heaviness of the downpour. The little waves, so lately jolly in the morning sun, were beaten flat by its power. As it cleared, we peered through drizzle to make out the steep shores and hills of Lantao on the port side, a view quite Hebridean on this grey morning.

About a mile offshore, we passed a line of nets suspended from great posts in the tide run. The high tide courses through these nets, allowing them to filter out the fish as it does so. This filter fishing can be very profitable but also risky, since a typhoon could sweep them all away in a few hours. The nets we saw were said to be the only ones in use in the colony. Some sampans were gathered around the poles, their crews repairing nets and sitting with the rain running off their great wide hats. They must have been soaked to the skin.

Along the Hong Kong shores, we often saw extraordinary fishing devices set on poles a little offshore. Four great bamboo masts suspend a square net between them and these are in some way hinged to the sea bottom so that they can be raised and lowered. A long rope runs from the tops of the masts to a little onshore platform, where there is a winch worked by a man with his feet. As the rope is winched in, the net, which has been lying on the sea bed, is raised vertically through the water encapturing shoals of fish. Stake nets of this sort are set in the corners of cliffs, on sandy beaches and well out in the estuary at Taipo, where the winch is erected on a separate bamboo tower placed in the water.

Tai O pier was set some way from the village which lay about seven hundred yards away up the small estuary of a stream coming down from inside the island. Several large junks and a host of sampans surrounded us. One of the latter transported us up the estuary to the village. On either side of the narrow channel where the river met the sea, lines of wooden shacks built on high stilts stood above the water. We passed up the little stream as if moving along a high street between rows of houses. In fact, that was exactly what we were doing. The shacks had wooden platforms in front of them and steps for descending into boats alongside. As the mad dogs of Englishmen paddled along in the rain, the kiddies on the platforms waved and grinned "Allo, allo, bye, bye". When the shore appeared at last, the stilt houses gave way to others perched on the edge of a steep, muddy and slimy bank. A small ferry was being punted to and fro across the stream connecting the two halves of the village.

Once ashore, the cobbled streets wound crookedly between single-storeyed wooden shops displaying their surprisingly fresh and clean goods for sale. In one shop, the owner showed us a little black bird like a starling, standing with a jaunty look upon a table. This was a talking bird, a crested mynah. Everyone tried to make it talk to us, the owner announcing, "This bird make small talk Chinese!" However, in spite of whistles, encouragement of all sorts, cajoling and bribery, the bird remained resolutely silent. I could swear it had a naughty Chinese twinkle in its eye.

In several shops, we saw the great bamboo hats the Chinese peasants and fisherfolk wear. We kept stopping to try them on to the great engigglement of numerous bystanders. There were several sorts of hat, each beautifully constructed from bamboo cane and leaf. The coolies use a conical version, often very broad, called the dai-mo. Boat women wear hats called tang-ka-mo, while country women have another type with a hole in the middle sporting a cloth skull cap and a cloth fringe all around its circumference. This is the shan-ha-mo. We tried on both the dai-mo and the tang-ka-mo but the problem was that the structures had no rim with which to grip the head. These can be separately supplied if wanted but there were none big enough for us.

Around the portals of the houses were pasted brightly coloured strips of paper on which were printed characters, charms or mottoes to keep away malevolent spirits and, near the landing place, we found a little brick shrine containing a fierce and colourful image – possibly the land god To-tei or else some divinity of the sea or river. Strangely, in this village of Taoist superstitions, we also located a small Jesuit school with a little white stone cross above a small hall.

We walked the length of Tai O, poking our noses into all sorts of odd corners; had a meal at a little café, watched by gigglesome children; saw the salt pans where sea salt is dried; stopped at the police station and were given directions for the coastal path to Tung Chung from where we were to take the ferry home.

The coastal strip below the hills of the roadless island was enchanting, although hard work with the path flooded and muddy in places. Mostly it was well paved and led up and down hillsides, along the shore, or across paddy fields. Repeated heavy downpours drenched us and when we came to a fast flowing stream, we could find no bridge. We went down to the shore, disturbing a vicious-looking snake in the bamboo along the way, and waded across at the shallowest place where it fanned out across the shore. In the heavy rain, the peasants were working the rich fields, wearing immense bamboo coats (Sau-yee) to keep off the downpour. Bamboo leaves comprising the coats were arranged like the feathers of a bird down which the water ran. The people looked like great ruffle-feathered herons stalking about the fields.

As we walked along this beautiful coastline, the peacefulness of nature and the natural peasant life surrounded us and I thought about some of the Taoist philosophical principles I had been reading:

"It is on the empty space where there is nothing that the usefulness of a vessel depends. We pierce doors and windows to make a house and it is on these spaces that the usefulness of the house relies. Just as we see what is, we should also comprehend the value of what is not."

Returning to the city was quite a shock. What an extraordinary city this is; the incredible quantities of merchandise in the shops; the open street stalls with their quantities of trousers, shirts, towels, combs, tools, films, fruit, sun-dried herbs and fish, ropes or rattan furniture; jewellers; watchmakers; umbrella manufacturers; ivory factories; curio shops; silk stores; tea and wine shops; restaurants and eating houses providing Cantonese, Pekingese, Malayan, Hawaiian, French, Russian, English or American dishes; hotels; brothels; cinemas; temples and dance halls, rowdy or riotous, silky smooth or jazzy and jiving! The Circus Berlin is set up on reclaimed land at Causeway Bay, there is a Peking opera at Queen's College hall. French, Japanese, Italian, German, British, Chinese and American films are showing in the cinemas and there is the ever-present gaiety of the street signs and lighting. Then there are the people; sweating coolies carrying huge loads on bamboo poles and wearing the great dai-mo hats; rickshaw runners pacing along or waving at pedestrians to get a fare; big American sailors smoking vast cigars with gaily dressed prostitutes in tow; elegant naval officers in rickshaws passing from cinema to night-club. Sometimes, we passed Chinese faces of such wantonness or cruelty that made the flesh creep. At other times, the beauty of the girls took one's breath away. There were also British soldiers returning from captivity in Korea blinking in the bright lights. Once in a restaurant, we came across a party of them. It was sobering, they had a haunted look of men who had endured more than anyone should. A truck from the Cheero Club took us back up to our mountain retreat.

I wondered where, in all this pullulation of human needs, desires, joy, tragedy and idiosyncrasies, one could find a place from which to see the Taoist value of emptiness within the city.

*

The Ascent of Big Hat, November 25th 1953

Chris and I went for a walk in the New Territories, that part of mainland China ceded to the British lying behind the city of Kowloon and stretching up to our frontier with the Communists. We started with the intention of ambling quite gently around the Jubilee Reservoir, a large artificial lake set between towering, closely-wooded mountains. It is approached through a narrow, cultivated valley, at the top of which is an enormous stone dam as massive and impersonal as the strength and weight of the water it controls. We found an infantry supply post quite shockingly badly camouflaged and we remembered that we were walking into a full-scale military exercise. All the troops in the New Territories were on a large-scale deployment exercise, testing all sorts of equipment usually hidden in various regimental glory holes.

Up beyond the dam all was peaceful and serene, the green hills shining golden in a warm sun, the rich fir woods along the shore and the restful blue of the water making a feast for the eye, while a light wind and the sounds of birds murmured in the fir branches. I had rarely heard so many bird voices at once in the colony. Perhaps it was because, along the whole length of the large valley, there was not a sign of habitation, not a single human being, no busy Chinese houses, villagers or bustling people. The valley seemed asleep, dreaming in its lonely beauty, a kind of lost world, aloof, wild and a little alarming.

At first the narrow path led along the lakeside through little pine groves, where Pallas' willow warblers flitted among the branches and a small flock of golden-green white-eyes flashed along the banks to dance about the foliage, like little jewels so intense were their colours, in a search for insect food. We found a tumbling stream running with a bubblesome chuckle over a rocky bed and, where it crossed the path, we rested. Chris washed his feet in the crystal waters while I wandered up a small track beside it to see what I could find. At once I was in a thicket of swampy plants, the foliage so dense it would have been impossible to penetrate it. Great ferns with huge palmate leaves dangled from a dense growth of shrubs and grasses and tall pampas towered upwards among them. The scent of eucalyptus arose from delicate, white-trunked trees and a spongy bank filled the grassy bed of a little valley. Where the ground was firmer the jungle thickets began in earnest. I heard some snatches of birdsong coming from a large-leaved bush and, after a careful approach, routed a couple of bulbuls. Then I caught a glimpse, between the leaves, of another bird, larger than a thrush, its brilliant gold and black plumage leaving me in no doubt, an oriole. I sat transfixed to watch it. A female appeared, greener and browner; there were some more musical notes and then they hopped away and the density of the foliage hid them from my sight. I felt as though I had penetrated some secret of the valley and, indeed, I had, for the last oriole should have left the country on migration quite a month previously. I walked warily back down the track to the path and consulted the map.

To my surprise, I discovered that we were more or less under the shadow of Tai Mo Shan, Big Hat Mountain, the highest peak in the colony approachable easily enough by jeep on its other side but rarely visited from ours. We wondered whether we might be able to climb it.

We set off happily enough down the path but soon discovered that the further we penetrated into the valley the wilder and thicker became the jungle and the steeper the hills on either side. It was very silent there, with hardly a movement on the placid surface of the lake. The bird calls were fewer now and the great, green mountain leaned over us. One side of the valley was half in shadow from the sun, an ominous shadow for it was climbing higher upon the indented slopes with every passing hour.

We lost the path in a river bed, where a rushing stream cascaded over boulders, bounding in rills and waterfalls from ledge to ledge. Little rapids surged between the grey stones and, in dark still pools, it seemed that strange creatures may have been lurking. Certainly they were lurking in my imagination because the place had a mute beauty and silence, half inspiring and half full of a prehistoric fear. Tigers have been known to enter these valleys and, at this season, it would have been by no means impossible to meet one. Leopards, wild pig and barking deer are also reputed to enjoy this habitat. It was with a little trepidation and an overworked imagination that I proceeded. Afterwards, Chris, too, said that on occasions he had found the secrecy of the place alarming.

Again I consulted the map. Having lost the path, there was only one way forward. We would have to scramble up the river bed. Leaping and jumping from boulder to shelf of rock and from wobbly stone to pebbly shore, we gradually moved forward. The tumultuous music of the river seemed to draw everything into a daze of sound. The banks were increasingly steep and precipitous, with little cliffs and enormous boulders; the jungle behind so thick that only animals could have entered it. It was tiring work and more so for Chris, for the leather soles of his shoes would not grip the inclined surfaces as well as the rubbery crepe of my sandals. Passing through a narrow gorge, we ascended the higher reaches of the river. Below us now we could see the still, blue lake, while a range of mountains rose in front of us closing in a half circle about the head of the valley.

After another interpretation of the map, we decided to branch left, up a tributary leading steeply and narrowly between the arching trees and shrubs of the jungle. This would, we hoped, bring us out on a track halfway up the hillside. The going was tough and exhausting for the boulders were even larger and often partly overgrown by thickets and the slope was increasingly steep. Sometimes we had to haul ourselves up the smooth face of a boulder using finger and toe holds. Often I had to take a grip on the rock and haul Chris up after me. Several times we emerged on a ledge, from which we could see the whole length of the valley behind us and the trail of the river cutting through the trees to the lake. Once a great blue and red bird with a long lolloping tail flew screeching a rapid cry from one side of the stream to the other. Vanishing as quickly as it had come, I nonetheless recognised that dramatic Chinese woodland bird, the blue magpie.

At last we found the path and, with lighter steps, walked rapidly along the side of the hill. As the trees cleared we emerged into a marshy, highland coombe, with the mountain on one side and the river some three hundred feet below. The vegetation changed again; from the damp soil sprang great clumps of different types of pampas and other delicate grasses that towered over us on either side of the path. There were more of the delicate eucalyptus trees and we rubbed the leaves in our hands scenting their fragrance. It was open country now and a light breeze hummed in the grasses. We began to climb the steep hillside at the end of the coombe and met some Chinese in hunters' clothes. There were four or five men, a couple of youths and three boys who had come over the hills from Taipo with dogs and guns looking for barking deer.

It was then that we made a mistake for, instead of turning left and scaling the steep, grassy hillsides to the rock-strewn slopes of the summit, we pushed on along the path which, to our annoyance, dived again into the valley, crossed the river, now only a mile or two from its source, and led us up the slope on the wrong side of the valley. To correct our error, I judged we should climb vertically to the higher ground and make for the hill pastures at the valley head. This became the most gruelling part of the trip; we had an unhappy feeling that night might fall before we got out of the valley for it was obvious now that it would catch us in the hills. I was trusting we would reach the jeep track before dark and be able to trace it safely down under the light of the moon.

The hillside became pitted with holes and ridged with what seemed to be the remains of some ancient attempt to cultivate the highland. It was cripplingly steep and the shadow of the hills had crept up the sides of the valley, leaving only the peaks in sun. At last, after what seemed an hour of scrambling over banks and half-hidden walls, we were able to walk freely along a tiny track to the head of the valley. Successfully above the jungles, the rocks, the swamps and the horrid, last clamber, we strolled light-heartedly breathing deeply of the hill air and rejoicing in the springy mountain turf.

At the head of the valley we reached the grassy crest of a ridge and peered over the side. A craggy valley without trees dropped some 2000 feet to the head of the Lam Tsun valley, winding its narrow way through the lower hills to Taipo and the sea. Looking west, over hills strangely called the Cotswolds on military maps, we could see the far-off hills of China. A group of shining, modern factories and the white observation towers of the border villages stood out clearly and, beyond them, a deep blue haze covering the land mass that reached all the way through Mongolia, Tibet, Siberia and Russia to Europe itself. We lay for a long time couched in the soft grass, gazing into that unfathomable distance, each locked in his own thoughts.

I became aware of a new sort of silence, not the shuttered, secretly oppressive silence of the valley behind us, but the silence of a great open space. The wind spreading little waves over the grasses seemed to come out of an immense nothingness, a huge fullness of sky reeling away domed over the world.

We examined the map again and set off up an easy incline to the summit ridge, disappointing because visitors coming by the jeep track had left their papers and fruit peel behind them. Even so, the view was overpowering in its vast distances. The whole of Hong Kong Island was visible, the city crawling up towards the Peak and the palaces near its top. The mountain of Lantao Island looked across a strait at us, its broken head seeming to nod in familiarity, and then, way out, we could see the shadows of other islands floating like clouds for the horizon was lost in the haze.

We tore ourselves away at last and, in the failing light, walked briskly down the jeep track. It was dark when we emerged from the silence of the hillsides into a collection of lamp-lit huts. We found a sign reading 'Officers' Mess' and were about to approach it when voices, broad Yorkshire and Scots, came out of a bush. It was a camouflaged bivouac. The mess was empty, although eighteen places were laid for dinner and, rather relieved, we entered the OR's cookhouse where a welcoming corporal served us a mug of piping hot, sweet tea. It was a homely and cheerful place and we enjoyed the men's friendliness greatly.

We had stumbled unknowingly into a Regimental Headquarters. The Regiment was on the deployment scheme and secrecy had been enforced. Even so, in fifteen minutes, we could have discovered most things about the dispersion of the troops in the area. I imagined none of the officers had supposed a spy would come over the mountain to find them out! If there had been any sentries they must have been entranced by the view for we never saw one.

A friendly jeep driver, by a rare coincidence the same one of whom we had asked the way earlier in the day, bumped us downhill to Tsun Wan. Dropped at the Regimental Aid Post, we walked on, comforted by the thought we had only three miles to go before reaching a bus stop. After a quarter of an hour, we thumbed a passing car and, to our surprise and shock, found ourselves seated with a staff officer, a full colonel, on his way back from a visit to the frontier. He was a keen bird-watcher and a great shot, an enormous Scotsman, wearing a huge tammy and kilt and a great pullover to keep out the night air. He was quite impressed by our exploit and conversation flowed most amicably all the way to Kowloon.

I found myself admiring these characterful infantry officers, so different from the technically-minded, office-bound majors and the pompous brigadier we were enduring in the Heavy Ack-Ack. Perhaps, even in war, flesh and blood are superior to remote control – more human, somehow.

*

The Monastery in the Mists

Orange blossom golden and white
falling from tight-lipped flowers
their fragrance is hidden in the song
of a tumbling stream.

Neither wind nor water
nor dancing clouds that dodge
the candle-holding mountains
could be more kind to Dai Tung Tzai.

A shy girl brings us scented tea
by the little stone bridge that jumps the stream
orange blossom for our delight
water to wash in from a bamboo pipe.

The stupa on the outcrop
sat mute and still
beyond its shadow the silent waters of the bay
and a green peaked mountain far away.

A woman sang in the bamboo grove
the wooden fish tapped pop pop pop pop
monotonous drone
cool summer eve

telling of Buddha, of peace, of the void
and the bamboo breeze sighed and sighed
Ormitopha Ormitopha
Koon yam poussa.

Looking south from Brickhill the long island of Lantao dominates the horizon. Undeveloped and roadless, the island is covered with forests and grassy hills and, along the bays and inlets, small villages snuggle under the mountains above shining green paddy fields. From our eyrie we watched the changing moods of the 'Broken-Headed Mountain', the twin-peaked summit of which rises above Lantao as a great mass of grey blue in the evening light. Sometimes long trails of cloud flew from its leeward side but often it was hidden in dense hill mist. The mountain had 'presence' in the landscape, bearing down upon the smaller hills and scattered islands, like a lord with an aloof and distant air, seeming to beckon us from afar. Hidden near the summit, we were told, lay a Buddhist monastery. One weekend Roger and I set out on a pilgrimage to visit it.

The island ferry boat took us out of the Hong Kong harbour into the choppy straits between the islands and the Pearl River estuary. There were a number of ports to visit, little townships full of junks and sampans, the focus of life on the several islands on our way. Sometimes we came inshore to a quay, other times we paused offshore and hosts of sampans, crewed by vociferous girl captains, came out to meet us and take passengers and goods ashore. Gradually we closed on the coast of Lantao, a large silent island, poorly populated, steep hills rising from near the shore allowing the cultivation of rice only within narrow valleys that ran a little way inland from the coast. Dense vegetation filled the upper vales and, behind the farmers' villages, thick little woods clustered hard by the houses. Where the brooks ran sparkling over the stones to the sea, luxuriant groves of elegant bamboo grew. In the evening light, the hills cast long shadows from their rounded ridges and the sunlit uplands glowed with a golden, grass-green colour in the sun – a shade quite different from the darker blues or pea greens of Europe.

Closely following the coastline, our little ship soon entered a narrow channel between the main island and a small one offshore. Here a wide valley came down from the lower slopes of the peak itself, opening broadly to a sand and pebble beach. A river tumbled steeply down to rush across a stony bed to its estuary. Wide paddy fields, brilliantly green with rice, lay on either side of it. We made out the houses of the village of Tung Chung set around the river mouth, an ancient place, once a pirate stronghold, and where there was still a crumbling fort with rusting cannon. A large sampan was pulling out to meet us and soon we scrambled aboard, squeezing between a little old Chinaman, with twenty or so very much alive frogs tied by their legs to a piece of string, and an immensely fat Cantonese gentleman, who at once put up his umbrella, an inevitable accompaniment to an outdoor excursion, since sun and rain are evidently equally possible and feared.

As the ferry chugged away, the oarsman, in the stern of the sampan, swung gently from side to side screwing the overloaded craft gently towards the shore. A calm fragrance hung in the air for a light breeze was wafting a sweet scent of vegetation out over the sea. With the sound of the ship's engine fading, we seemed enveloped in a sudden silence; evening was falling; the bustle of the day was over; smoke from evening fires mounted in slow spirals above the village and a tranquil mood, exactly as in a Chinese painting, seemed to be settling over us. Our companions were happily contented to be arriving; the boat was full of the gentle jollity of the Chinese and we laughed our way to the shore.

We still had a few hundred yards to go when we heard an unusual sound, a soft booming that hummed on the wind for a second and then was gone. Three times we heard it. Several of the people in the boat had noticed it too and glanced up at the mountain. It was the great gong of the monastery, we were told, actually a huge bell, taller than a man, that hung in the upper room of a building. It was inscribed all over with prayers and, at certain hours, an attending monk would swing a clapper to hit it and its deep, bronze voice would go thrumming out on the wind, echoing down the valleys and, on still days, carrying several miles out to sea. The bell's sound carried with it all the prayers inscribed upon its surface. Some said that every time it was rung the torturers of Hell ceased their work for a moment. We listened to hear it again but now there was only the sound of the wind and a cockerel crowing somewhere in the village.

Immediately on landing, Roger and I set off walking quickly across the paddy fields, winding our way along the narrow foot-wide dykes between the tiny, swampy fields. We quickly found ourselves climbing steeply through bamboo thickets and shrubberies of bushes and graceful trees like acacias. In a small village, we were amused to pass two youths sitting casually astride a shrine to the Earth God, To Tei Kung, no more than a little altar with a boulder upon it representing the deity and set, as is usual, below a shade-giving banyan tree.

The path led us into a thick jungle obscuring our view of the loops in the path both below and above us. We emerged alongside the upper reaches of the river, now a clear flowing stream tumbling from boulder to boulder near the track, and paused for a rest at the edge of a little mountain hamlet, set within a wooded cleft in the mountain not far from the bare face of the summit slopes. Here the houses were strikingly large, two-storeyed with balconies opening to the view over the tree tops to the sea. Later, we learnt this was a Buddhist settlement around a cell of monks and that people came there for retreat or a holiday.

The scraggy pines grew more infrequent as the path began to wind across the bare, boulder-strewn flanks of the mountain. Out at sea, curtains of white mist were passing northwards and, from time to time, long streamers of it trailed along the slopes lingeringly and swirled awhile about us before floating on alone. Sometimes the summit would loom above us, bare and rocky, only to be hidden at once in swirling fog. We were entering the domain of the clouds, a fluid, eddying landscape of hills and vapour; sometimes great caverns would appear in the mist and we could see, as if at the ends of white corridors, the distant, sunlit peaks of China. Often the path disappeared in vapour and we groped forwards, looking out carefully for every turn in the trail. As we went on, the views below became more and more infrequent, occasional glimpses of a shimmering sea. The fresh air, wet with the evening mists, was chilling and we stopped to don a sweater apiece.

On rounding a shoulder of the mountain and approaching the high point of a col, we came across a great stone arch, silhouetted nakedly against the darkening sky. Solitarily situated among rocks and scree near the top of the pass, it gave the place a powerful atmosphere. Coming close, we could see it was painted white and that there were great black Chinese characters incised upon it. We stood below it, listening to the wind and gazed up, puzzled, at the writing. Then, to my surprise, we found near the bottom of one column an inscription in English. Three terse phrases lay one above the other:

"TO THE GREAT MONK – SING WAI"
"THERE IS NO TIME"
"WHAT IS MEMORY?"

The words were so unusual, so unexpected, that on reading them I was shocked. There was a momentary gap in my thinking and feeling, as I tried to fathom their paradoxical power. This was my first confrontation with a text that summarised Chinese Buddhist insight completely and the question it asked not only perplexed me deeply but was to go on rankling, under the cover of my daily activities, for months to come. It came as a revelation to realise that here was a perspective that asked the very questions that seemed to have been deliberately avoided in my religious education, questions which, in recent years, had concerned me more and more and would not go away. A sudden silence was filled with the sound of the light wind and, below, the mists parted to give a momentary glimpse of a small junk heading out to sea.

The gateway opened to a hollow in the hills, almost like an ancient crater now filled with vegetation. Rich, grassy meadows covered its floor and there were several cultivated plots. Around the edges several little shrines, small pagodas with spires and stupas, sat about on knolls of their own. Several cottages loomed dull white in the evening light and a larger building was set among trees with an arched gate before it, not unlike the one on the hill. We pressed forward eagerly to the Po Lin monastery of Ngong Ping.

Passing through the great gate, we entered a little courtyard where several men were standing dressed in grey habits. They smiled courteously, inclined their heads and pressed their fingertips together before them in a greeting. We were taken to a small room, where a large, jovial monk in a brown habit received us with smiles and a deep, rumbling voice. We were soon to learn that he was the 'Secretary'. A scrawny, ill-dressed, little man with a squeaky voice, a scraggy neck, great affability and a modicum of English emerged, as it were, from behind a panel and asked us, "You take tong-cha?" We said we would love Chinese tea – without milk but with a wonderful flavour. "You like blekfast – six – seven – eight – nine – ten of clock?" Everyone was smiles and grins. We were clearly oddities here and the monks' sense of correct hospitality only just curbed their extreme curiosity. Everyone was positively dying to get a look. A row of nodding and smiling heads faced us and the little man – the Chief Accountant – rattled off introductions all round. Suddenly, in from the dusk, came a taller, unusually-attired Chinese. He addressed us at once, "Good evening, gentlemen! I also am guest here. I am Mr Sun. Who are you?"

He had a clear, ringing voice full of strength and character. His remarkably handsome face held a pair of piercing brown eyes, friendly and strong. "You take tea now. You sit down. You will eat later." His tone was such that his interrogatives sounded pretty well imperative and all we could do was to obey.

Mr Sun was a writer, especially of film scripts. He hailed from Shanghai which he had left when the Reds approached and he had had to leave his wife behind. Mr Sun carried a great, heavy stick and always walked with reliance upon it as if it tired him. A gay little skull cap fitted snugly on his round head and he smoked a powerful, aromatic tobacco in a deep hooked pipe. He was taking a three month 'holiday' up at Ngong Ping to 'concentrate' upon his story. He loved the peace and quiet of the monastery, he told us. He showed us his writing, pages and pages of closely-written characters. His English was good enough for everyday matters but he did not tell us very much about his writing.

"You take hot bath – yes!" A charming youth was fetched, who led us to our room, a long, wooden attic, lined by a row of boards set upon trestles. Upon these lay mats, smooth, wadded mattresses and a blanket. Around each bed space hung a muslin mosquito net, so that each bed looked like a miniature four-poster, complete with white curtains. We wondered if they were dens for spiders and centipedes and, with some trepidation, we examined them with the light of a little oil lamp. All was clean, however, and the room smelt beautifully of wood.

We were taken to the bathroom, simply a couple of dank cubicles, lit by a guttering oil lamp and containing basins of hot water and stools. We sat on the stools, washed our feet, soaped ourselves and finally, *faute de mieux*, poured the water all over ourselves to feel mightily refreshed. We saw two enormous mosquitoes lurking in corners and rapidly fled back to our room to dress.

It was very nearly dark and the monks had begun their evening service. Some fifteen of them processed steadily round and round the courtyard, chanting a repetitive melody with a lilt measured to the tread of their feet.

"Sigamouni Bo, Sigamouni Bo, Koonyam Boussa, Detsang Boussa, Omitopha, Sigamouni Bo..." on and on.

It was a strange song, even though musically very simple it stirred some not easily definable feeling. I had never heard the like of it. There was an accompaniment from the leading monk with a small tinkling hand bell. In the quiet mountain air, the reedy chanting seemed to emphasise the timelessness of nature and the unusual life of men who lived, it seemed, out of contact with contemporary history. Only much later was I to learn that the monks were chanting the names of the Buddha and Bodhisattvas as mantras of faith and power.

In the shrine room of the Buddha, which filled the greater part of the main building, guttering oil lamps were being lit. Through the windows, we could make out a great dark temple with many hanging tapestries in narrow strips like early Victorian bell pulls. On the ends of some of these hung small bells with high, insistent tones and, the next day, we were able to see their elaborate needlework and the many characters and charms worked upon them. In the centre of the room stood two glass cases, the larger containing a shining, golden Buddha with lesser deities surrounding him. One of these, representing, we were told, Kuan Yin (Koon Yam in Cantonese) the Goddess of Mercy, a beautiful piece of silverwork, had many arms stuck out in a frill around the head. Numerous drums, gongs and 'wooden fish' lay about the room. The latter are hollowed blocks of wood, vaguely fish shaped, which, when tapped, emit a hollow clopping sound, which deepens in tone with the size of the instrument. As the monks processed and chanted, I had the impression that the pale ivory Buddha, in the larger of the glass cases, moved in the guttering lamplight almost as if it were breathing. His inscrutable face gazed down upon us with – was it pity, scorn, love, or vacancy? A diamond, set deeply in his forehead, flickered.

The chanting ended and the monks filed into the hall to kneel on hassocks in lines radiating out from the Buddha. There was more chanting, a great shower of tinkling bells and then it was over. At the back of the temple, near the staircase to our quarters, was a further entrance. Three golden images stood here, side by side, above a small altar by the door. Yellow lamp light flickered upon them and the statues seemed alive with the beauty and lavish splendour of the ornate workmanship.

We were treated to a very good vegetarian supper of rice and vegetables, delicately flavoured tea and, to finish, hot, wet face towels with which to freshen ourselves and toothpicks to play with. When we had eaten, Mr Sun took us for a little walk just beyond the gate towards the paddy fields. He kept his eyes glued to the path all the time, warning us of the snakes. He told us that the lights of Macao were visible from a nearby knoll but that it was "very dangerous to walk out there at night". Mr Sun and the monks clearly considered the night to be given over to snakes and evil spirits. We retired early, Mr Sun admonishing us to lock our door tightly and to pull our mosquito nets taut because of the snakes. He showed us a back window through which a great snake, four inches thick and immensely long, had once crept in during the night.

As I lay inside my mosquito net, knowing no insect or other creature could creep in upon me, I felt a deep repose and pleasure, a sense of being at home. In spite of the simplicity of the wooden boards, the thin mattresses on which we slept were silky to the touch and very comfortable. The night air tasted cool and delicious, with a flavour of late September in England. High upon the mountain, we had escaped the heavy, airless humidity of the nights down in Hong Kong. The Broken Headed Mountain is about 3000 feet high, so I supposed we were at about 2000 foot altitude.

Soon after 5 a.m. I was awoken by movement below our room. Mr Sun had put on his light and visited the lavatory. I made good of this advantage and meeting him there, he bade me good morning. He told me that, before long, the dawn service would begin. I was shivering in the morning air. The whole place was in a deep stillness, not a sound anywhere. Roger lay on his bed like a comatose dog.

Soon I heard a mysterious, tapping noise far away on the other side of the building. 'Clop clop clop clop.' 'Clop clop clop clop.' It came closer and passed below our window. I could hear the swish of the monk's robes and the pad of his sandals. The sound faded away around the building. The eerie tapping in the silent before-dawn air had a quality that made one's hair stand on end. I realised it was an awakening call but also felt it to be a frightening away of evil spirits before the service began. Soon there began a distant, measured rumbling of gongs away in one of the buildings. One by one deeper-toned gongs joined in and the sound swelled louder and louder. Little tinkling bells began to ring, their notes piercing the deeper thunderings of the gongs. The hand beaten drums chimed in, together with the rattle of variously toned wooden fish; the noise swelled to a crescendo and fell away. Suddenly the chanting started, rising and falling like the swell of the sea, now loud, now soft and all the time in a gentle, swaying rhythm that set my toes moving.

I knew I would never forgive myself if I just lay there listening. I slipped on my plimsolls and crept down to the back of the temple. The three images were glowing again in golden lamp light but beyond them all was shrouded in darkness. I crept along to a side window. Before me the massive back of the larger Buddha obscured the view but, between the dangling tapestries, I could see the figures of the monks kneeling or standing facing the Enlightened One. Some were drumming with their hands and tapping the wooden fish. It was very dark and I could see little, so I crept around the flank of the building, trusting to luck as far as the snakes were concerned, and emerged through a circular "moon gate" into the courtyard. I crept almost into the pool of light before the open door, from where I could see the ivory Buddha and the monks before it, one officiating before the altar.

Suddenly, a chow dog in the doorway looked in my direction. It pricked up its ears and, almost at once, the courtyard became a turmoil of barking and yelping dogs. I turned and edged my way out of the courtyard, expecting to be attacked at any moment. All was well however and I reached my room feeling a little shamefaced at having caused such an uproar. Anyway, the barking soon quietened and the chanting went on louder and louder until everything was going at once in a sort of triumphant hymn; voices, many baritones of a reedy quality led by a ringing tenor voice; gongs; drums; bells at full volume. When it quietened, the original swelling chant took its place. I lay in my mosquito netting and listened until I was lulled back to sleep.

After a delightful Chinese breakfast, served again by the charming youth, whose shy smile could best be described as the precise opposite of the Buddha's, we were shown the temple and the various finely wrought paintings and calligraphy. There was one room off the courtyard that particularly intrigued me. It seemed to be a kind of small hall or study for there were hassocks on the floor and around the walls ran a stone pew upon which, at intervals, cushions were placed. As I passed the window I noticed what appeared to be a life-sized image sitting just out of the light coming in from the window. I looked more closely and realised that it was, in fact, a young monk. He was sitting with his legs crossed, the soles of the feet upturned upon his thighs and his hands resting together lightly between them. His back was upright but not rigid and his head inclined slightly forwards. His eyes were shut and his face completely relaxed, expressionless, serene. I watched him closely, strangely drawn to him with an emotion akin to awe. His breathing came and went so slowly, so slightly, that he seemed not to move at all. The Buddha posture gave him an air of detachment, of distance, of separateness from the world of men, from life even. He seemed most like the mountain itself, filled with an impersonal, unengaged power meditating upon its own centre. The words on the gate came back to me, "There is no time. What is memory?" What indeed could memory be without time? What could time be without memory? What was memory?

What was time? The questions spun in my mind and I pondered over them near the window for some time before I drew myself away.

We said goodbye to Mr Sun. He was busily writing in his room and told us he was a Christian. He had with him a great black Bible all in Chinese. He looked forward to seeing us again whenever we might come. We paid our lodging fee and then walked out regretfully across the plateau to find the path that would take us down the mountain to Tai O, at the end of the island. Once more the great view opened before us, patches of cloud drifting across and dappling the pale blue sea with dark shadows, between which silver shivers ran. The wind had dropped and the tall mountain grasses stood still about us, their delicate heads curved against the sky. A feeling of vast space and distance enveloped me with that extraordinary peace of mind that sometimes creeps under the edges of my skull when contemplating such a scene. As the clouds drifted alone and serene over the hills my eyes followed them; I felt that everything in my life and in the world around me had fallen still; that it had always been so; that nothing had ever happened nor would happen and that it would be thus from everlasting to everlasting.

Chapter Nine

Sai Kung Patrol

Into the woods

Early in December I received orders to 'stand by' to take a patrol into the mountainous county of the Sai Kung peninsula. I was at once thrilled by the idea and began examining the map. Sai Kung is a large lump of the Chinese mainland forming the northernmost area of the Colony's New Territories, that parcel of land rented by the Chinese to us until 1997. It was totally remote, covered by range upon range of bulky mountains, split by steep-sided valleys and cut off from the rest of the colony by deep inlets of the sea. Between some of the mountains lay small plots of rice paddy and attendant hamlets. As yet there were no roads in the interior; footpaths wound up and down from col to valley cutting desperate capers with the contour lines.

I went to the Army HQ in the city for a briefing. I was informed of the area to be patrolled and told to visit all the villages within it, checking whether any returned deportees, communist soldiers or strangers of any kind were lurking there. I had also to check that no illegal wolfram mining or excessive timber cutting was going on and to prepare a report on the lives of the villagers, following certain specified lines of enquiry. Our mission was to provide a short-lived military presence among the most cut off villages of the colony where intruders could easily be hiding, to give medical treatment where needed and to establish friendly relations with the village headmen, showing that the Government had some interest in their welfare.

It took me a day or two to plan the operation and collect the men, signals and other equipment, weapons and medical supplies needed. I had a sergeant, two bombadiers, eleven men, a RAMC medical orderly and three Chinese police representatives, one of whom was my interpreter. We were to carry full "Korean" marching order, our food in heavy boxes, a jerry can of fuel for a fire, a 62 wireless set, two heavy batteries for the same, and a great camp kettle for brewing meals. I took a revolver and a few rounds, while the men had a rifle apiece, the NCOs carrying stens. We had enough ammunition to slaughter the entire neighbourhood!

I did not expect any trouble. There had been no reports of Communist infiltration into Sai Kung and the patrols were usually a matter of routine – a kind of scouts' outing. Nonetheless the patrol of the previous month had spotted a party of deportees trying to sneak back into Kowloon. An exhausting forced march across the mountains had cut them off but the deportees then made for some junks on the coast and it seemed they might escape. Patrols are under strict orders not to shoot unless attacked but, on this occasion, the accompanying policemen thought differently. Their corporal grabbed a sten and fired a burst in the air. The lieutenant in charge was horrified but then delighted to see the deportees surrendering. He marched them back to Kowloon and the patrol was duly fêted by the authorities. Every few years such an incident occurred, so we, too, had to be prepared for possible excitement.

We started out the Sunday before Christmas and drove in a three-tonner to the small fishing village of Sai Kung, where the army had a battle school for infantry bound for Korea. We were taking the only road into the area – 'Hiram's Highway', a miracle of military road-making, so narrow that traffic could only go one way at a time, with twenty minute up periods followed by twenty minutes down. The track twisted between cuttings, edged around vertical drops, looped the loop around little valleys and hurtled again up a rise. We reached the police station without mishap and met our policemen, three round-faced and grinning little men. Their inspector, who treated us to a drink, was no doubt the most influential person in the area.

It was a hot afternoon and under our heavy loads, sixty to seventy pounds each including badly-balanced boxes of tinned food, everyone was soon sweating and panting. The mountain slopes, dotted with small fir trees, alternated with sharp little gullies, where small rivulets bubbled and jumped over grey rocks, the water, fresh and clear, tasting sweetly. The track, paved with huge slabs of stone, led us into the hills. My men struggled up, weirdly bent under their loads, two of them carrying the heavy wireless set slung between two poles. Gunners were not so highly trained as infantry for this sort of task and we found it was slow work; the men, tired from their weekend debaucheries, needed frequent rests.

After a map-reading consultation with my new police corporal, an excellent man with good English, I decided to head for a dot on the map called Wong Chuk Shan – Green Bamboo Mountain. We paused along the way to test out our communications and, to the signalman's horror as well as mine, discovered that the microphone was not working. The spare one failed too and the outlook was bleak – no contact with base. Nonetheless, I decided to push on as fast as we could to establish our base camp. I sent one bombadier, a man of vast strength carrying twice the load of the others, and the police corporal on ahead to talk with the headman and borrow a barn or some shelter to cover us during the cold night.

Late in the afternoon, we topped the crest of a ridge and gazed into a long valley sheltered from the wind by thick woods. The sounds of birds came up to us and, at the far end, stood a group of houses. I led the way quickly down through terraces for hill rice cultivation but, as we entered the trees, the path became precipitous and soon we were all stumbling about with fatigue, dropping the heavy boxes every few yards.

The school-room of the village had been given over to us for the visit and, as we arrived, the villagers stood around in a reserved but not unfriendly manner, while the children were wide-eyed with amazement. As soon as the tea was brewing, I set off with the constable and a gunner on a forced march back over the hills to the police post. We travelled light and soon covered the distance. Having borrowed another microphone, we scrambled back over the mountain in the failing light. It was dark when I got in to find my bed roll ready on the stone floor, a most inviting prospect.

I was up before first light and, while my sergeant and a bombadier prepared breakfast, I shaved in the cold water of the village stream. With the men fed and ready, we set off. I took the main patrol with the police corporal, while the sergeant led the others on a rather easier route. My plan was to cover the northern area in one long day's march travelling entirely around a large mountain, Ma On Shan, and visiting a sizeable iron ore mine.

Carrying only our personal arms, ammunition and water bottles, the going was easier and we made good speed. At a solitary little hillside farm called Ngong Ping, a farmer greeted us with a smile and twinkling eyes. Out came the little benches we were soon to know so well together with bowls of Chinese tea, delicately scented and refreshing. Every house along the way seemed to be keeping a kettle continuously on the hob to greet a weary traveller. In one village they called the tea 'Italian', although why I could not find out.

I questioned the farmer through the police corporal. Had any strangers been seen in the vicinity? Was there any sickness on the farm? Was the harvest good? Have you a police rifle? How many people live here? He was most obliging and seemed happy to entertain us.

We approached the small shantytown of the iron ore mine down a narrow valley. Ugly community sheds clung to the rocks. Huge boilers were heaped with steaming rice and hundreds of Chinese, looking very different from the villagers, stared blankly at us. The hillside had been carved into cliff-like tiers, five galleries running round the sides of a quarry in the hill. Along each of them ran a rail track and men could be seen riding on wagons up the slight inclines. Rock was being hacked from the cliff faces and piled into the wagons. More rails, vanishing into three great holes below the hillside, revealed the entrances to underground shafts.

I had a long chat with the chief clerk in the main office. There were many workers employed here, mostly refugees from south China, Hainan in particular. They received five dollars a day (six and three) for their labours. Their families lived in the little shantytown and the men rarely left the desolate hill for a visit to the brighter lights of Kowloon. There was an excellent dispensary, staffed by a doctor trained in Europe. The manager arrived, appearing charmed to see us. In excellent English he said "Ah, but, of course, you may see the mine! Here is my foreman. May I introduce Mr Chung. He will show you around."

I set off with the police corporal, my medical orderly and Mr Chung, leaving the patrol relaxing under the watchful eye of a lance bombadier. On the floor of the chasm, men were sorting rocks into three piles, good, medium and poor ore. This was determined by estimating the ore weight, by swinging the rocks in a basket slung on a short length of rope. The heaviest rocks contained the most ore and were blueish in colour, bright and shining. Entering the shaft, we moved forwards into darkness with drops of water dripping from the roof all around us. There was a strong smell of cordite. The far end of the shaft was lit by electricity and we inspected the boring device. The technique was to bore a narrow hole into the rock at the face and insert an explosive charge and fuse. The 140 foot shaft was then evacuated and an explosion set off. In this way some forty tons of ore could be mined in twelve hours at one face alone. The manager gave us a truck to take us downhill on a private, gravel road to the coast, where the ore was being loaded on to a small steamer from a jetty. Along the little waterfront stood a number of warehouses and dwellings; once a month a steamer sailed direct to Japan. We took a sampan and began a series of visits to the villages of the flat coastal strip bordering the wide Tolo harbour.

*

Wind and water

The villages of the interior were lively little places filled with friendly people, whose welcome never ceased to delight us. Around them spread the paddy fields, in mid-winter freshly ploughed but, in spring, filled by a glue of wet mud and water, brilliant green with the sprigs of newly growing rice. The village plan was almost always the same, the houses placed together in a characteristic pattern expressing the beliefs of the villagers.

Several rows of houses stood one behind the other, all opening the same way, away from the hill behind the village and out towards the open view. Often only the front houses actually had a view, the others peering into the backsides of the row in front of them. All apertures opened forwards and the back wall of the village had no windows. Often a group of houses were clustered together to create a minute hamlet of several homes, again with a windowless rear and opening on to a small courtyard. Behind the village, there was almost always a thick tanglewood or a steep well-forested hillside. Sometimes, where the gradient of the hillside was steep, the houses were spread out along a contour with the track running along in front of them. The tanglewood behind the houses was especially important, we were told, even lone houses being positioned in this way. The idea is to prevent the entry of ghosts.

Just as cats rarely cross an open space but prefer to run with their sides to a wall, so the villagers like to have a wood behind them as a protection. This is because ghosts can only move in straight lines. In the tangled wood they soon get thoroughly confused and withdraw. A frontal approach leading to entry to a building is foiled in another way. Wide screens are placed inside an entrance, so that an approaching spirit, being unable to turn aside, is reflected back out again. Often these screens or the doors themselves carry paintings of the Door gods, protectors who, likewise, eject an approaching demon or ghost. Mirrors, too, are especially protective, since ghosts see themselves in them and get terrified. Dragons on the eaves of the houses counteract the effects of bad siting and scare away evil beings.

The view in front of the houses must be as perfect as possible with Dragon or Tiger shaped hills poised in the scenery, ensuring peace and protection. All these features produce the most marvellous landscaping effects; houses and villages beautifully positioned to take advantage of surrounding natural features. We were encountering the practice of Feng Shui meaning 'wind and water'. Specially trained geomancers are called upon to study the landscape around any building project.

The forms of the hills, the directions of the watercourses, the positioning of roads and bridges were all held to influence the 'breath' or 'Chi' of the landscape, the flow of universal chi moving through a location. Feng Shui is the art of adapting the residences of both living and dead to the local currents of this energy so far as possible. It is the geographical expression of the Taoists' search for harmony with the Tao of things, the 'way' or nature of the universe. The positioning of graves, which form a focus for ancestor worship, was equally significant. The overall result had clear-cut material benefits; these hamlets were marvellously sheltered from cold, wind and typhoons, while their inhabitants enjoyed the most wonderful of views. To us visitors, every arrival was a joy.

The open space in front of a village is the equivalent of a village square in England and, on arrival, we usually gathered with the villagers there. I always asked the police corporal to lead the way into the villages, since the arrival of a Chinese face naturally palliated the shock of what was to follow! Amid scenes of enthusiasm, the police corporal would call for the village headman.

Dogs barked madly, young men came forward, some eagerly, some shyly, to greet us. Often women and children ran to hide in the darkness of their houses but some of the kiddies always ran forward in delight, whooping and laughing, so that the others would soon follow. The arrival of the headman was always a sign for more respectful behaviour and, since his house was often the largest in the village, benches would be brought out of it and bowls of tea, "cha", served for myself, the police corporal, the medical orderly and sometimes for the men as well. Seated on the bench of honour, with the corporal on another and the headman facing us, I would then initiate talk to obtain our information.

While we were talking, the medical orderly got to work. If he spotted a child with sores or anyone with cuts, boils or skin infections he would treat them at once. He had a reassuring manner and, as he clowned about with the children, he revealed a jollity which amused everyone, laughter following him around wherever he went. The police were soon swapping stories expansively with the young men and bashful maidens tentatively approaching the MO with questions. Our meetings were gay, little affairs which everyone seemed to enjoy.

Sometimes we came across terrible conditions; a little girl with a scalded leg, with the skin broken open and suppurating; a man in Wong Chuk Shan with gangrene from the ankle to the knee, the whole leg black and peeling, with two angry purulent sores. He was quite ignorant of the seriousness of his condition and three times I got the corporal to make him promise to go to the Sai Kung dispensary within three days. There was a handsome little boy with swollen neck glands, to whose father I gave a chitty of introduction for the dispensary and an old lady, with such a twinkle in her eyes, whose feet were cracked and swollen with fluid, in a manner that led us to suspect gangrene.

In all villages there were complaints of malaria and one little lad was very seriously ill with it. I had to explain several times that the disease was spread through mosquito bites and emphasised the importance of using nets at night for sleeping. Although we often saw them in the villages, it did not look as if many people used them. Often we left behind a quantity of Paludrine tablets. Since many of these would end up being sold on the black market for a profit, we gave them only to actual sufferers and to the headmen themselves for communal use.

On the second day, we arrived back in Wong Chuk Shan in good time and it was a delight to rest awhile in this pleasant spot. It was so high in the hills that the houses were more spread along the contours than those lower down. The headman occupied the highest house and we were amazed at how his attitude and that of the villagers changed, as we started handing out some of our excess food as "gumsah", gifts. Tangerines, brilliant orange against dark lanceolate leaves, were in season and a couple of lads climbed a tree bringing down handfuls of fruit for us.

A mountain stream tumbled down a narrow gorge between the houses, where we washed in a pretty pool overhung by great ferns and shade-giving trees. As it got dark, little salamanders appeared from under the stones and swam about in the light of our torches. One of the gunners was keen on biology, so he and I caught some and put them in our mess tins, to the extreme amusement of the men when they awoke in the morning.

We had set up our base camp in the local school, itself part of a miniature village, the buildings forming a square, with a narrow court in the middle and a wood behind. The school-room itself was the central room in the front, facing out over a valley of paddy fields. The other rooms were the homes of families all opening onto the central court. In the middle of the back row of rooms was a small temple, inside which two apparently identical images faced the entrance, surrounded by a miscellaneous assortment of disciples. After some discussion with the villagers the corporal told me it was Ngai Ching but sadly I failed to discover anything about it. Perhaps the deity was the local village god but the collection of disciples made this unlikely and, anyway, we found a similar shrine in another village. At either end of the narrow inner court were two cow byres. Every morning, out would come the animals to feed in the outer court on great bundles of rice hay from the stores (see diagram overleaf).

Every morning and evening, we set up our wireless in the outer court and, surrounded by gaping children, listened to the whistlings, buzzings and screamings that accompany any attempt to communicate in this way. The hills made reception difficult so, one night, I sent two signallers up to the top of the hill overlooking the village. It was dark and they had not returned, so, with another gunner, I set off to give them a hand down the dangerous paths in the darkness. The set and its batteries were very heavy and any slip could mean disaster to equipment or limb. We went warily up among the hillside trees flashing our torches along the ground and into overhanging branches for fear of snakes. The fireflies played with us all the way, cruising

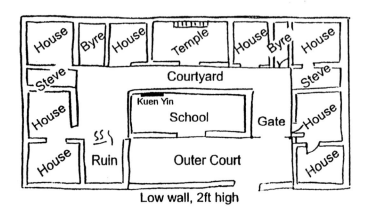

House | Byre | House | Temple | House | Byre | House

Steve

Courtyard

Steve

Kuen Yin

House

School

Gate

House

House

Ruin

Outer Court

House

Low wall, 2ft high

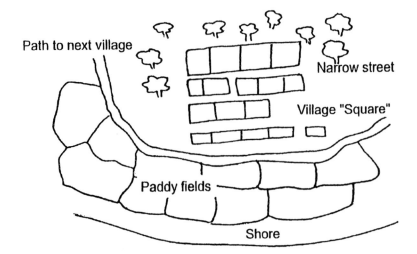

Path to next village

Narrow street

Village "Square"

Paddy fields

Shore

out of the forest like little white sparks or sitting still on a leaf or rock, like glowing eyes. Every evening they had cruised about us as we sat around our fire in the outer court. The luminescence comes from a group of patches at the rear of the abdomen, which flash on and off as the insect wills.

We found the signallers well above the tree line and brought them back without mishap, arriving in the village to a chorus of yapping dogs. The villagers went to bed at sundown so we must have disturbed them, but we had seen no ghosts nor had the police who, like the villagers, rarely moved at night without great torches.

We all relaxed around our evening campfire and, after the hard day's walking, gloried in the sweet night air of the mountains, the twinkling stars, the silent night and the incomparable moon sliding down the heavens and casting a soft light on the distant mountains, the flat-lobed leaves of the papaya plants and the wood along the hill. As the fire crackled and glowed I listened to the life stories of the gunners.

My signalman had fought with the Ist Welsh Regiment during the war and, afterwards, became a whaler in a catching vessel. He told us stories of the chase, the strange sounds of the ice floes, the albatrosses gliding by, the penguins clowning about on the ice. He told us of carousals in South Georgia and of a visit to remote Kerquelen Island. Yet he had got tired of that life and reinlisted in the infantry. Finding himself stuck in Aden and loathing it, he joined the Artillery and came to Hong Kong. He was loving the patrol; a man of action, he found sitting on a gunsite painful. "Sitting up there on the bloodee mountain I might as well be in my coffin, you see!" he said, his Welsh accent bringing a lilt into his voice.

My sergeant had originally been an aircraft fitter on a carrier during the last phases of the war and, after a spell in civvy street, he found he could not settle down. He tried to get back on to carriers again but, for some reason, he failed and joined the army as a second best. "I look like doing twenty-two years now," he said, a trifle regretfully, I thought. I wondered what it was that drew these old warriors back again and again to the military life.

One of the brightest gunners was little more than a boy, with all the energy of a wild colt in spring, the helpful sort, full of enthusiasm, interested in far too much and quite unreliable. He jammed a wad of cloth in a village rifle while trying to clean it and it took me half an hour with an improvised ramrod to clear it. Both he and a signalman want to join the SAS and go parachute jumping into the trees of Malaya.

When the men had turned in, I would sit on the terrace wall gazing out over the moonlit valley. The whole landscape seemed magnified and distorted by the night; the mountains leaned down over the valleys emanating power; moonlight glowed dully on the heavy, pewter leaves and pendulous fruits of the pawpaw; the thick tanglewood breathed around the houses; the stream chuckled over its stones and salamanders; someone was snoring in the house; a cow defecated and the dried hay let forth a sweet odour of cattle urine, as it lay drying on the stone slabs. One or two of my men turned and moved, rustling their mosquito nets. A baby cried in a house across the stream. Fireflies drifted past, ghosts' eyes between the leaves, the branches and twigs, flying silently past my face and, drifting on a small breeze, were wafted up over the corrugations of the roofs and away, flashing tiny, occasional lights above the valley. I felt the place pressing down upon me in its own silent contemplation. Spirits were abroad, drifting over the paddy fields and around the houses and brushing me with a feather touch of the windless air. The valley seemed to be murmuring with the silent memories of centuries. I thought of the rooted lives of these village people; the unchanging lives of their ancestors; those bottled-up bones in the hillside jars, washed at certain festivals with the waters of the stream from which they once had drunk. Nothing seemed to have changed here; cock crow; dog bark; the movements of cows; children's laughter; disease; acceptance of old age, well-tended; the silent brooding of the hills over life and death alike; the rhythm of the year; harmony; Tao. The spirits moved around me, invisible, intangible, understanding, gentle. A pewter pawpaw leaf shifted in the silent air. I sat for a long time thinking and not thinking, keeping harmony with the chi, a silent meditation.

*

Coming down

On our last morning, we awoke to find half the village standing about outside the school with immense trays of steaming hot food smelling deliciously. Sadly this was no gift. They wanted to present it to the little shrine of Koon Yam (Kuan Yin), the Goddess of Mercy, that decorated a wall inside the school-room. We hastily shifted our things and I sent the men outside. The Chinese entered, lit joss sticks and kow-towed several times to the shrine. The food was laid out before it and selected portions placed on the shrine itself. A great chain of Chinese crackers was hung from the wall outside the house and lit with a match. The valley exploded with a rattle-like machine gun fire, sparks from the crackers shot about all over the place, children went mad with jollity, pocketfuls of crackers appeared and the village was filled with rifle fire, battle raged around the houses, over the stepping stones of the stream, under the pawpaw tree, up on the terrace of the headman's house, children and young people throwing fireworks in a gay abandon and, all the time, the deafening rattle of the immense cracker chain near the shrine roared on. Not a ghost remained for miles around. Pieces of food were handed to me and then the villagers bore the trays triumphantly away for a long morning's breakfasting. The air was cleared of all malevolence, sunlight danced like the children among the paddy fields. It was the day of the Festival of the Winter Solstice.

We started off on our homeward trek through villages gay with frivolity. I sent the sergeant one way and I took another, in order to visit two different localities. We met in the afternoon at an appointed rendezvous. I noticed the sergeant's bombadier was missing. The sergeant told me he had gone off but would be back shortly. I was pointing out that this was scarcely in the orders, when the character appeared on a far-off mountain side swinging along at a tremendous pace. He was a great, red-headed thug of a man, good humoured and with a reputation for eccentricities. He had been in the army for years. He marched into camp and presented me with a bottle of Coca-Cola.

"Glad I'm on time, Sir – 'fraid I wouldn't make it! Brought yer some refreshment."

"Where have you been, Bombadier?"

"Kowloon, Sir. It was like this see – Sarge here let me off for a bit of free time. So I made it, Sir, there and back. Three hours, Sir!"

Intrigued, I could not stop myself.

"But, Bombadier, we shall be there tomorrow, so what's the hurry?"

"Nah – that's asking, Sir, that is. It came over me sudden like to see the popsy. A week in these 'ere 'ils tickles yer up a bit, you know, Sir. I thought a bit of the old one-two would do me good!"

The patrol was rocking with delight. The bombadier's feat was indeed astounding. In a little over three hours, he had climbed the hefty range of mountains between us and Kowloon, found his girl, had a session, bought some Coca-Cola, climbed back over the mountain and was indeed on time at the rendezvous. I congratulated him on his virility and pointedly told the sergeant to make out a charge sheet, if there should occur the slightest opportunity. The bombadier was as good as gold for the rest of the trip; the most energetic and peculiarly helpful bombadier for whom one could have wished.

We spent the night at an old army camp on a summit above Kowloon. The city lay below us shimmering its jewels and we sat up late watching the lights and talking to base over the radio. We had a little rum with us – for medical purposes – and some of us celebrated our return. In the early light we came down through clouds to the city. It was Christmas Eve and the men, fitter than ever before in Hong Kong, were "raring to go, Sir". We signed off amid cheers and jollification at Battery Headquarters and I set out for Brickhill and what I imagined might be a night's rest.

Chapter Ten

Christmas and a New Acquaintance

Festivities on a hilltop

The camp was in a state of high excitement. Speke, one of the drivers, was drunk and wandering about the camp, with a Chinese broom between his legs, pretending to be the Wizard of Oz. Mulberry, who I had retrieved from a police station only a week before, had smuggled whisky into the camp and had spent the morning dodging the Troop Commander, slipping into a latrine now and then for a 'wee dram'. Another gunner had a whole cache buried just outside the perimeter wire and, despite the orders forbidding it, as soon as the TC left for Christmas in his hotel, the liquor started to flow with alarming rapidity.

Our noble Cook Corporal had arranged a Christmas party for the evening. It was a marvellous show, decorations all over the gunners' mess hall, jellies shivering on their plates, cakes in mounds and everything seasonal to please. The camp rocked with carousing gunners displaying their linguistic abilities to a nicety. We three subalterns served at table and there was riotous fraternisation. One bombadier, with his arms around my neck, was calling me John when "Good old Crook" was called upon to make a speech. I climbed on two chairs.

"Gentlemen!" Loud cheers. "Having just returned from the wilds of China – " Riotous cheering. "I can think of nothing better than to join you all here!" Dramatic, prolonged cheering and the subsidence of Crook. Toast after toast we drank with gunner after gunner. I had just returned from the patrol in the New Territories and had eaten nothing since breakfast. Soon I could hardly see straight and retired to the calm of the MI room with Drabble, our medical orderly, only to find a neatly laid up table, complete with brand new wine glasses and bottles of sherry, port, brandy, whisky, beer, cigarettes and an ashtray. It was not for me to spoil his kindly show. I selected his best whisky and, having opened it with due ceremony, we drank it like a liqueur from the wine glasses.

My signalman from the patrol joined us, rolling with beer. Drabble quickly hid his spirits under the table and draped a towel over his range of some twenty beer bottles. 'Sparks' was well away.

"You know, shir – you and I – do a patrol to Mongolia – shee the world shir – blasht them Chinks – you and I shir – jolly good patrol shir – you know shir – you're a horror – escushe me but I'm drunk!"

One by one, it seemed, the gunners rolled in to see us; the whole camp and even one of the guard must have been tipsy.

It was amazing how quietly everything went off; no fights; no broken windows; some remarkable things came to the surface, the gunners telling me things they would never have said at other times. They told me what they thought of the sergeants. I discovered they had a nickname for the Troop Commander – 'The Flapper'. We subalterns seemed to be their favourites. I was surprised and indeed very moved by the expressions of affection several of the gunners showed towards me. The Cook Corporal complimented, "The best officer I've ever worked under!" Everyone seemed happy to use my first name as if I was an old pal.

I realised how deeply within themselves the men judged their officers. My policy had always been to encourage through influence and suggestion rather than through loud orders with no expression of understanding. I endeavoured always to make a man feel it was he who was important and that, although I might be directing his work, I was, nevertheless, more a friend than a superior. I tried to deal with the men as human beings not as numbers doing set jobs. I never felt different from the men as a being apart; essentially they were my brothers and no different, except in upbringing and their individual points of character, from myself.

I had some mince pies to absorb some of the spirit, but it was a hard job to retain control of myself, let alone keep the others from falling down the hill and hurting themselves. Eventually, I walked to my room in a straight line, congratulated myself on having a head for whisky and fell instantly into a deep but somewhat circulatory slumber.

The sergeants woke us at seven fifteen on Christmas morning and we went around the camp throwing Chinese crackers into the billets and dishing out tea laced with rum. Roger and I then zipped down in the car to the cathedral for Christmas Communion – very peaceful after the riotous celebrations in camp.

At breakfast, our mess was attacked by the gunners with firecrackers and battle royal ensued. One of the REME men climbed on the roof and dropped fireworks down the chimney. We retaliated with a stirrup pump, finally directing it so well as to soak his matches and wash him from the roof. The sergeants came to drink in the mess. The Battery Commander and Troop Commander both arrived and we all went down to serve the Christmas dinner to the men. The Corporal Cook had again done wonders with the turkeys, chickens, stuffing, two sorts of potatoes, green peas, cauliflower, Christmas puddings, blazing away in flaming brandy, and lashings of brandy butter.

Then it was off to the sergeants' mess, brandy-dries running like water and the Battery Commander talking shop for an hour with a loquacious sergeant. I got fed up. At 3 p.m. we got our own lunch. By this time the soup was cold but the main dish still perfect. The commanders had left for town and the cook was deeply offended. I mollified him with extravagant praise and this, coming from the camp's messing officer, at last made him happy.

Suddenly my mood changed, tired of drink, feeling cynical and depressed, I retired to my room, and, to my surprise, wept. Somehow, the innocent debauchery of the gunners seemed infinitely pathetic. I reflected on the way too much drink tended to make me feel the sorrows of the world and its veiled futility more than usually strongly. I supposed it was that, in that condition, I could not produce arguments to shore up my otherwise sometimes shaky faith in living.

After a shower and a good wash I cheered up and we three subalterns set off for Kowloon for the Battery Commander's party on Stonecutters Island. It was quite a success. We played roulette with counters and I left feeling ready for a visit to Monte Carlo.

About twelve thirty, we crossed the harbour to find a great glow in the sky and a huge pall of smoke hanging ominously over the whole of Kowloon. I realised at once that a shantytown must be on fire and, knowing how sad a sight it would be, I was against going near it. The others, still in festive mood, seemed to think the occasion a kind of

Guy Fawkes Night and even my acid remarks did not lessen their adolescent desire to see a spectacle.

We could not get very close for the police were blockading the streets; riot squads, wearing tin hats and carrying truncheons, were out in force in case of trouble. The fire brigades from all over the colony seemed to be converging on this one spot and, indeed, there was need. In the centre of Kowloon there were several low hills, the Nine Dragon hills, which were smothered by shantytowns; row upon row of decrepit, wooden buildings like chicken coops, garden sheds and shacks, all propped back-to-back, higgledy-piggledy, without any plan. Thousands of the Chinese poor live there, coolies and the many destitute refugees from Communist China. One of the hills was ablaze, flaming from top to bottom with towering billowing masses of black smoke and sparks twisting skywards, while a rain of ash and still-glowing particles fell around us. Shack after shack dissolved in flames, horrifying tongues of fire reaching fifty feet or more skywards, spewing smoke and crackling sparks. The fire was closing on the built-up area near Nathan Road and all the fire-fighters could do was to contain it among the shacks.

The streets, empty of their usual bustle, were filled with dazed Chinese standing about in numerous groups, like men watching a funeral and a weird, grieving silence pervaded them all. Refugees were hurrying away from the fire; ragged men and women with clusters of kids, all carrying great bundles of clothes and a few items of furniture, the only belongings they had left in the world. A sewing factory had been evacuated and men hurried past, dragging the metal sewing machines, scraping them with a shattering noise along the pavement. It was frightening, ominous, awful.

The Hong Kong Police, steadfast as ever, had all movement under strict control and their show of strength and purposeful activity was impressive. It was Christmas night and thousands of the world's poorest people, in one of the world's most overcrowded cities, were now entirely destitute. My companions had sobered. It wasn't so funny after all. We drove away in silence.

*

Yannang

By the end of November, I had began to experience a restlessness and irritation at the too few contacts I was able to make with Chinese people. I wanted so much to enter their society and be allowed at least an attempt at understanding their lives. Yet, with the shortage of free time and limited introductions, it seemed I never would be able to make headway.

One or two of the Hong Kong newspapers published contributions in English prose written by Chinese students. They published the prize-winners' short articles, stories, descriptions of experiences, definitions of friendship and suchlike and I took to reading them, thinking I might, in this way, stumble across someone interesting. I made one attempt at a contact and spent a very dull evening with a young Chinese, who knew nothing of his own culture and whose general attitude resembled that of a totally uninspired schoolboy in England. The only entertaining thing about that visit was that he lived on the top storey of a large house to get into which one pulled a wire in the street to ring a bell outside a window. Then the key for the flat door would be tossed down to the road. All we did was to go to a cinema.

I was almost giving up hope when, one evening, I read the following article, which resonated with my own recent experience.

FIRE AT NIGHT

It was a moonlit night when I walked along the path on the hillside. The sky was high and clear, the moon bright and round; its silvery light pouring over the trees so that their green leaves glittered.

My mind was fully occupied with the beautiful scenery when suddenly I saw a column of smoke rising at a distance in front of me. I ran forward to see what was happening. As I drew near I caught sight of flames shooting out from one of the huts on the slope. "Oh Fire!" I cried out. I lost no time to render assistance and ran as fast as I could to ring the fire alarm.

The fire brigade arrived soon after but several huts were already in flames. Rescue work began at once. Several hoses were shooting water into the flames while two others played on the surrounding houses to prevent the fire from spreading. At the same time some firemen with wet towels covering their noses, hurried into the smoking huts to help the people out, away from danger.

The people were in a state of alarm and anxiety, confusion reigned in the village as the crying, shouting and sound of falling fragments filled the air. Children cried for their parents while parents ran shouting for their children.

As the wooden huts were very dry and the roofs oiled with shellac the fire spread with the most dreadful rapidity. The strong wind fanned it so that the flames darted out like golden dragons from the windows and doors into the air. The moon was concealed by thick black smoke. The water had no effect and the firemen could not save the village from ruin though they tried their best.

The poor refugees saw their homes being destroyed but were helpless. An hour later the fire died out and there remained only the black messes of ruins. Each family sat huddled together with its baskets, boxes and clothes facing the razed houses in great misery. The dreadful fire was to them a serious disaster. They were now homeless.

On the higher slope, there stood the white buildings. They seemed peaceful and quiet in the silvery light while their owners slept safely in comfortable beds. Oh! what a contrast it was.

I read the article several times. It seemed to catch the atmosphere of the occasion vividly and to show great empathy for the suffering of the refugees, often crowded in unhealthy shantytowns around the city. I was struck by the precision of the writer's observation and his ability to present it in terse but reflective sentences. The style gave the text a detached tone with a slightly dreamlike quality. To say "My mind was fully occupied with the beautiful scenery," suggested an introspective awareness different from, say, "The landscape was beautiful under the moon". The writer was contemplating the spectacle, even as he described its horrors and even though he was, to a limited degree, a participant. The last paragraph observed the social inequalities of Hong Kong and the fate of unfortunate people in such a curiously detached and accepting way that I was touched. It could only have been written by a person of some maturity of mind, awareness and reflective sensitivity. I felt that the article was in some sense distinctively Chinese and that a British writer would not have used English in this manner. As a piece of student prose it seemed remarkably good.

It was signed Yiu Yannang, with an address in the most densely populated area of Victoria. I resolved to write to him suggesting that we might meet and talk. So it was that, one evening, I walked along the front of the Hong Kong Shanghai Bank to meet the writer. In front of the bolted doors a young Chinese was walking up and down, alone. I introduced myself; we shook hands and strolled off together to take coffee in a nearby restaurant.

I felt at once that there was something appealing and delightful in his company. He was quite tall, about an inch shorter than myself, slimly built and he moved gracefully with alertness. Tastefully dressed, he wore a blue blazer, a red tie and grey slacks. It was difficult to guess the ages of Chinese but I would have said he was anywhere between seventeen and twenty-five. He was in fact nineteen.

Yiu's conversation was at once rewarding. While his English was not without faults, he spoke with little accent, with good pronunciation of words and with an intelligent use of a wide vocabulary. He told me he was learning English, Mandarin Chinese, Philosophy, Literature of both China and England, Geography, European History and basic Science at his college in the city. With the exception of topics concerning China, the subjects were taught in English and, because of the difficulties this posed for the students, the leaving age was high, around twenty for the few who were to go on to higher education.

We made ourselves comfortable in the café and he began to tell me about his life. He was a native of Hai Mun, a large coastal village north of Hong Kong, where the dialect was that of Swatow. Living now in Hong Kong, he also spoke Cantonese fluently. His father, Yiu Mingsing, had run a trading business between Swatow and Hong Kong. He had owned junks, some for fishing and some for the transportation of goods, and also some farming land. He travelled regularly on business between the two ports, where he retained offices. During the Japanese occupation of Hong Kong he had remained in China but the family had had to escape from the village when Japanese soldiers arrived.

Yannang had come to Hong Kong by junk for a holiday and, during his stay, the Communists took over his village and he preferred not to return. Later his mother and one of his sisters had also reached

Hong Kong but his father had to remain in Hai Mun. All his ships and land were taken away from him. As a landlord, albeit a small one, he was subjected to continuous persecution by the Communists, as were so many others at that time. He emerged virtually destitute. Yannang, meanwhile, was accommodated by his father's former business associate, whose son later married Yannang's sister. This "uncle", Chan Wingtak, was a kind man offering help not only to those to whom he was connected by reason of business or family ties but also to other villagers from his district. Often he was himself in some financial difficulty as a consequence of his generous heart.

"Life is very difficult, is it not?" said Yannang with quiet resignation, uncoloured by any tone of frustration. He seemed determined to enjoy and value life, even if it was not good to him as it was to some. We discussed how we should spend the evening together. He ruled out of hand the idea of visiting a cinema.

"It is much better to walk around and talk," he said. "To sit together and see a film when we have barely met would be too absurd!"

We wandered through Victoria, visited the Hong Kong Products Exhibition in Kowloon and, finally, I took him for dinner to Jimmy's Kitchen, one of the small, more fashionable and comfortable European restaurants with a pleasing atmosphere and excellent service.

We settled ourselves at a corner table while Yannang looked around with an astonishment that was amusingly naive. "All foreigners!" he said. I glanced around hurriedly, expecting a bevy of Spaniards or a bunch of Teutons, but all I could see were some rather dull English colonial businessmen with their very ordinary wives, one or two smarter military couples and a group of Americans, whose very noticeable wives had voices that seemed crossed in love with foghorns. I realised that, while I now accepted the mixture of English and Chinese in Hong Kong as natural, both being for different historical reasons equally 'native', Yannang only perceived Chinese as native and all Europeans, whether English or not, quite foreign. I then found that although he had read about English meals at school he had never before eaten one. It was Boxing Day, so I ordered turkey with stuffing, sauce, cauliflower and potatoes, followed by Christmas pudding with brandy butter. I also ordered glasses of Rhinegolde for each of us.

Yannang at first tried to use his fork as if it were a chopstick and he had to copy my own movements carefully before he could lift anything from his plate at all. While I had found my first experience with chopsticks infernally difficult, I had never thought a knife and fork could pose comparable problems too.

"You know Chinese food is always cut up prior to serving," Yannang told me. "It is really very strange for me to cut up the food on my plate!"

He enjoyed the wine but was surprised to find it served cold. "Chinese rice wines are best served hot," he told me.

After a while he asked me, "Would it be all right if I push some food on to your plate. In China this is a sign of friendship and I would like to do it!" I had to say that this was not the usual practice in a European restaurant.

We talked about religion. "Have you one?" I asked.

"None at all," replied Yannang, as if the whole business was quite pointless and really not worth worrying about. To this realistic Chinese it was living that mattered; anything that might come after could not be known so why be troubled by it?

Relaxed from our meal, we went wandering in the shadows of the arcades hung with their brilliant neon signs. We passed a lavish prostitute who made eyes at me.

"I think most of the soldiers in Hong Kong live bad lives," said Yannang.

"Hmm," I replied. "I'm afraid most do."

I realised that Yannang was a good person with a sensitivity for rightness in human conduct and relations. He revealed a kind of innocence that was not merely refreshing but something I found myself respecting. The soldiers, indeed, spoke of little else other than women and, among my brother officers, our ears and tongues were continually fouled by asides about the ladies of the streets, the pox, homosexuality and the vice dens of the city. Yannang, partly because of his youth, but mostly because he had already judged these things irrelevant to a good life, was free from such concerns. I suddenly felt that this innocence might become abused in my company and I feared my own earthy mind. Yet, it was clear that he was a realist too and by no means ignorant of the extent of the sex trade in Hong Kong.

I could not tell how well he had enjoyed his first European meal for he was scrupulously polite and I was afraid its oddity might have been too much for him. The subtlety of the intermixture of cultures in Hong Kong intrigued me. Yannang with his almost faultless English, his European dress and his school-scrubbed appearance had never before handled a knife and fork.

As we parted, he said "You are the first foreigner I have known as a friend."

Chapter Eleven

A Chinese Tenement

An evening visit, January 31st 1954

One evening I met Yannang outside the vehicle ferry. He said, "Tonight you come home with me." I was delighted since never before had I entered a Chinese home as a guest.

"My uncle says it is too poor a place for you to visit and that he has nothing to offer you but, since you are a friend of mine and I know you want to come, you are most welcome."

I said it was happiness not wealth or poverty that counted and that good conversation was better than wine or food. So we began our evening with a classical Chinese exchange and set the standard for the occasion.

We walked past the colourful shops of Des Voeux Road, gay with lanterns, decorations and displays for the forthcoming Chinese New Year. We came upon a steep little stairway leading up between shops, climbed over the rubbish littering the lower steps to the third floor and paused outside a front door opening off the stairway. A shrine to the Door God was set into the wall, bright with crimson paper and good luck writing. Joss sticks smoked before it and others were stuck into the woodwork around the door.

"It ensures that only good luck can enter!" said Yannang.

Somebody opened the large letter box and looked at us; the door was opened and in we went. What had once been a large room was divided into many cubicles and only the rear end of the tenement belonged to Yannang's people. We entered the living area, which already contained a sizeable party. 'Uncle', the head of the family, was gambling with three friends at a small table, playing with small Chinese cards with figures I did not know upon them. A pile of coins and dollar notes lay beside each man. The merchant rose and shook hands, bidding me welcome. He spoke a few words of English, since he had at one time lived in Shanghai. Several women and children sat around talking or sewing, the kids round-eyed and curious. I was not introduced to any of them. A young student appeared, apparently another nephew of the merchant. Studying English in the city, he spoke it well, although not so clearly as Yannang. Kut Lok, "lucky happiness", was a bird-like youngster with bright eyes and a merry glance.

Against the wall was another shrine, gaudy with crimson paper and containing two brilliant silver and gold paper images. One of these was the protector of the household and the other a kind of policeman who regulated the lives of the household.

"Yesterday we had a small festival," Yannang explained "The Kitchen God went back to visit Heaven and deliver his report on the behaviour of the family during the year. He will return on New Year's Day, when we will set up a new image in the kitchen shrine. We gave him a very good send-off, so that he will give us a good report. You know, for two days all the Kitchen Gods are in Heaven so we can do what we like!"

I asked him which members of the family believed these stories.

"All the women believe them and it is they who maintain the shrines and the correct observances. They have no education and this is part of their traditional life. My uncle and other men enjoy the stories but we do not believe that the events they portray really happen."

The women stayed at a distance, preserving a reserve. I never discovered who was the old man's wife nor who was his concubine. Judging by the number of faces travelling in and out the room there was no lack of talent.

The evening passed in a wonderfully leisurely way; no complex etiquette to observe, for, after the introduction, the elders carried on gambling, the women sewing and Yannang, Kut Lok and I sat talking around a business desk; folk stories; cultural contrasts; unscientific philosophies and the interpretation of poetry. One of the children brought us tea and I was treated to a glass of Lai Chi wine, earthy and strong, from a poisonous looking preserving jar where the fermenting liquor swilled around the ancient fruits. Yannang brought out an old cough mixture bottle and we each had a glass of Benedictine!

Yannang had a big book in large Chinese characters, the Tao Te Ching of Laotse. It was exceptionally obscure, he told me. Many of the characters were rarely used today, so it was a difficult book to understand. He read it because it made him think. He translated a few paragraphs for me and I offered to bring down Waley's translation to see if we could penetrate the more difficult parts.

Kut Lok enthused about the origin of characters.

"They were originally like Egyptian hieroglyphics, picture drawings of objects but as writing evolved so the characters changed."

He drew the ancient characters for a house, a tree, a ship and put them beside the modern versions. There was a clear resemblance but one could not imagine the object designated from the present-day version, whereas it was possible to guess it from the original.

"You see, a character often acquires a metaphorical meaning so that it is not always easy to follow an ancient script."

Yannang showed me the books he was reading, *Pickwick Papers*, *Nicholas Nickleby*, *The Mill on the Floss*, *The Three Hostages* and *Kidnapped*. We talked about Bardell versus Pickwick, the life of Dickens, highland scenery and the Hebrides and then he brought out a tattered copy of *The Golden Treasury*. Thumbing it through, he found Keats' *Ode to a Nightingale* which he asked me to read. I knew it fairly well and gave a careful rendering. Then came the inevitable barrage of questions. What was a dryad? What was Hippocrene? Why did the poet use thees, thous and thys? What was the metaphysical implication of some phrases? My friends revealed a scholarly love for interpretation and language. I had to think hard for Keats is by no means always easy to explain.

Out came some notes on English scansion and here I had to tread warily for, although I love poetry, I have never used or treated scansion seriously and, in my own efforts, I rely on an intuitive feeling for assonance and dissonance rather than versification. I was amazed at the knowledge and persistence of these boys, their interest and depth of understanding. Yannang was particularly quick at sensing the meaning of the more abstract matters we discussed. He had an alert mind, which I had not entirely appreciated earlier because, at first, he had conveyed the impression of casual enjoyment of life whatever it might bring him.

The merchant was engaged in the import and export of fishing nets and tackle which he used to obtain from Swatow. Kut Lok's people were fishing net makers in Swatow and could carry on normal life under the Communists since they were not "landlords". In Hong Kong, the exiled sons of fisherman and landlord study literature under the same roof like brothers. There is a Chinese parable, "Once there was an old man who lost his horse so that he became most distressed. Soon after it returned, accompanied by others. Who knows what is good luck or bad for each in time may lead to the other".

I asked Yannang if he could concentrate on his studies in so crowded a room.

"In the daytime it is normally fairly quiet here but, whenever I can, I take a rug and pillow up to the Botanic Gardens and read there. It is a beautiful place."

Out the back and down the steps a crowd of highly vocal people were practising songs from Chinese operas, cymbals clashed, gongs, rattles and drums strummed wildly. Nearby some people were playing mahjong and a continuous rattle came from the table as the players slammed their pieces down. In the front tenement, the wireless was playing swing, every now and then an English disc jockey changing the music. Chatter and laughter was all around, except in our corner where it was quite peaceful, doubtless with respect to the gambling fraternity and the scholars discussing philosophy!

A journalist I once met at Ngong Ping monastery thought that the stability and happy appearance of so many Chinese under adverse conditions has to do with their upbringing. A child is carried on mother's back or, if she is busy, then on the backs of older children, brothers or sisters. Kids of five or six hurry about with the lolling baby strapped to them. Babies are not left alone for hours in prams or alone in the lonesome dark of rooms at night. Somebody is always with the child and, as it grows, it meets so many people that all the sharp edges of character are worn smooth. The children of the boat people can handle sampans alone at five or six. Commonly one sees a kid of six or less manfully rowing with the great stern oar, almost as heavy as the child, swinging the little craft from side to side across the water.

The crush of humanity brings a certain security but, for those who wish to study or think for themselves, this massive pullulation of people, so characteristic of China town life, can be depressing. I was soon to learn the extent of Yannang's reaction to it.

*

Cross-cultural vision

To walk and talk with Yannang, visit his home, meet his relatives, look at his books, sit in the room protected by the family shrines and offerings to gods while the old men gambled and mahjong rattled was an entry into a new life. Any European can see these things from the outside but to participate in Chinese life in their company gives a new insight and constitutes a challenge. The effort and strain is often considerable, although unnoticed at the time. It would be easy to offend in some breach of etiquette, to do or say something repugnant in Chinese eyes.

I have no doubt the Chinese react with aversion to some of our habits, just as many Europeans are revolted by Chinese spitting. Until one is accepted as a friend one is no more than an outsider, but, once a friendship has begun, thoughts and feelings merge and mould themselves in a mutual harmony. One has to advance and retreat, straighten out knots of language, laugh at misunderstandings, solve puzzles about what a chap is called, where to sit, the correct way to eat, how to be open or maintain reserve in the company of elders. There is a continuous focusing on how to fit into another world. Alone with the Chinese there is only intuition, mutual respect and a will to understand that can help one through.

The Chinese are proud people, outwardly reserved and living in a city where old colonial attitudes are still only too evident. Yet, once friendship is formed, barriers quickly fall. When I left the tenement I thanked the 'old man' very copiously and genuinely for his invitation and he, who had had an ear in our direction all evening, I warrant, shook hands and told me I could return whenever I wished. Yannang looked as delighted as I felt.

Up on the hill the Troop Commander cannot understand these trips of mine. "Dirty, foolish people!" he mutters, "All firecrackers, din and smell!" Many of my brother officers are disparaging about the Chinese simply because they have no wish, being as self-satisfied as Cheshire cats, to understand them at all and lack any sense of the compassion needed to feel at home with a strange people. For this there has to be love.

Often it is difficult. I cannot yet understand my own reactions to these immersions in another world, different, yet also so similar, to our own. I come away exalted, treading on air, knowing the barrier of race no longer hinders me, that I too have been accepted by others simply as myself. Yet, sometimes, a gesture or the fall of light on a face causes a kind of mental twist, a sudden wish to flee such queer company, to be alone to adjust oneself. Although I try to believe I have no race consciousness, yet these occasional twists occur and I feel I am not yet truly at home. In others such twists cause race hatred, bad feeling and spite.

Of course it might be easier as a civilian. I have met a number of men of real knowledge of the East with the right attitude to racial contrasts. Brook Bernacchi, the famous Hong Kong lawyer, and his mother have adopted a refugee lad of fifteen and are bringing him up as their son. I do not know where he comes from but he is a jolly, energetic boy. Such action cuts across European aloofness in Hong Kong and Bernacchi's courage reaps reward in their relationship. To see Bernacchi at his mountain farm in Lantao with the boy riding his horse and chatting in his native tongue with the villagers, while his guardian talks high politics and Buddhist metaphysics with his welcomed guests, is an inspiring sight.

In the ranks of regular officers and most subalterns the lack of interest in the world around them, the obsession with cricket or squash, the clique-mindedness, the public school bias, a niggling class and racial attitude – all this makes me vomit. I will never say a man or a race is superior or inferior to another, merely that they are different. My criteria for civilisation are happiness, mutual understanding and goodwill, not metropolitan railways or poetry recitals in upper rooms. A friend reproved me saying I was a lover of the "noble savage", to which I retorted that there was no essential difference between the humanity of a villager and a city bank manager.

*

Chinese New Year, February 4th 1954

The streets were thronged with people, everyone with pockets stuffed with firecrackers; in at the windows of cars they went, under the tyres and feet of passers-by, flashes, showers of sparks, popping, crackling and exploding in alarming detonations. Outside some of the shops dangled enormous decorations fitted with artistic lanterns, whirls of roman candles, bright signs and writing. In front of first floor windows hung great composite crackers in long streamers, their explosions throwing off smaller missiles into the roadway where further crackings and bangings sustained the racket.

Some stalls were selling New Year cards with little envelopes marked with the double Hei character for marital bliss and Tai Kut for 'Great Luck' in which gifts of money are put. Yannang in make-believe said, "You must imagine I am older than you and married. You are perhaps my nephew. Here is a New Year remembrance for you," and he gave me a little red envelope containing a ten cent piece. I thanked him with correct effusion – doje doje sup fan doje.

Along Bonham Strand West the Chinese traders had formed an association to make their streets especially attractive. Great wickerwork lanterns hung outside the shops, parchment colour with huge vermilion characters written on them. Each front room was decorated in a traditional manner, with the long shop counter laid with cloth on which stood bowls of flowers and fruit. Often a great vase held aloft a cherry tree, its leafless branches bursting with little pink flowers, like butterflies clinging in spring to unsapped twigs. If a tree fails to bloom before the festival it is an unlucky sign so the growers have to take special care before supplying their customers. Great scrolls hung down the walls depicting mystical mountain scenes with gaunt trees, swirling mists, high perched temples, vast chasms and extraordinary bridges. Some depicted mandarin scholars in their grandiose clothes, stately and magnificent.

In one front room a band with singers was in full voice singing songs Yannang recognised as hailing from his home area near Swatow. We ate in restaurants far off the European track, where I was greeted with many noddings of heads, smiles, "allos" and chuckles. One evening we had a dish of Yeung Chow Chou Fan, fried rice with prawns, scrambled eggs and diced meat and followed it with a steaming bowl of snake's meat – stringy but highly flavoured complete with arteries and veins and swimming in a tasty, thin gravy.

A beggar came round and, giving a reserved bow, placed a little piece of red paper on our table. We rewarded him with a fifty cent piece for which he again bowed and thanked us. He left us the paper, on which a golden god brandishing a great whip rode a rampant golden lion. It was the God of Wealth. By giving alms to the old man we had invoked the god to bless us in the coming year.

At these restaurants there is a curious system of ordering and paying. The waiter takes an order, which he then shouts at the top of his voice to the cook standing by his stove, with the foodstuffs hanging on hooks around him. Once finished, one simply gets up and walks to the door. The waiter, who has noted the number and type of dishes eaten, shouts again, this time to the cash desk where we make payment. The noise is terrific with some twenty waiters all bellowing orders and bills at once. Apparently they use a sort of code – 'one week' meaning seven dollars for example.

Outside, several fortune tellers sat at little tables illuminated by oil lamps. Most of them had palmist drawings or sketches of physiognomies and cranial shapes on boards beside them. The most entertaining was a gentleman with a small cage of birds. For thirty cents a bird would answer any question which another bird would check by performing an exact repetition of the behaviour of the first. A sheet of paper lay before the cage upon which was a pile of envelopes. The first bird hopped out and chose one. In each was a sketch, depicting a particular Chinese story which the soothsayer used to answer a question. After the first bird had made a choice, the second was brought out and chose identically the same envelope. Quite impressive. I was to have two wives, the first by October. The Chinaman gleamed at us, the little crowd chuckled at his remarks, which may well have been more colourful in the original tongue!

Chapter Twelve

Rank and Friendship

Military exercises

By the middle of winter, life at Brickhill had become a matter of routine and, with better opportunities for enjoying my free time with Yannang and other Chinese friends, the army life ceased to pall and the gun site became the centre of a small world, in which I officiated like a minister.

The weeks passed easily; two or three training practices every seven days; educational and training courses; occasional inspections and sudden cathartic visits from the CO. A second firing camp was held in which the troop excelled all others and, together with a good record during a three day scheme, we were satisfied that we were probably the best trained and most operational troop in the colony. The Battery Commander was pleased and directives from regimental headquarters became fewer. Whether we were in fact the best was really irrelevant; we considered ourselves so, without snobbery, and the result was an extraordinarily high morale.

The men were remarkably free: after work hours they went climbing on the cliffs, reading in their bunkers, doing gymnastics on an apparatus created by the cook corporal, or, again under his expert tuition, practising weightlifting. Most evenings we had a bathing parade, greatly enjoyed by officers and men alike. The only difference in the water being that, statistically speaking, the officers were less likely to be pushed off the raft in the bay than the men were.

Out of working hours, the Troop Commander, whose technical brilliance was the chief cause of our military success, was rarely with us. Our regular army subaltern was a good disciplinarian but young enough to appreciate the national service's attitudes of his two brother officers. In off-duty hours the camp became a sort of Butlin's for soldiers. Saluting still existed, of course, as did the hierarchy of rank but it had become a matter of tacit agreement rather than of discipline. Everyone knew everyone else so well that any 'bullshit' would have amounted to farce. Nonetheless, any troublemakers were bounced severely and our guard mounting parades continued to be strict, amounting to an evening ritual linked to the setting of the sun. The long shadows of the men moved across the little parade ground, the stiff figure of the inspecting officer sliding between them, a plump sergeant trundling behind.

A kind of mutual respect had grown up among national servicemen of whatever rank and we formed the majority on site. The camp very much acquired a national service atmosphere, slack in off hours but enthusiastic and hard-working at other times, with many of the men expressing a moving loyalty to the gunsite. Regular soldiers, with the exception of one or two older sergeants, played in with us and the result was a strangely happy collection of men, none of whom could have said exactly why they were so contented.

We had our family troubles, of course, but, in general, things went well. I felt contented among good friends and came to appreciate our isolated mountain life, where I could both direct and serve others even apart from military duties. This surreal army atmosphere was only occasionally troubled by the intrusion of some pompous, high-ranking officer.

One week I had to take a reading and comprehension test for those men with no educational qualifications. I got them to read a simple passage from some story, firstly to themselves and then aloud to me. I would take the book and ask them to tell me in their own words what they had read. This was one way of grading the men for a new educational scheme being introduced in the colony.

I was amazed and shocked by the showing of most of my gunners. A few of the gun numbers could not read at all, some could pick out only the shortest and simplest words, others could read but not pronounce and, again, a few could read but failed to understand what they had read. This was an eye-opener for me because all these men talked with ease, made sense of their lives and appeared moderately intelligent. In fact they were illiterate. We set to work sending them on schemes to provide them with a basic education.

Gunner Barry had been my senior generator attendant for weeks. I wanted to promote him to Lance Bombadier for he was a useful person who could do well. For a long time he was reluctant. "Well, ah must think it over," he would say. Finally, I broached the subject directly saying that I had mentioned the matter to the Troop Commander. We were standing by the generators, looking down the precipitous valley to the grey rocks of the shore.

"Ye know, Sir," said Barry, "Ah don't think ah'll take it. Ye see Sir – it's like this. If ah become an NCO then ah'm no longer one of the boys. Ye' got to be in with your muckers in the army, Sir. Muck in with the boys, that's wot ah say. Ye can't do nowt else. 'Ave a drink at the NAAFI, a bit o' cunt in town, but ye mun do it with yer pals, Sir. Nah, if ah became a bluddy NCO ah'd be different – Sir – not one of 'em. It's awright for them as likes it but not for the likes of me. No Sir, thank yer very much, Ah'll stay with me muckers!"

And he did. I, too, had lived in a barrack room and could appreciate this intense desire for solidarity with his friends but I realised that the origins of his decision lay deeper in his history, in his northern working-class origins, the distrust of 'they', the authorities, a fear of becoming one of 'them' cutting him off from 'us'. He was neither a dominant nor an aggressive individual but he was both efficient and assertive. I wondered if desire, dominance and aggression were needed to break the bonds of 'usness'.

For some reason Barry and Trill, the other generator attendant, took a great fancy to me and would frequently ask me to "Cum an 'av a drink with the boys, Sir." I knew that there was a point at which familiarity became destructive of respect, so the situation here was a tricky one. I found a solution in the fact that when I was duty officer it was possible to 'drink with the boys' in the NAAFI in uniform, when the others were relaxing in mufti. This meant two things, firstly the wearing of uniform emphasised the necessary rank distinction and the fact that one was on duty meant that one could not touch more than a pint or so. This was well understood by the soldiers' extraordinary instinct for the correct social relationship required by an officer in a particular mood. One evening, however, Barry and Trill came up to the officers' mess with a bottle of beer and a mug for me. Fortunately, I was alone.

"Ave a drink with us, Sir," said Barry. "It's all on Trill here – ye see it's me bluddy twenty-first fucking birthday!"

"Barry," I said, closing the door of the mess gently behind me, "congratulations and many happy returns!"

"Hep – and many 'appy returnsch!" added Trill.

We sat on the steps outside the mess and they poured me out my beer. Barry was not so very drunk but the beer had loosened his tongue.

"'Ere's to you, Sir!" he said, "Our best bluddy officer."

We drank and I toasted his birthday. Barry leaned forward confidentially.

"Ye know, Sir, the trouble with you is y're too fucking eddicated. What's the use of bluddy eddication if it stops ye mucking in with the boys. All you eddicated chaps're the same, always thinking or reading books, talk, talk. Don't ye ever 'ave a girl, Sir, go on the booze 'an get proppa sozzled. That's our life an it's a good un – it keeps yer well cleaned out. When ye with the lads ye can 'ave some proppa fun. On yer life, Sir, ye can!"

I told him a little about books and reading but he was not impressed.

"Tell ye wot, Sir. When it's yer birthday, jest ye let Trill 'ere an me know an we'll take ye on a booze and show ye up Gobblers. Clean ye out it would, Sir, proppa like. Come in with the boys and we'll give ye a good time. Jest ye let us know, Sir!"

I returned to the mess thinking there was a lot of sense in Barry's philosophy. I felt they were right, that I was missing something. But what to do?

At the backside of the city of Victoria there is a narrow gully containing a stream that tumbles down steeply into the city from the upper levels. Alongside the brook, a path climbs out of town winding between thick bushes. To the gunners the place was known as 'Gobblers' Gulch'. Here they would repair on Saturday evenings in search of a 'popsy' for a 'knee trembler' in the bushes. Often going in groups and having found a willing girl, they would disappear with her among the bushes among the rocks near the stream. Tossing up for first go, they would carry out rites proper to the occasion. They had a superstition that the chap who was 'first in' never got VD, whereas the second fellow, should there be any such risk, usually 'caught a dose'. Occasionally, by way of a change, they would seek a 'brown arser' instead but this was usually referred to with bated breath, not because it merited disapproval, but because it was a rarer and more perversely exciting procedure.

One evening Roger and I walked 'up Gobblers' to see what we could. All we noticed was a group of figures some way off the path and a couple of mincing girls, who made eyes at us as we passed. At the top, however, where the 'Gulch' comes out on to a residential road, we met several of our gunners about to come down.

"Ah ha – good evening, Sirs," they chorused with ribald amusement. "Having a good time?"

We gave them of our best repartee and went on.

It was extraordinary how popular we were in camp next day. "Had a good time last night, Sir?" "Saw you up Gobblers, Sir, was she a good 'un?" and so on. The camp approved strongly of what was evidently seen as a demonstration of normal virility by its officers. It seems that British soldiers believe all officers to be impotent, chinless wonders. Our supposed exploit bore useful fruit.

I once asked our cook Corporal the meaning of 'Gobbler'.

"Well, Sir, you know, it's what happens when you have a six and nine."

After a little encouragement I understood.

"Of course you can't do that in the Gulch, Sir. You have to get her to take you to her room for that."

Gunner Collinson was a very nice boy. He played tombola in the NAAFI all Saturday and was never drunk. He was also saving a lot of money every week. One pay parade he said to me,

"Sir, may I draw out my savings next week?"

"No reason why not, Collinson, but what do you want it for?"

"Well, you see, Sir, I shall be going back to Blighty soon so I thought I might get a few presents for the folks."

Next week Collinson duly disappeared into Hong Kong with some three hundred dollars in his pockets. The story did not emerge until later when the camp was agog with it and Collinson a hero. Wearing his best suit he had strolled nonchalantly into the grandest of Kowloon hotels, a most impressive building, functioning as the air line terminal and the centre of a social order normally well beyond Collinson's reach. Entering one of the bars he had a drink and waited for what he had been told would happen. A svelte Chinese waiter approached him.

"Are you waiting for anyone, Sir?" he asked.

"Well, not exactly, I was just wondering–"

"Of course, Sir. Well, there are British, American and French planes in this evening. I dare say one of the hostesses might like to oblige – er – for the usual consideration."

"Naturally – perhaps you might like to arrange it for me."

"No problem, Sir – and which nationality was it?"

"Ah – French, of course," said Gunner Collinson.

"Room 291, Sir. In half an hour. I'll let you know when you may go up."

So it was that Gunner Collinson slept with a charming French air hostess in the most famous of Hong Kong hotels. Asked what it was like he would smile dreamily and say "Sir – It was lovely." A penniless but happy man.

We had limited transport and on Saturday afternoons a single three-tonner was used as recreation transport, taking officers and men alike down to the city. At midnight, everyone reported back to the truck for the journey home. It was a fantastic if disgraceful sight. Across the great car park of the services' Cheero Club, groups of sozzled gunners would appear, some singing at the tops of their voices, some supporting a vomiting companion, and others more exhausted, "shagged to the wide".

Greetings would be effusive and officers avoided but, as there was only one seat next to the driver, it was frequently necessary for one of us subalterns to board the truck behind. We were usually greeted with cheers, Christian names and long-winded tales of the evening's exploits. Off went the truck swaying out of town, two or more men vomiting over the tailboard, "spewing the ring". Loud singing echoed along the shuttered streets, pavement popsies receiving piercing whistles and catcalls.

Occasionally a man became aggressive and was surrounded by his fellows, the more sober gathering around the officer, isolating him from the more drunken individuals. A sergeant or NCO was usually present to keep a semblance of order.

One day there was a serious row in camp. One of the more temperamental bombadiers, who had been under some stress, threw down his jacket on being given an order. It was a refusal to obey – an 'I'll soldier no more' incident. He was marched off at once to the guardroom where he spluttered apologies to every officer who approached him. The difficulty was twofold. Apart from this incident, he had a good record and, in spite of his temperament, he was a jewel of a character. His case was tried at the Battery Commander's orders with the Troop Commander and me as witnesses. The Bombadier apologised profusely, confessed his attachment to the site, to his friends. It was the happiest time he had had in the army, he said. He couldn't bear to leave it. To the surprise of us all, he began to weep like a child. The embarrassed Sergeant Major marched him out and we adjourned to allow him time to recover. The BC looked at us and asked for our opinions. We were indeed loathe to let him leave the camp since his usefulness lay not only with his efficiency but with his good influence on the men. In addition, although we were shy to admit it, we had been affected by his protestations of affection for the site and his life there.

He was marched in once more. Apologies again; "Dunno what came over me, Sir. Blubbering like a baby." The BC then launched into a merciless dissection of his character, delivered with a savage iciness, yet with the air of a rather disillusioned father rather than that of an Officer Commanding. The analysis was accurate and I respected the BC's performance. According to the Manual of Military Law, the man ought to have received an unpleasant sentence and reduction to the ranks. The BC decided to give him a second chance and, after dire warnings, his case was dismissed. The BC told us all to forget it.

On another occasion, I was nearly stuck through with a bayonet. It was an unpleasant Saturday evening with all other officers and sergeants out of camp. I was Duty Officer and only a single senior bombadier remained as Guard Commander. At Guard Mounting Parade this bombadier behaved rather strangely and I realised he had been drinking: yet he was coherent and mounted the guard without error. On the parade, however, one man, whose rifle was poorly cleaned, was ordered to parade before me some time later for further inspection.

He was brought to me by a very junior lance bombadier. The rifle had not been touched. I was launching into a torrent of corrective abuse when, to my discomfort, I noticed the man draw his bayonet from his belt and conceal it behind his trouser leg. I knew this man well from the patrol, a trusty old soldier. I altered my tone and enquired whether he was all right. I then saw he was swaying on his feet and quite drunk. He made a slight movement with the bayonet, which was at once seized by the lance bombadier and wrestled from him. Without further ado, I had the man under close arrest and locked up in the guardroom.

The disciplinary problem posed by this event was not simple. First, if it came out that my guard commander had also been drinking then both he and I would have been in serious trouble; he, for not having controlled a member of his guard, and I, for not having dismissed him before the parade on a charge of being under the influence.

I called the Guard Commander up to the mess and, seeing his thoughts were still cloudy, treated him to a strong, black coffee. I decided not to mention his 'state' and he was soon 'right enough'. I decided to charge the potential bayonet sticker with drinking on guard duty rather than threatening an officer, thus avoiding an awkward enquiry. In any case, I liked this man and did not want to see him before a court martial. I was later to find out that he was, in fact, a developing alcoholic and that little could be done for him. He asked to see me and apologised profusely, being at great pains to make things up generally. I advised the TC to transfer him to another troop as soon as possible.

And then there was the outing of Gunner Mulberry. He was my favourite Gorbals' 'die-hard' straight from the Glasgow slum. Mulberry rarely left camp, preferring to save his cash and get quietly sozzled in the NAAFI. Whenever he did venture forth, the whole camp held its breath.

One evening the whisper went round, "Mulberry's going to town!" and everybody anticipated the inevitable sequel. Mulberry's mind did not run particularly on women; he preferred rickshaws. He and his mucker, McTavish, would drink a bottle of Scotch together and, with some extra beery fortification, they would hire a rickshaw and set off on a wild carousal, singing and roaring through the streets. Suddenly they would stop and, amid mighty oaths, drive the unfortunate coolie into an arcade. McTavish would then grasp the shafts of the vehicle and off they would go again weaving dangerously in and out of the traffic with a lordly Mulberry in the back waving a bottle. Always it ended up the same way, a free fight on the highway, bruised policemen and a locking up in jail. Around one in the morning the sleepy Duty Officer would take the call and get ready to prepare some defence for the morning's magistrates court.

*

The Chinese view of the Army

Unsurprisingly, the British 'tommy' is not popular among the ordinary Chinese of the colony. Some men leave camps on a Saturday with the deliberate intention of causing trouble in the streets, assaulting stall vendors, rickshaw coolies and the like. One of my gunners reckons that well over half the men in camp go out with prostitutes, some of them as frequently as possible, prices varying from a ten dollar fuck in a shantytown to large expenditure in hotels. There are, in addition, numbers of small boys willing to oblige at ten cents a go; talent is nowhere lacking.

Chinese, generally, have standards of behaviour as strict or stricter than ours. Under normal conditions, only a girl of low moral repute will act as a prostitute but, today, under conditions of extreme economic need, many have taken to the profession and this is not severely condemned. Indeed, some of the girls are very kind to the men and exercise a good influence on them. There is an underlying need for love and 'Suzie Wong' relationships of charm and delight sometimes develop. The provision of Prophylactic Aid centres for the armed services in the city keeps the incidence of venereal diseases quite low. The men prefer to use these rather than contraceptives which are generally considered a spoil sport.

I have heard a British 'tommy' walk up to a coolie shouting "Out of my way you yellow-livered, slant-eyed, bastard!" If I had not been in a car which started off across a traffic crossing at that moment, I would have had the military police on to him. The average Chinese are slight in build and naturally quiet, normally not seeking trouble. The men tend to exploit this. It would do them good to come up against more redoubtable adversaries, as they would elsewhere in the world.

The troublemakers are part of a British social problem. They come usually from the toughest deprived areas of urban Britain, the Black Country, Liverpool, Glasgow. It is these men who set up incidents that create bad feeling. Although they enjoy their disorderly nights out, most of the men are peaceful enough. The soldier is in surroundings quite unnatural to him; some of them would be problem adolescents at home let alone here. Talkers and bad mouthers in camp have an insidious effect. Bad barrack-room influences lead decent men into trouble, even when it is only to 'see what it's like'. Those who behave with decorum may become objects of barrack-room ridicule. Sometimes they invent plausible stories to cover themselves.

In China, a soldier is traditionally the lowest of the low and the behaviour of British troops comes up to expectations. Even so, men often expressed a real liking for the Chinese. Those who hated the "yellow bastards" were in a minority. In general, the men know through experience much more about the Chinese than do the officers to whom, isolated in their clubs, their existence was an irrelevance. Some soldiers, who had established relations with Chinese families, were full of admiration for them and there was an occasional marriage. Men who crossed these social barriers were usually quiet, thoughtful types who had picked up a smattering of the language and developed real friendships.

My batman, for example, was an expert on the life of the junk people in Aberdeen, the boat people who roam the seas around Hong Kong. Gunner Hughes was one of twins who became friendly with the brothers Lai who were our washhouse cleaners in camp. They invited him to their home in Aberdeen, where he made friends with a school master and a police constable and where he sat in on English classes trying to learn Cantonese in reverse. Gradually, he began to spend all his time with his new-found friends, walking down to Aberdeen alone as soon as the day's work was done. He learnt many things, Chinese carpentry and fishing techniques, but spent most of his time with a family talking with them. I met him once at a Cantonese opera in Aberdeen and noted how totally he was accepted by the folk of the township. Some of the men said he had a mistress there, a story he found it useful not to deny, but I do not think he had. He had simply entered another world and was happy in it. Hughes was a quiet person with little education but perfect manners. The Troop Commander said he had "gone native".

One day, when he had been laying out my 'blues' for a Guard Mounting Parade, Hughes asked me if he could borrow my copy of Arthur Waley's translations of Chinese poems. Next day, a gunner told me, with awe in his voice, that Hughes had spent the whole evening reading it and was copying some of the poems into a notebook. I talked to Hughes and found that his interest was a very spontaneous one; he could not say why he liked a poem. Certain of them struck him as revealing something and these he would copy down laboriously.

Hughes told me he would be heartbroken when he had to leave Hong Kong and his Chinese friends. He seemed to have fitted entirely into the nearest equivalent of his own "class" within Chinese small-town life: neither he nor his friends knew much about the intellectual culture of the Chinese; his friendships were practical, down to earth; he enjoyed folk tales, odd customs, the Chinese atmosphere. It spoke somewhere to his soul.

*

Operation Night Watch

To test the operational quality of the colony's air defences we had a three day exercise, manning the radars and guns continuously day and night. British and American planes flew sorties over the colony during the day and, at night, a *Sunderland* flying boat cruised around in order that we might practise engagements upon it.

We organised the troop into a series of watches but, whenever there was an "alarm", everyone had to double on to the equipment. We were fully manned in between thirty seconds to a minute. At dawn and dusk, we ran local defence schemes, manning the trenches around our perimeter and sending out small patrols which tried to infiltrate the camp. On one occasion, Hughes and I got through the barbed wire by crawling up a drain and succeeded in 'blowing up' both generators and ammunition. We had crawled some thirty yards in darkness up a very steep slope taking at least a quarter of an hour. Everyone was startled as our 'fire crackers' went off loudly in the half light of dawn.

Morale was exceptionally high. There was some grumbling but it was good-natured and, what with our little games of sabotage and the occasional air raid, interest was well sustained. Although we only had a total of eight hours sleep, divided into four periods of two hours each, it was a surprisingly happy time.

It took a scheme like this for me to realise what a self-dependent unit we were. At night we were surrounded by the dark hills and sea, giving us a lonesome feel that seemed to reach the men. Each one had a clear-cut job to do; operating the radar; manning telephones; laying the guns; spotting aircraft; looking out for saboteurs. Everyone did well and the apathy so common on a bad day was absent.

Humour and good leadership sustained our work. The Troop Commander was absent, so our regular subaltern provided the military knowledge and experience which Roger and I lacked. We treated the whole thing as a game and, by enjoying humorous situations with the men, creating laughter and smiles and by teasing those who were fed up or fatigued, an atmosphere of comradeship spread through the troop. We all felt responsible to one another. This feeling of togetherness within isolation is difficult to define. In spite of sleeplessness everyone seemed "chuffed".

The 107 set began to buzz. The telephonist, at the AAOR board in our control room, adjusted his headset. The wireless crackled, "Peter Ricksha Peter Ricksha Peter Ricksha. 12345, 54321. Able Baker Charlie Dog Easy Fox. Broadcast Broadcast." The voice droned monotonously into the control room. As Duty Officer, I turned the knobs, adjusted frequency and waited.

"Hallo all sites Jig. Hallo all sites Jig. Message. Duty Officer to phone. Officer to phone. Acknowledge. Jig 1? Roger. Jig 2? Roger. Jig 3? Roger..."

One by one the gun sites acknowledged and the duty officers listened in. One by one they repeated the message back. Our telephonist giggled at the calculatedly blasé voices of the officers, contrasting sharply with the brisk tones of the control set operator. One site was asked to "read back" – there was a pause. Regimental Control sounded irritated.

"Jig 6 Jig 6 read back message now." A long pause then a hesitant gunner voice came on, "Wait one!" There was a spluttered exclamation from control. Our telephonist giggled. Jig 6 had dropped a bollock. There was no Duty Officer there. Ha Ha.

"Jig 6. Jig 6. Repeat back last message."

"Jig 6. Duty Officer here." A voice thick with sleep. "Send your message."

The message was sent. Another pause "Say again!" Laughter rang out in our control room, everyone was wide awake now. Finally Jig 6 got the message and the set went silent.

Alive, humming with sensation, the silent night brooded around us, the wireless buzzing, yet mute without voices. Over the hills lay the telephone lines like spiders' webs, the operators waiting for the next alarm. The radar paraboloid spun round and round, reflections flickering. Inside, on the screen, lay a neat picture of land and sea for some fifty miles about us. Our invisible beam was tickling the masts of junks some twenty miles offshore and fondling the shapes of islands. The Radar Telephonist in the Control Room was plotting the junk positions on a board. I watched him. At last the picture was complete. "Red – go to bearing," I ordered. The radar stilled, the telephonist snoozed. Yet the air was vibrant with a kind of humming, radars, predictor, wireless, wires a hundredfold quivering with life, uneasy tension.

I strolled outside, climbed the steps to the command post and leaned on a wall facing the sea. With the moon riding high, swift silver-tinted clouds cast patterns on the wrinkled sea. Distant islands rose steeply from the waters, black mounds seeming to move up and out of their settings. Moth-winged junks, shrouded in the dim twilight of the moon, sat barely moving on the water, silhouettes dark against the night-grey sea. The morning fleet was moving seawards silently, not even a fisherman's voice. Sometimes a sheen of moonlight ran in a crescendo of wind patterns across the waves, a faint sound of waters washing the feet of the cliffs below.

Moon and space tell strange stories and my drowsy mind could neither think nor criticise. Here was a crystal moment, the great view, the dark, portentous hills, the shrouded sea, the secretive movement of the junks. In timelessness I gazed at the sea, gathering shreds of light to see more clearly the shapes of islands, hills and bays, the butterfly shapes of boats. I neither knew nor cared who those men may have been. Their presence was enough. Maybe they would be there always, sailing towards the horizon. Perhaps they had been there even before I had come.

I returned to the control room. No one had moved. Suddenly a great clatter on the telephone. I grabbed the receiver.

"Jig 4 Duty Officer."

"Jig 4 stand by – operations operations!"

I crossed the room, pulled down the alarm bell switch and checked my watch. The sound of running boots, shadows of men crossing the door between me and the sky, fifty-five seconds. Not bad. The lines were tested.

"Red. How do you hear me?"

"Radar lines loud and clear, Sir!"

"All guns loud and clear."

"Roger all guns."

Bombadier Wilson was operating the radar set, a gentlemanly type, precise with a scientist's vision, a draughtsman and photographer, my senior operator and a reliable NCO. He had just set the range selection switch to maximum and we were scanning out beyond the Lema Islands across Lantao and were picking up clutter from the Communist islands off the mouth of the Pearl River. To the north, we peered over the mountains into Chinese airspace. A few junks appeared off to the south, the specks of light remaining on the screen a few seconds after the strobe had passed, repeating the echoes returning along the axis of the beam.

Reducing range, we had a closer look around Hong Kong. Suddenly a bright spot appeared, elevation about five degrees, couldn't be a ship. Wilson flicked over the switches, master control to 'locate' and brought the range step on to the target. He locked on, the dials started swinging around, range and angle steady but the bearing dial turning steadily, a crossing target.

"Red following, bearing 50 at 6 angle 5."

"Red track." This from the control room.

"Red on target."

The target disappeared in clutter and we lost it. Yet there it was. The *Sunderland* was off from the sea and flying out for us. Later we picked him up again, tracking him well out to sea. He seemed off course for he flew straight over the Lema Islands which are communist. Locating him again at 34,000 yards we tracked him into the harbour area. Things were going very well.

I returned to my room for two hours of precious time off the set. It was five in the morning and at 7.30 a.m. I was again on duty. I slept like a dead dog.

After 'stand down', the NCOs found all their beds neatly laid out on the roadway, turned down for immediate occupation. Somebody had decided that not all sabotage should be imaginary. I suspected the REME mechanics but didn't say anything.

Chapter Thirteen

Just Talking

One evening Yannang and I were leaning on the rails of a pier on the Praya. We had with us a great book of pictures which Yannang had brought for me to see. Each page carried a Chinese painting, some famous, some less well-known, and every one gave us new ideas to talk about. We became so engrossed in conversation as to be almost oblivious of all else. The tide flowed under the pier; the sun set; neon lights began to light the oily water with patterns of green, red and blue; a party of rowdy American sailors, carrying on with gaily dressed Chinese girls, departed in a launch. We talked on and on.

I had never known this kind of talking, a conversation of the soul rather than the intellect. We described feelings and states of mind, evoked by the pictures, with an intuitive understanding of one another that seemed to transcend the barriers of culture, race and language.

One evening, we climbed to the Upper Level, a narrow road ringing the Peak some way below the summit. In a sheltered corner of the hillside, with jungly woods around us, we found a little stone table, its top smooth, polished and marked with a Chinese chessboard. There were two seats beside it. The hours once more sped by while we talked of beauty, the essence of life, Christianity and Buddhism. Using twigs for pieces we had a game of Chinese chess. Dusk fell as we strolled down to the bustle of the town. We usually ate in simple Chinese restaurants or teahouses avoiding the high prices and culture of the European restaurants.

There was a kind of poverty in what we were about, a disregard for the frippery and thrills of the city. We rarely visited a cinema. Our enjoyment was in conversation, an open-ended discovery that went beyond outward form. It was simple, cost nothing and there was a lot of gentleness. These conversations were profound, reaching beyond the insight of most of my friends. There was a seeking to understand one another and a certainty of its accomplishment. Like an ephemeral butterfly at a choice flower that might be frightened by a sudden movement, I found in it a sort of compassion that I dared not try to probe.

Another evening found us up on the Peak again. The whole, vast city lay below us, brilliant with strings of beads of light, flashing, dancing, quivering in the haze. Ferry boats weaved across the harbour, a liner hooted, the murmur of traffic and voices came up to us. It was a warm night and again we talked for three hours, oblivious of all except the shadowy light on each other's faces, the glow from the city below and our long, long talk.

"Look at the lights of the cars, they are so small from here," said Yannang. "The rich people look so important in the city in their big cars and expensive clothes, yet, from up here..." He left the sentence unfinished.

He told me about his home in Swatow. When times were kind, there had been much coastal trade and his father's junks were laden with cargo. When trade was poor, the junks went fishing but, when times were exceptionally hard, they all had to live off the land. There was no question of moving food around China, it was local produce or nothing.

"It was like that when the Japanese came. Our land saved us. There was a terrible famine and many of the peasants died. Only those, whom the land could feed, survived. In my father's house the Japs discovered firearms. They did not like it and they burnt down our house. I remember being dressed hurriedly as a farmer's boy, torn clothes and a broken bamboo hat and a stick over my back. All the family hurried from the village and I can remember passing along our street, hearing the crackling of flames and the smoke as they burnt our house."

"We walked by night, hurrying along small paths. It was a long journey and I was very tired. I was about nine then.[*] At last we came to an inlet of the sea and we were rowed secretly across in the moonlight. I recall the quiet dipping of oars in the water. On the other side we rejoiced in throwing off our peasants' clothes and

---

[*] Chinese begin counting age from conception so Yannang was actually eight at the time.

hurried to meet my father's brother. We were in a country not yet occupied by the Japanese."

"The Japanese only occupied certain coastal areas around Swatow and did not penetrate very far inland. When the war was over, my family returned to the village and I spent some time there. I came to Hong Kong on a holiday and I was here when the Communists took over China. At first I was very unhappy. I wrote a long letter to my uncle and to one of my friends. It was an inspired letter. I have not been able to write like that lately. I complained about the evils of society, the sin, wickedness, the corruption. Life in Hong Kong is cold, harsh, money-ridden, grasping. You will not have been here long enough to know this fully. Most of the police indulge in petty corruption and take squeeze money for most things. It is very difficult to be a good person here. So I have turned my back on this ugly life and look to nature."

"Do you love the world?" I asked him.

"No, not the world but I love nature. Society seems corrupted. Innocence has left it. There are not many good people. It is all money, careers, business prospect, a scramble for living. So few understand their lives."

He looked down at the city below.

"They rush and bustle, the countless thousands, the poor, the coolies, living from one dollar note to the next, from one meal to the next. Their minds, which are meant to understand, achieve nothing: there is vice and squeeze and toil. My idea is not shared by many."

We looked down and listened to the roar of the city. O Jerusalem!

"So, you see, I always like the quiet places, the mountains, the mists and the trees. There I find peace and consolation."

We talked about Buddhism and Yannang remarked that he had often thought about becoming a monk.

"A real monk high up in the mountains. I believe that after many years it is possible to realise something. Perhaps it does not take so long. If one thinks rightly, something can be seen. Of course, most monks are not like that for they do not have the power to live the right life and they fall back into worldly things. They become concerned with ceremonies and appearances and there is nothing in that, nothing in their superstitions, their false Bodhisattvas. Few monks hold to the high ideal. They mistake ceremony for practice and forget the silence in the hills. The doctrine is difficult and most are too stupid to understand it. The Buddhist idea is very high, too difficult for most of us. It means getting away from the world and, as you know, all Chinese love their families. If I became a monk, I could not bring up a family and that is natural life. I should fulfil life, not deny it. For me, I do not think I can attempt that life. Even so, there are some who find something by a monastic way of living. I believe that is so."

I asked what he thought of Christianity.

"It is a very good religion. I mean in the sense of being a good organisation. It does a great amount of practical good, teaching health and hygiene, raising the ways of living of degenerate people. Christians are very friendly, they welcome new friends, and Chinese, you know, are often stiff and formal, until you know them well. Christians seem to override this. Yet, I don't like Roman Catholics. Like some Buddhists, all they seem to think about is ceremony and incense and chanting in Latin. Protestants are better because they do not try to tell people what to do and do not have such fixed dogmas. Their ceremonies are simpler and in local languages. Mainly I like Christians because they are practical."

"What do you think of Christ?"

"He was a great teacher, a very great one, like the Buddha maybe, but human like the rest of us. Once, in Swatow, I lived in a house with four other students. One of them was a Christian and we talked a lot. He used to tell us that Christ was the son of the one God and that he had risen from the dead to become a judge whom we had to ask for help in life. This student told us many such mysterious things but I did not believe any of it. The great thing about Christianity is its kindliness and good works. I may join a Christian society because then my children will have a good education."

"Have you read the Bible?"

"Only small extracts. I want to read it. It is one of my great wishes, because the English is so very excellent."

"What then do you think of the Christian God?"

"There is no god like that. The world is a great mystery and, if you ponder the mystery, there is no need for a god. In nature there are so many things, birds, animals, sea, land, the stars, all moulded together in a great and wonderful rhythm, a kind of harmony. The old Chinese, you know, called it the balance of Yin and Yang, spirit and matter, force and resistance, positive and negative, male and female. It is so expressed in one of the oldest of Chinese books collected by Confucius around 400 BC – the I Ching. But it is very mysterious, too difficult for us in everyday life."

"Well then, what is the cause of all this?"

"Cause? Well, we do not think about a cause. The world is. It is a wonderful mystery. Nature is a secret in which lies the strange harmony of which we all form a part."

We fell silent, conscious of the night about us, the slight chill of the mountain air and the chirruping of a cricket somewhere in the darkness. It was indeed a mystery and beautiful beyond expression. Was it really worthwhile, I asked myself, this striving to explain, this scientific search to which I was so deeply wedded?

The question had to come. "What do you think happens after death?"

Yannang turned to me, a smile on his face. "Nothing. It is a long sleep with no awakening. It is the great peace we long for. Yes, it is like a sleep, yet it is nothing."

A sadness came over me at his reply, even though it was an answer to which I too, by a different route, had also come. It was the way he said it, with such faith in both life and death, their co-presence in the universe, that moved me so. In Yannang there was such an acceptance of the harmony of all things. There was no sorrow in his voice, no passionate wish for an afterlife. Death lay before him as an idea, something to be regarded as everything else, a thing in itself, a fact. There was no fear, no regret, a tinge of sadness and a wonderful acceptance.

The night became very silent as I looked at him, wondering what the great faith that made him understand so much could be and where it had come from. I had a feeling of finality. There was nothing more to be said. An unutterable beauty was there. All desire for anything else faded away. I was happy in this gentle, perceptive company.

I asked myself, how is it that Yannang alone, in these last challenging months, has made me think and think hard on a level I have not known with any other friend. With most of my friends, I felt I could go further than they in any metaphysical talk, drawing on my own feeling and experiencing a certainty that I could refute any argument I contended. Sometimes I would sweep into a merciless torrent of talk, which only a few could perceive as really a kind of fog. With Yannang I found myself with no wish to excel, to show off knowledge and brilliance, as if conversation was an intellectual competition, a game of chess with words and ideas. With Yannang I was learning that words were the façades of feeling.

Yannang was not especially brilliant nor especially handsome. His health was poor and he suffered from the effects of earlier malnutrition. Yet he had a surprising persistence. While he did not appear forceful or dynamic, his gentle almost shy approach was like the water that wears away mountains.

"I do not want riches or great success because they spoil one's true nature. I want to live a simple life. First I must find a way of earning enough income. Then I must see to it that I have enough time to sit quietly in the country and study, perhaps then I can write something too. It is a vain wish of mine, but I would like to write about English things in Chinese and Chinese things in English. I would like to go to a university but I would have to win a scholarship outright. Then again I would have to stay two more years at school and I am sure my uncle cannot keep me that long. I am afraid my wishes are vain ones. I shall never be able to do all I would like but I shall try."

"Do you want to be famous?"

"Only a little among my friends! Look how busy famous men are, always rushing about in a way that ruins the natural life. My chief idea is happiness. If we can find happiness then all difficulties settle themselves."

"Isn't that perhaps a little selfish?"

"Maybe, but first we must find the way for ourselves and afterwards lead others onwards. The Buddhist monks of China say that, once he has found the way, a great man will not keep it to himself but turn and help others less fortunate. This is also a Christian idea. In helping others we find further happiness."

"But isn't happiness the opposite of sorrow? Do they not both exist together – necessarily? You cannot find happiness alone without sorrow."

"That is not quite my meaning. Indeed both sorrow and happiness are real and inseparable opposites but the true happiness I mean is different from either; it understands and transcends them."

Yannang said to me, "I do not talk about these things with my other friends. Somehow you manage to understand better than most.

An idea comes up and then another. They flow along. I do not talk like this as often as I should."

"We certainly seem to have thought about very similar problems and, in spite of our so very different backgrounds, have come to understand much the same thing."

"Yes. It is so extraordinary. We have known each other for so short a time and we converse in a language that is not my own yet we understand each other's deepest thoughts."

"It is a strange chance that we should have met at all," I said.

"It's a miracle!" said Yannang with feeling.

"When I first read that newspaper article of yours there was something in it that pleased me. You know I had been watching that page for weeks. It was only this one article that seemed to cry out to me. I recall you were comparing richness and poverty, not as a moralist but like a being upon a cloud looking down from afar – simply observing, detached even while you were present."

"Yes – you see it was the moonlight."

Some conversations run out of words.

"Will you ever come back here, John?"

I hesitated. How could I answer with the world poised about a razor's edge?

"Perhaps," I said. "Maybe I shall want to teach here, to work in the university, but so much depends on the situation in the world. If the frontiers of China ever open again I shall come back at once. I would love to go to China and you could come with me."

"Yes."

We returned to our own thoughts.

Chapter Fourteen

Beginner's Mind

One hand clapping makes a sound
in the land where flying geese
move forward in the same place
and the winds of time
fluxing and refluxing at a constant rate
strum a strange kind of differential analysis,
where consequence is inconsequence
and blind logic, drowned in the spirit bottle,
lets loose the joyful goose.
In the upside down dance
the world is still
moving in a flash of lightening's speed
and the silent watcher
heeding the spectral junk on darkening waters
climbs downwards for his tea.

The Zen Quest, May 26th 1954

My visit to Ngong Ping Monastery had rekindled my interest in Buddhism, which had begun while reading Christmas Humphreys' book on the subject[*] during our voyage out East. I had felt a considerable sympathy for many Buddhist ideas and could not dismiss them as easily as I did most of the metaphysical notions of Christianity. As a biologist with an interest in evolutionary theory, mystical notions in the interpretation of life seemed to me as out of place as Yannang too had averred.

---

[*] Humphreys, C, 1951. *Buddhism*. Pelican books.

One day I expressed my interest to Ma Meng. I was visiting his home near the university and he mentioned the matter to his father, Professor Ma Kiam, a much revered man of letters in Hong Kong. The old man was taking a kindly interest in me and had already shown me some wonderful classical paintings. He wrote a letter of introduction to Yen Shiliang, a businessman who had trained on retreats with the famous and very Venerable Master Hsu Yun, the key teacher of Zen Buddhism in China early this century. Yen Shiliang, he told me, was a most lucid expositor of Ch'an and, if I could join his discussion group, I would learn much.

I guessed that a young English army officer would not be the type of person Mr Yen would expect to have in his group, especially since I knew no Chinese. He responded kindly to the letter of introduction, however, and invited me along. I started attending the weekly meetings. There were two Chinese doctors, several businessmen and Mr Yen himself. We met in one of the doctors' consulting rooms where we had tea and talked.

Yen Shiliang was discussing the famous Platform Sutra of Hui Neng who lived between AD 638 and 713. The Sutra has two parts. The first purports to be a biography of this famous master. He was an illiterate woodsman who, on hearing some words of the Diamond Sutra chanted by a nun, immediately perceived their significance and had a moment of deep insight. He sought out the teachings by going to a monastery. The insight he had gained spontaneously turned out to be more profound than that of any monk there but, for a long time, the abbot of the monastery could not acknowledge this for fear of evoking the jealousy of the monks. The story is a wonderful account of human failings, doubts, self-judgement, sloth and intuition. After Hui Neng won a competition in which a single verse of insight was required, he was secretly given transmission and became the next patriarch of the sect. He had to run and hide from persecution by other monks but eventually emerged to teach. The second part of the Sutra contains his teachings.

Mr Yen read a passage from the Sutra in Cantonese and then put it into fluent English for my benefit. Although most of the participants knew some English, I was the only European present and felt this effort to communicate to be a very kind gesture. Mr Yen then launched into a personal commentary on the text.

Our discussions focused on the method of obtaining the central Buddhist experience – the state of enlightenment. To the Theravadin school of Ceylon and Burma this is only attained after many lifetimes of diligent self-discipline and abstention from all the attractions of this world. In China and Japan, the Zen school, called Ch'an in Chinese, emphasises a form of insight, which is a sudden recognition of the ground of all objective and subjective phenomena. This insight is believed to constitute the core of the Buddha's discovery. Such a realisation is, at first, merely a glimpse of the basis of mind beyond the personal constructions of the self, but, later, it provides a security of mind which cannot be touched by circumstance. To attain this insight there must first be awareness.

Awareness cannot be an object of striving nor can it be treated as a goal because, when this is so, the mind is divided. Attachment to an idea of what it might be and an ambition to succeed in something not yet understood constitutes a serious error. In the appropriate awareness there must be no discriminatory thought, no clinging to belongings, place or form, no desire even to become aware, for so to desire is to prevent realisation, by splitting the mind between what one is and what one wants.

Mr Yen paraphrased the story for us.[*] The Master had asked, "Think of your body as a tree and your mind as a mirror held by it. How will you preserve its clarity?" He was using the metaphor of the mirror for the condition of awareness that is simply a direct appreciation of what is, without judgement or obscuration by thought.

The senior monk had answered, "I would clean and polish the mirror keeping it free from all stain and blemish. I would feed and prune the tree, keeping it healthy and keeping both free from dirt and harm."

When Hui Neng heard of this answer he blurted out, "But – but – there is no mirror, there is no tree. Where does the dirt come from?"

The master made no comment at the time but he knew Hui Neng had the deeper insight. Hui Neng knew from experience, as, of course, did the master, that when awareness was present, there was just a vast spacious clarity with no intellectual content and that concepts like mirror or tree had then no meaning.

---

[*] For the actual story of the poetry competition between contestants for the robe and bowl see the translation by Wong Moulam, *The Sutra of Wei Lang (or Hui neng)*. Buddhist Society, London 1953.

The senior monk typified what is called the Gradual School focusing on persistent effort to attain cleanliness, to reach nirvana, to understand truth, to become an Arhat – enlightened. In this approach there is time, there is the aim to reach a goal. But all these methods and goals are no different from ideas about Heavens and Gods. They are wishful projections of the mind filled with desire for another state.

"Intentions and goals," Mr Yen told us, "are complementary to one another and express the desires of the self. Without intention there is no goal, without a goal no intention. Should one of them be satisfied, the other disappears. If you reach heaven without understanding desire, a vista of further heavens soon arises. This is the wheel of suffering driven by beginningless desire."

He went on, "Gradual change and slow modification remain within the midst of conditions. This is not a fundamental shift, no bursting through the bounds of fate set upon us by our environment and our conditioning. There is no direct realisation of the ground. Gradual paths remain relative to conditions and hence continue to express them.

"You must know," he continued, "that the realisation of the truth is unconditional, outside convention, swift, sudden, like a flash of lightening through cloud, the abrupt opening of a door or the sudden dropping of a bucket. Such flashes may be brief and barely noticed but they are the first steps to total light.

"Let me tell you an old story," he went on. "When Dhamo (Cantonese for Bodhidharma), the founder of Ch'an in China, first appeared before the Emperor he bowed low. The Emperor told him about how he had given gifts to the poor, to monasteries and in support of the teachings and wondered what his merit might be, merit to secure him a beneficial rebirth. The Emperor asked whether he had any virtue. The reply was immediate, 'None whatsoever.'

"Understandably, the Emperor was both hurt and surprised.

"'What then is the first principle of Buddhism?' he cried.

"'Vast emptiness,' said Dhamo.

"The Emperor, not understanding and doubtless feeling exasperated, demanded testily, 'Who then stands before me?'

"'I haven't the faintest idea,' said Dhamo."

Yen Shiliang explained, "In this dramatic manner, Dhamo, who was speaking from inside his realisation, tried to show the Emperor that the presumptions of the mind are a hindrance for in its very thinking it sets up conditions. Thoughts consist of attachments to objects or ideas; any such attachment will prevent the realisation of which we are speaking. It is not possible to become aware of the 'nothing that is something' if one's mind is puzzling over the 'something that is nothing'!

"So often we gasp at the beauty of a view or practice a meditation that brings us to stillness of the mind: for a moment the mind is poised on the brink of awareness and then some thought creeps in, sticking it to a prior understanding as glue might do. The whole purpose of Ch'an is to topple the self over into a sea of awareness if only for an instant. It is this loss of self-reference, that is essential. One may find that a timeless second reveals that time itself is empty of self. There is no way to such an experience. It either happens or it does not."

One of the doctors objected, "It is all very well to speak of the uselessness of the gradual approach, yet even the Buddha himself went though intense training, asceticism and learning."

Mr Yen paused. "Yes, that is true but there is a qualitative difference between the gradual and the sudden. The Buddha became aware that great learning, much reading, wise talking, even ascetic practices, all comprised mental activities supporting a personal view of the self which, merely circles around a central conceptless awareness. When he gave up his attachment to self, he immediately found the peace and enlightenment he sought. The Buddha revealed the manner in which such things are made real to one in personal experience. He never said that his exact words should be followed to the letter.

The basis for becoming aware can perhaps be prepared for in some ways; reading the teachings, for example, and comprehending them; or practising meditation, but if the mind is focused by an intention which necessarily centres on the self, no awareness arises. This is why Dhamo and the Patriarchs emphasise the uselessness of the scriptures in this regard. The way requires a sudden leap under the guidance of the master which comes about in its own time. This is passing the Gateless Gate or walking the No Way Way. Learning and understanding of worldly matters are only stepping stones, not prerequisites. An illiterate can uncover enlightenment."

Another time Mr Yen pursued the notion of stepping stones further. Even on the faster path it is often only little by little that we advance.

"A businessman once asked a monk to show him the Way. They travelled together for a long time, over high mountains, through fertile valleys where the rice crop was rich every year. After a while they hit upon a desert. For days they wandered seeking to cross it. At last the pupil cried out, 'I cannot go on. I no longer see a path. It is impossible. We must return to the security of the last frontier fort.'

"'Right!' said the monk, 'we will stop right here. See, there are trees around us.'

"At once an oasis appeared around them with a large hotel by a shining lake. They stayed for a month and one morning the monk asked, 'Do you think you have found the way? Are you happy here in this beautiful oasis?'

"'Yes,' said the man, 'I feel as if I am well on the way and in this place I have found much happiness.'

"'So well and good,' said his guide. 'It is time to continue the journey.'

"Once more there was only the whine of the desert wind eddying the sand over the dunes."

So it is, Mr Yen told us, with all forms of worldly happiness and learning. After reading a book; after some material achievement or career advancement; after living a while in a happy place, one has to beware of stagnation. Real insight always lies in the flux of things, in a moving on. It is no good building up treasures on earth 'where moth and rust corrupt' or becoming fixated on certain places or teachers. This goal of Zen, which is no goal at all, lies within and beyond such things. It is time to move on.

"Even if you met the Buddha and stayed with him learning great wisdom, there would come a time when you would have to leave him and carry on alone. It is you who have to make the discovery, Mr Crook, whatever the Buddha's discovery may have been to him is of no use to you. These discoveries are lonely matters. When you are crossing a river do not get attached to a stepping stone. These explorations always involve enquiries to which there are no answers on the original level of the investigation. Pause a moment within the question and without moving from it: lo – the solution is found within the problem itself."

One Monday, I arrived in good time, before the room had been cleared of patients. Mr Yen had arrived too and we had Chinese tea and some of his home-made cakes together. He had had some extracts from the Sutra typed up for me in English by his own translation. This was a great help and I was touched for all the books were otherwise available only in Chinese and quite unintelligible to me.

We discussed that part of the Sutra where the Fifth Patriarch calls his successor-elect to him in the dead of night and passes to him the robe and bowl. He imparts to him some of the vital teachings especially the line from the Diamond Sutra: 'Use the mind empty of projecting thoughts.'

"The projecting, thought-filled foreground of awareness is anything produced by the bias of one's conditioning which creates interpretations of what one hears and sees. Such interpretation distances one from an immediate experience. Sometimes this is called the influence of 'Me and Mine' because such conditioning is always related to one's personal wants and to the maintenance of an image of oneself.

"When you look at a drinking glass you assume the image you have of it to be really there but, when you look away, how do you know it remains or has any reality at all? This 'reality' resides in an inference which continues after perception. The connection between 'what is' and 'what is seen by the mind' lies in inference and inference inherits all the projecting background of our personal and collective past. The glass is only such because of its functional use, its social meaning, its manufacture according to specification. Seen otherwise, it is a silicon compound which, when we shift our frame of reference to a physical vocabulary, is of a certain atomic structure floating in space. Yet the immediate apprehension of the glass in my hand is direct, immediate. There need be no interpretation. I drink the wine!

"To see reality in direct, uninterpreted awareness, mental and personal bias and the very image of one's self, which you may feel to be so important, all need to drop away. If we tinge an object with what we expect or would like it to be, it becomes a social confection. Without such a tinge, things in Zen are seen naked, just as they are. And this applies especially to your very own understanding of yourself, to your proud self-image. You see, Buddhism is a kind of psychological nudism!

"When the Patriarch was teaching him this, Hui Neng found it matching his personal experience and exclaimed: 'Who could have expected that the root of mind is originally naked of self and pure?

"'Who could have expected that the root of mind is without thought of either becoming or extinction?

"'Who could have thought that the root of mind was without self yet self-sustaining?

"'Who could have expected that the root of mind cannot be shaken or changed?

"'Who could have expected that the root of mind manifests all in all?

"When you experience the root of mind yourself, Mr Crook, you will be able to confirm this, expressing it not in the same words but in your own. Such an expression, however it may take shape, will tell a Master that you know for yourself. This communication may then lead to a transmission of the teaching; that is a mutual acknowledgement of understanding between master and practitioner. The root of mind is simply the experience of being without judgements, criticisms, valuation, discrimination. We may simply call it 'awareness'. What awareness is aware of stands immediately before it. No interpretations project themselves upon the clear space."

I felt this connected with something I had known before in my life. How, though, was I to experience it again?

*

Exactly so

During our group discussion that evening I raised a question that had been bothering me. In the Prajnaparamita Sutras the No Soul doctrine of the Buddha expands into an insight revealing the emptiness of all things due to their impermanence. Yet in Buddhism there is also the idea of self-reincarnation.

"In Buddhism there appear to be two tendencies, the idea of no soul and the idea of personal reincarnation. If there is no soul how can there be reincarnation?"

Mr Yen argued that there was indeed no soul in the European or Christian sense of that word. What was thought to be reincarnated was the totality of unexpended causes left behind at the end of a life and which have their effects in the next, settling upon the unborn child in the womb, the child itself of course being biological reincarnation.

"If, then, at death all bones, sinews and flesh dissolve to dust, atoms, energy, nothingness, how is it that this little package of unexpended causes retains its identity?" I persisted.

And that was as far as I got. Until then we had had a to-ing and fro-ing of question and answer but now Mr Yen shifted to a different tack.

"Who could know the answer to that?" he responded. "Whatever clever speculation we may enjoy, the only answer to that question lies within yourself. Who knows? Who could know? My dear Sir, who are you? What are *you*? When you look at your own unexpended causes and their origins perhaps something can be found. Do you not recognise in yourself themes that come from a very distant past, before you were born? Only the enlightened can solve such a paradox and perhaps the solution is not communicable. Orient yourself first towards the central experience and then perhaps the issue may become clear, or the question perhaps unnecessary. The premises are mistaken so there is no answer on the plane of insight. You are too much attached to reasoning and puzzling things out. Only the direct experience counts."

Defensively, I remarked that I had asked not so much for myself as to comprehend the Buddhist teaching on the subject.

Mr Yen's eyes twinkled with a rapier-like humour.

"My dear Sir. If you ask for the sake of knowing the doctrine you are still asking for yourself!"

We all laughed and agreed that question and answer were fair ones. Somewhere, however, the Buddha had said that such questions tended not to edification. Only a direct knowing counts.

"So," I said, still trying to clear the matter up. "The question is of no importance because it does not matter whether one believes the *anatta* doctrine of no soul or the notion of reincarnation or either or neither. In fact it does not matter whether one calls oneself a Buddhist or a Christian for, in reality, names have no ultimate meaning. They are just contextual expressions in particular cultures, relative themes functioning as social conventions bolstering personal security. Belief and opinion are of no importance if the true knowing is there, or at least the apprehension of its possibility. Words and arguments matter not a jot if one knows."

I had asked out of a sense of befuddlement and a slight irritation. Mr Yen held me with a look.

"Exactly so," he said.

Then it seemed I had answered my own question and a feeling of exhilaration, of escape from the meshes of definition and seeking to understand, came over me. Strangely enough the answer really did seem to lie in the problem!

I felt my questioning had put Mr Yen on his mettle for he seemed very pleased with the evening's talk and thanked me for my contribution. Everyone seemed very satisfied and we all went out chuckling in the polite Chinese way.

These questions were more subtle and difficult than those of any conversation I had had in England. Rarely had I found myself outmanoeuvred in a discussion of religious or psycho-metaphysical matters. If there was a shift in viewpoint to be made, it was usually I who made it. Usually I was able to persuade or at least hold my own in such discussions. Indeed I must have been an insufferable student. At university I used to attend Christian meetings and wait until the speaker used the word God. I would then ask him to define God, remarking that without a definition I could not see how his talk could proceed. Basing his talk in conventional assumptions, no speaker was ever able to answer me.

Here I am up against a very different interlocutor. I can argue, with ability and precision, the premises and inferences tidily related, and Mr Yen will follow me, give a partial answer along the same lines and then, suddenly, with a look and a few deft phrases of equally clear reasoning, he sweeps all my contribution to one side. Lo and behold, the conversation has entered another dimension, still the same subject, still logical, yet in a realm in which only he is master and in which I can only hover along behind, trying to follow his fluent discourse and the extending reach of his mind. It is all very good for me!

The two doctors are in much the same position as I. Mr Yen sweeps them along just as neatly. He is a past master at conversation, never getting into an argument yet always bringing his viewpoint home with sound reasons. What is new for me is the way he calls on the intuitive as well as the intellectual intelligence. It is this which gives his words such added power and makes them fly.

These Buddhist ideas do not rest on logical reasoning alone. Reason only "circles about and about for evermore" bringing us back in through the door through which we went. He seems to speak justly when he says "One either knows or one does not." So far this knowing is however only within his dimension, not mine. It is as if he suddenly uses an entirely fresh verbal 'conjugation' which shifts the whole context of a conversation into another register.

One of the regimental subalterns, with whom I discussed these ideas, calls them all "false dreams and vain imaginings." Maybe so, but then what isn't and who is to judge? The whole subject calls for a kind of empathy that very few Westerners seem to have. Yet some of my Western acquaintances here, who have lived long in the East, seem familiar with it, Professor Kirby, Mr A.C. Scott and Brook Bernacchi seem to move easily in these dimensions. Only a few of my younger army friends have any idea of what I am talking about. Mr Yen tells me that Europeans have from time to time attended his meetings but not often. Certainly I am twenty years younger than most of the participants who go there now. Yet I find it difficult to say how old Chinese people are. Mr Yen might be thirty, he might be eighty. What is time and where is memory? What was Mr Yen? What is Mr Yen?

Plate 24. *(above left)* A mountain gate to the monastery.

Plate25. *(above right)* The reception, Polin monastery, Lantao Island, 1953.

Plate 26. *(above left)* Roger at Polin monastery.

Plate 27. *(above right)* Mr Sun, Polin monastery, 1954.

Plate 28. *(above left)* Police and soldiers: Saikung patrol, December 1953.

Plate 29. *(above right)* Resting on patrol, Saikung.

Plate 30. *(above left)* Getting the radio to work, Saikung patrol.

Plate 31. *(above right)* Headmen and villagers, Saikung.

Plate 32. Ladies of the village, Saikiung.

Plate 33. Village kids, Saikung.

Plate 34. *(above left)* Stilt houses and chanel to landing place, Tao O, 1953.

Plate 35. *(above right)* Landing steps with sampans.

Plate 36. *(above left)* Junk fleet setting sail.

Plate 37. *(above right)* Sea going junk.

Plate 38. View over junk fleet and towards Lantao, Brickhill.

Plate 39. Junks near Castle Peak. Hull cleaning, 1954.

Plate 40. *(above left)* Yiu Yannang at Castle Peak monastery.

Plate 41. *(above right)* Yiu Yannang and moon gate.

Plate 42. *(above left)* The monk Mun Yiak conversing with Yiu Yannang

Plate 43. *(above right)* Mun Yiak: a portrait.

Plate 44. Altar in Mun Yiak's temple room.

Plate 45. The many armed Koon Yam, Mun Yiak's retreat, Castle Peak.

Plate 46. Second Lieutenant John Crook RA. Brickhill, 1953.

Chapter Fifteen
Palaces and Temples

The home on the Peak

I took a forty-eight hour leave and spent the Friday night with Chris at his friends' house right at the top of the Peak. The master of the house, a short, rather scruffy little man, with beetling eyebrows and a bald pate, is head of one of the major Western banks in the city. His wife is a friendly, motherly sort of woman, a philanthropist interested in social welfare and especially in Hong Kong's Leprosarium on a lonely island off Lantao. Husband and wife are both OCHs, Old China Hands, who have lived in the Far East, including Japan, for a long time. During the war, he was in Shamshuipo prison camp, while his wife escaped to Australia and thence via Panama to Britain.

The elegant single-storeyed villa stands on the knife edge ridge of the Peak and commands vast views across the harbour, the hills rolling away into China and, on the other side, Apleichau Island, Brickhill, Stanley and the distant Lema Islands. A glance from any window is an inspiration; the first thing to be seen, set in a huge perspective of sea and mountains, is miles away and far below. During the winter months, a chill mountain breeze mutters outside and a warming fire splutters and chuckles in the hearth. In summer, when the big windows stand wide open, the whole place becomes an airy palace.

The spacious sitting room is comfortable but not lavishly decorated. Sherry, Dubonnet and wine are available from an obsequious Chinese servant, at the touch of a bell. At first I felt quite uncomfortable. As I was thinking of the poverty-ridden tenements in the city below, the servant addressed me. "What time will Master want tea in the morning? What kind of breakfast does Master want?" He reminded me of the genie in Aladdin's lamp.

The servants are a people apart in this household, not to be included in conversation, joked or smiled with, humbly abiding in their own quarters. This is an upstairs-downstairs world, where the chauffeurs, butlers, wine servants, waiters and amahs know their own place. If they are discussed at all, it is with a paternalistic kindness which subtly emphasises the difference between we and they. Out here the OCHs behave like British gentry of the last century never having experienced the socialist revolution that followed the war. Hong Kong has never known the idea of a redistributed income.

To my surprise I found that the master of the house, in spite of his great experience of the East, had no interest whatsoever in Eastern culture or indeed anything that we could detect outside the field of banking and economics. When he heard that Chris and I were intending to spend Saturday with a Chinese friend visiting Taoist temples he thought it "most odd". As for Cantonese opera, "Phew, once was enough for me!"

When the subject of Buddhism came up, he let loose a string of conventional misapprehensions and things became a trifle strained after he had produced a tirade against the Reform Club and I mentioned I had lunched with Mr Brook Bernacchi in his mountain retreat on Lantao.

Bernacchi believes that representatives from the Chinese classes should have a say in Colony policy. The Reform Club is a vehicle for such ideas. I had to agree with my host that such ideas entailed some risk at the present time of international chaos and the Korean War. Hong Kong Chinese, at present, have only a limited political consciousness and it seems unnecessary to fan flames of possible political discontent. However, in broad terms, I was on Bernacchi's side.

I had some support from our hostess who knew Bernacchi's mother and admired the son's independent line. She also liked Chinese drama and art, but criticised Europeans who became so Easternised as to lose touch with their own culture. I was on safer ground discussing the education system, provincial universities, Oxbridge, the public schools and grants for degrees. Even so, my visits to temples and tenements branded me in their eyes as 'unusual', to say the least.

Of course the beds were luxurious and the sheets so smooth that I slept in a more relaxed way than I had for months. I had felt positively unclean on arrival and a good bath did wonders. It seemed a long time since I had experienced 'civilisation'.

*

Temple tours

On Saturday afternoon, the master of the house very kindly lent us his car, a huge fawn Humber, with a uniformed chauffeur in a peaked cap. We picked up Yannang in Aberdeen and spent our time driving around the island, visiting temples in Aberdeen, Shek O and in Causeway Bay. Yannang was delighted by the comfort of the cushions, armrests and car radio and we had a long talk about 'human pride', one of his favourite topics. It was rare for us to converse in such luxury.

It was Ching Che – the Feast of Excited Insects, a kind of early spring festival. On this day, a lordly dragon who has been hibernating since the autumn raises his head and knives and pins should not be used for fear of cutting him; insects revive to fresh life; the sun is blessed for his vitality and it is a day for augury, paper sacrifices to the gods and for invoking the Yellow Tiger.

Having entered Aberdeen Temple, we were immersed in a cloud of incense. The two life-sized and moronic-looking stucco guards, who flanked the doorway, let us in without assault or battery and, crossing a small hall decorated with paper streamers and gay lanterns, we approached the high altar. Huge joss sticks glowed before it, spirals of smoke ascending to the roof; smaller ones smoked in the sand box nearby and candles of many sizes illuminated a row of colourful divinities. It reminded me of Christmas.

In the centre stood Ting Hau,[*] the Queen of Heaven, much loved by fisherfolk. Centuries ago, during a pitiless tempest, she had stood on the shore pointing at her people's boat which alone, out of the fishing fleet, returned to port. She is considered one of the most benevolent goddesses in the local pantheon. Her image sat behind an ancient, dusty curtain pulled sufficiently apart to reveal her squat

---

[*] Cantonese.

figure, an expressionless face, a dirty doll's dress and a hat covered in cobwebs. Before her, on the altar table, sat two minor deities, clothed alike in rich but dirty clothes and representing a minister of the Sung dynasty and a King of the North. On either side of the table stood two life-sized and heavily-robed figures with fierce bulging eyes and multicoloured faces, each carrying a great club. These were Ting Hau's guardians, All Seeing and All Hearing, between whom no evil can pass undetected. Flanking the main altar were two smaller ones. The one to her left was for Ting Hau's parents; the one on the right consisted of a table on which were arrayed many carved figures, each symbolising one of the sixty years of the Chinese imperial calendar. In the centre was the image of a well-decorated horse for this is the Year of the Horse. There were also pictures of Liu Jo and the merciful Koon Yam (Kuan Yin), one of the Buddhist Bodhisattvas displayed in this Taoist temple. Near her was a wickerwork arch with a tiger painted on it. This was the Arch of Safety through which all those facing tribulation were invited to walk. Women facing childbirth, for example, may, for a suitable fee, pass through this gate to ensure a successful birth.

Standing in a side chapel was an altar to the 'Doctor Fairy', Wong Tai Sin, a famous physician of an early dynasty now deified for his good works. There was great activity near his shrine, a pious-looking, bespectacled priest, dressed in a rich red robe and a yellow undergarment, was murmuring an indecipherable chant to the accompaniment of a drum, a brass sounding plate or cymbal and a brass bowl with a high ringing tone. A flute player joined in at intervals. A well-dressed woman, with a rather fidgety child, knelt before the altar. She gave the priest a piece of red paper on which were written her address and the name of a sick relative. These were solemnly intoned to the deity by the priest who knelt at the altar, banging on the sounding bowl. He then rose to his feet and, followed by the woman and child, walked three times around a table before the altar where the joss sticks burned, still chanting and now banging the cymbal.

On the opposite side of the temple a white tiger in *bas-relief* glared from a wall. The whole reredos before him was covered with green, paper horses. An incinerator stood in front of the tiger where paper offerings of animals and other objects were being burned, their platonic forms ascending in smoke to the heavenly jungle. Across the floor of the hall a green dragon faced the white tiger and, although it was not his day, someone had stuck a piece of lettuce in his mouth. The worshippers were insuring themselves against ill fortune in the coming year.

We motored around the coast to Shek O, a beautiful and rather solitary village, set between high hills and sea at the far end of the island. Near it is Big Wave Bay, one of the few places in Hong Kong where ocean rollers come in to the shore. It was a grey spring day with the horse-hair trees bent before the wind and an early swallow was resting among the dunes.

The little temple at Shek O was again protected by two life-size Door Gods painted on two wooden panels just inside the entrance. Evil influences, which cannot go other than in straight lines, cannot enter but we, with human cunning, sidled around to the side. The interior was dark and Ting Hau set back behind deep folds of curtains. Great banners bearing paper decorations stood about for use in processions, each one a floral tower with gods nestling among the blooms. Across the top of the altar was spread a beautifully embroidered cloth with the donor's name in large, bold characters.

As we motored on round the island, Yannang entertained us with the story of the Door Gods.

"In the days before history became scientific the seas of the four directions were ruled by dragons. They were brothers and they had marvellous powers over the wind, waves and typhoons. In particular, the East Sea dragon had been commissioned by Heaven to administer the beginning and ending of the rains and he did this through his knowledge of secret charms.

"Now it so happened that a famous wizard had researched these charms and come to understand them. When the East Sea dragon heard about this, he was naturally disturbed and turned himself into a man to check up on the story. Meeting the wizard, he tested his powers and found the story was true. The wizard had indeed discovered how to control rain.

"The dragon became livid with rage. So angry was he that he broke all the laws of Heaven and rampaged so furiously at the bottom of the East Sea, shouting out all the magic he knew, that a dreadful typhoon struck the land. The land was flooded, many people killed and, since the wizard had not predicted it, his reputation was ruined.

The dragon curled himself up in a rock grotto and smirked with self-satisfaction.

"The powers in Heaven were not pleased, however. The dragon had exceeded his brief. 'He has broken our laws,' they fumed, 'The punishment must be Death!' Now it so happened that the executioner in Heaven, one of three spirits of a famous Minister of T'ang times, had a second appointment as executioner for the Emperor of China. Naturally he could not be in two places at once.

"Rumours travel quickly under water and, when the dragon heard about this proclamation, he was a trifle scared. 'Coo!' said he, 'what do I do now?' The Emperor was having one of his favourite dreams when the dragon appeared to him and fixed a bargain. At the time when the execution was supposed to take place in Heaven the Emperor would make sure the executioner was engaged in his palace. Unfortunately, on the appointed evening, the Emperor played chess with his ministers for so long that he became tired and took forty winks. In a split second the executioner shot back to Heaven and the dragon's head lay gory on the block.

"But the spirit of the dragon was not vanquished. It went roaming loose over the housetops. The golden crows cackled at him from the eaves of temples and, every time he tried to enter a house, the horrible sight of himself in a mirror startled him. 'I shall haunt the Emperor who deceived me,' he thundered, and set off for the palace.

"The Emperor saw the grasses bend and the trees sway as the dragon spirit approached. 'Oh Dear!' he said as the dragon's breath nearly boiled him in his bath. His ministers and augurs appointed four generals to guard the emperor, two for the windows and two for the doors. The Emperor, having been nearly boiled, was unwell and stayed indoors while the generals guarded him day and night. As time passed and there was no relief, the generals became exhausted. The window generals fell ill so the palace windows had to be boarded up but the Generals of the Door, Wai Chi Kong and Ching Jau Jin, stood firm.

"The ministers and augurs met together. 'The generals must have sleep,' they said. 'What can we do?' They hit upon a brilliant strategy. A famous artist painted life-sized portraits of the generals which were set up in the doorway. The dragon never discovered the trick and could never get inside; the ministers became famous; the artist so rich he forgot how to paint and Wai Chi Kong and Ching Jau

Jin each slept very well. Whether the Emperor ever went out again does not seem to be recorded.

"Of course anyone can copy a painting. That is why the Door Gods keep out evil influences from our homes and temples, however poor they may be, even to this day!"

The largest Ting Hau temple, beautifully decorated outside with elaborate wood carvings and figures of glazed china, was situated on a raised terrace in Causeway Bay. In front of it stood great incinerators where offerings to the sky were burned and stone tigers stood about looking slightly foolish. The layout resembled the temple in Aberdeen but the offerings to the White Tiger were more prolific. In front of the altar large bowls of sand supported the many burning joss sticks and, as at Aberdeen, there were pictures of Koon Yam and a Goddess of Fecundity. A peculiar clay pagoda stood before the main altar and, before the door of each of its seven storeys, stood a little Aladdin's lamp burning brightly, the Seven Stars Lamp, but Yannang did not know its meaning.

On Tiger Day one of the festivities was 'beating the spirit out of the devil'. Little paper tigers constructed around bamboo slips were on sale at stalls near the temple together with a 'Devil beating and Temple Visiting Kit'. This comprised pieces of folded paper covered in strange designs, the original meanings of which lie way back in time and are now forgotten. A collection of small sticks was used to beat a piece of paper representing the devil, while the paper tiger stood by, a joss stick burning in front of him. Outside the temple several groups of women had gathered to engage in this vigorous activity.

I bought myself a tiger and a kit. At once a crowd of grinning Chinese gathered around, including an amazing old man with the longest grey beard I have ever seen, huge bushy eyebrows and twinkly eyes. There was an animated discussion and I asked Yannang what it was about. He merely remarked that they knew I wanted the objects as curios and not for use in the temple.

There were several methods of augury available. One was to shake a tube of many little sticks before a god. When, eventually, one of them fell out, it was taken to the priest who interpreted the character drawn upon it. Alternatively, you might toss two moon-shaped pieces of wood, each with a flat and a rounded side, into the air. Depending on how they fell, so one's future was foretold. To ensure accuracy these tricks should be repeated several times over.

I found these Taoist temples infinitely curious. Chinese people are amazingly superstitious in the most elementary way. This cult of dressed-up dolls, fortune telling and future fixing seems quite out of tune with the sublime reflections of the ancient Taoists of the Tao Te Ching or the writings of Chuang-Tse. For centuries the Taoist philosophy vied with those of Confucianism and Buddhism in China but, for a long time co-existing with primitive village cults, it finally faded into them. There is still a pope of the Taoist cult, the Chang Tien Shih or Heavenly Leader but no educated person takes him seriously. I am sure Mr Ma would rather be found dead than seen nosing about a Ting Hau temple!

Chapter Sixteen

Taoists and a Yogi

He had a wind's walk
the old man of the hills
the grotto dweller who was daft
they said – or drunk
from the more cynical.
On the air's own nectar
I supposed, or the gushing streams
that fed the year-round flowers
in the unending spring
of the rain mountain's life,
or the sunshafts through the holes
in crazy-paving mists
that coil like woolly snakes
from the loquacious sea.
One day rocks will fall
before his cave hiding
from the curious world the skeleton
of one who knew
there was no time
nor is–

I came up to the mess after work and sat watching the slow falling of the night; distant sounds hung heavily in the breathless air; Chinese music in Heung Kong Chai; a drowsy generator's mutter and the undertones of grasshoppers; pine trees with their thin candles in pointed parallelism reached for the sky, a scent of resin drifting past like incense; a cricket chirruped a song and, above the slowly rising mists, a pendant silence, like a half-fallen wing, held its breath, waiting.

Out at sea, dark islands rose in silhouette from the placid, white expanse of water. With soft footsteps the night was falling, an evening vapour disseminating from shadowy places, coming through the grasses, the foliage of the trees, out from the crannied rocks, seeping over the valley, which the night haze darkened first. The western faces of the hills went black against the sky and, one by one, the eastern faces too lost shape, trees, rocks, dwellings becoming dim, obscure and merging all the time. This was the hour when particulars are lost, the numina appear, a crouched tiger, a maiden's breath passing like a sigh, the nodding hill, the threatening hill, the rolling sombre hill. At last the waters, too, copying the slowly changing sky, grew dark and dull, dying a little until, in some small corner between the rocks, a first star glimmered. Suddenly, I was bitten by the first gnat.

*

The Man Mo Temple

Down in the city the street was crowded, coolies trotting along with heavy loads slung across their shoulders. Stalls in obscure corners were poorly lit by irregular street lamps: small oil flames, guttering from the tops of old squash bottles protected from the breeze by glass shields, cast patches of light for the letter writers, fortune tellers, sweetmeat sellers, lucky money and paper offering stalls, vendors of quack medicines. On the evening before Ching Ming, there was little hurry in the street although the coolies, toiling to earn another cent, never slackened their pace. The street was gaudy with sound, especially from loud music up in a tenement where someone had died seven days before.

On the pavement outside the house stood a sombre iron incinerator, like a night watchman's shelter, and, in front of it, a large paper house of two storeys and open balconies filled with furniture, tables, cupboards, beds and a maidservant. Next to the house lay two paper trunks and two paper bridges, four feet high and seven feet long, complete with paper lamps and paper people crossing over. Up on the second floor, revelry was in progress and outside the windows 'spirit-calling' signs rustled in the slightly moving air. Today a ghost was coming home to receive his heavenly inheritance.

Yannang and I watched as a paper horse went up in flames before us to become the old man's spiritual steed. Soon the house, his heavenly home, the trunks, his heavenly belongings, would go the same way, the fine smoke drifting up over the roofs of the houses and around the eaves of the nearby Man Mo Temple. The bridge signified his kindness on earth for, in the old days, to donate a bridge to one's village was the height of patronal piety. In heaven, the paper bridge would enable him to cross the river of Hell.

Beyond the Door Gods, it was dark inside the Man Mo Temple; some priests were lolling asleep in chairs near the door and someone was curled up on a mat. Moving around to the left of the hall, we passed a rather crude picture of a Bodhisattva floating on clouds, holding what appeared to be a pill of immortality. Yannang slowly translated a notice on a wall nearby, a list of commandments and advice for avoiding evil by doing good. Flickering oil lamps cast long shadows between the statues of the guardians near the central altar and, in dark corners, dim outlines of gods and tables of images were vaguely visible. Below the main altar a small, open oil lamp guttered, maintaining the health of the Earth God in his lowly position. Above us, among the beams of the deeply shadowed ceiling, something scuttled along the boards.

A curious mood came over us in that place. It seemed unbelievable to me that, out of all the countless places upon earth, I should be at that moment there in that temple with Yannang for company. His translation became slower as if it was no longer required. He faltered and there was a kind of tension in the air as if each of us had become aware of an unique moment. Among the strange shadows thrown by the lamp light, the special quality of our friendship, the miracle, Yannang had called it, this coming together from the ends of the earth and from such contrasting backgrounds and personal histories, seemed to strike us both. It was then that the magic came again and, afterwards, the evening remained unique in the same way. We seemed lost, walking the Chinese streets we cared not where, drunk with a kind of happiness. What are these moments, so rare and precious, so full of unsaid understanding, so all-sufficient, when nothing, other than their reality, is desired?

Suddenly the electric lights went up. Brilliant with colour as if taken from a Christmas tree, light bulbs blossomed on all sides of the altar before us. From his pedestal Pau Kung, a symbol of Chinese justice, looked down on us, black-faced, gorgeously robed, throned, crowned and surprisingly well dusted. The chief priest, or was he the chief cash collector, hurried forward.

We could now see that the Man Mo temple was considerably better off than the poor little Ting Hau temples along the beaches with their grubby little god dolls. Pau Kung, an ancient imperial minister, was really quite impressive. Behind the image, in a curtained recess, stood another figure, about four feet tall, said to be older than Hong Kong itself for it had stood in a village temple long before the British came. In front of Pau Kung stood a smaller copy of this old image evidently used in processions. On either side of Pau Kung stood two robed officials, his servants, and, in addition to an assembly of pewter joss-stick holders, candlesticks and bowls, there was an odd hand mirror with paper stuck across it as in a multiplication sign. The priest informed us that this symbolised the powers of yin and yang, the innate twin powers driving the universe. By carrying it, Pau Kung could enter Hell to discover the answer to any problem. We found a sinister wooden guillotine shaped like a hinged axe in the form of a yellow striped tiger. In olden times such an instrument in metal was used to cut off the heads of criminals.

The chief gods of the temple, Man and Mo, stood above the central altar, splendidly arrayed with numerous attendant godlings. Man is a god of literary skill, Mo is helpful to fighters and a promoter of honesty. Surrounding the two gods was a collection of carvings depicting the doings of the eight fairies, said to be ancient and made by a highly skilled craftsman.

We found another seven stars lamp. This one was not constructed like a pagoda, rather the seven lamps simply stood open upon a metal frame. The priest began to be useful.

"Once upon a time," he told us, "there was a chief minister of the state of Shu [AD 181-234] whose name was Chukwa Liang. He was a skilled early scientist and military commander. When the king died, Chukwa Liang took control of the state and tried to conquer the state of Wei to the north. During the last of six attempts he became ill and, wishing to extend his life, he invented the magical lamp to ensure it. But one of his generals, on rushing into his room to bring news and ask for orders, blew out the lamp in his hurry. In a few days Chukwa Liang lay dead. Today this lamp symbolises the hopes of all of us for a prolonged life!"

On the walls near the Pau Kung altar hung a group of very old scrolls, paintings in beautiful detail of enthroned Bodhisattvas of which there were also a number of images in the building. We asked the priest why so many images of Buddhist origin were present in a Taoist temple. He told us it would enable a larger number of people of differing beliefs to use the temple. "And," added Yannang, "so to pay more temple dues!"

Next door to the Man Mo temple is a similar building, housing a Chinese physical culture club. Inside it four men, two teachers and two pupils, were working in pairs. One pair seemed to be dancing, creating postures of poise and grace, followed by rapid movements and leaps with various whirlings of arms, each set of movements ending in a well-balanced, stable posture. The other pair, the teacher being an old man, were practising defensive postures, careful, balanced positions that could withstand attack from any direction. The old master would make movements which were at once copied by his pupil. Sometimes a stance would be held for many minutes to achieve stability and strength.

This sport is known as Chinese boxing which, however, also includes high kicks and judo-type throws as well as fisticuffs. It is not however like jujitsu, where the opponent's misdirected energy is allowed to encompass his downfall, for here aggressive attacks are also allowed. The flaying arms are used to hit the opponent as well as to knock aside his blows.

The men were slightly built but extremely wiry and supple. There was no show of brute strength and animal ferocity but rather an obvious joy in poise, balance, speed and stance. It looked more like ballet than boxing. Yannang told me that such training today is mainly for physical exercise but that it was used formerly as a fighting skill and that many of the throws and blows were potentially fatal.

*

A song

Back in the tenement we spent time translating Yannang's favourite song. The music is romantic and the words lyrical. Chinese words are monosyllabic and tonal, capable of great subtlety when sung. Our version in English cannot capture the original feel but we enjoyed our attempt.

A Proposal – The song of a suitor at Khan Ding

Each year there is a horse race at Khan Ding. The track runs up the mountains and through clouds to an inland sea. Here everyone enjoys a night-time party with music, dance and lovemaking. It is very romantic in the mountains with the light of the moon on the snow. Everyone hums this song.

> *Mountain climbers are riding,*
> *Grey mists Khan Ding are hiding,*
> *Night on the hill in the star land*
> *And dancing in the firelight's glow.*
> *The Moon, the Moon, shining –*
> *There's dancing in the firelight's glow.*
>
> *The maiden daughter from Lee*
> *O see – how beautiful is she!*
> *Watch her movement, how she dances*
> *Son of Chang she quite entrances.*
> *The Moon, the Moon, shining –*
> *Son of Chang she quite entrances.*
>
> *What delight see how she dances*
> *How the starlight her grace enhances!*
> *Wealthy lands her father holds*
> *Hei Ding's daughter, fall such chances!*
> *The Moon, the Moon, shining –*
> *Hei Ding's daughter, fall such chances.*
>
> *Maidens all the world delight,*
> *Young men's hearts are set alight.*
> *The gay pursuit, the sweet desire*
> *This globe itself seems set afire.*
> *The Moon, the Moon, shining –*
> *This globe itself seems set afire.*

*

Swami Yogi

The Indian community of Hong Kong had invited Swami Yogi, a famous Hindu practitioner, to stop off in the colony, on his way to a World Religious Conference in Japan. Many Indians live in Hong Kong, forming a small but thriving business community. I attended his lecture on world unity in the rooms of the University Alumni Association in Queens Buildings and found myself the sole European present. Most of the audience, of around a hundred people, were Indian, large men with huge introspective eyes, long Aryan heads and often a fine physique even when tending to corpulence. Most of them were wealthy traders and a few appeared artistic or intellectual. They had an earnest air about them which I liked. A few Chinese had also joined the throng.

When the lecturer arrived, everyone rose in silent respect. His Holiness was dressed in a huge mauve turban, flowing fawn and mauve robes and, on his forehead, sat the scarlet mark of the Hindu faith. He was a short, thickset man with a square face, aquiline nose, a thin-lipped mouth running in a straight line above a determined jaw. His narrow eyes were so deeply set it was difficult to make out their expression. His flesh had a womanly appearance and his age may have been anything between sixty and one hundred! In repose he seemed remarkably expressionless, blank yet contemplative. There was a certain power latent in his curious face. When he spoke it was with a rich, commanding voice impelling attention.

In introduction we were told he had begun life as a chemist and before the war he had studied in Germany. In later life he became dissatisfied and joined the priesthood, soon making his name as a religious leader. In recent years he had felt increasingly estranged from ordinary people, sensing that religious feeling was disappearing in India. He retired to the Himalayas, where he meditated for long periods in the silence of the great peaks. Returning with new confidence, he taught his doctrinal viewpoint directly to ordinary people, avoiding the old sanctuaries of Brahminical thought.

A bowl of joss sticks was placed before him and, while he was being presented with a garland of paper flowers, the room filled with the sweet tang of Indian incense. When he rose to speak he closed his eyes and seemed to concentrate for a minute. At first he spoke slowly but, gradually, the speech came faster and faster until a great flow of words flooded the room. He smiled as he talked and his dynamic diction held attention.

It was a strange lecture, difficult to follow because of the noise of cars outside and his pronunciation. From time to time he lapsed into Hindi or gave Sanskrit quotations from scripture. I gathered the following to have been his viewpoint.

Astrology has revealed that world and cosmos move in great cycles of many thousands of years. History is a great flux of events often influenced by hidden currents of human thought and feeling rather than specifically by the deeds or sayings of leaders who, nonetheless, may mould such currents into social movements. We are currently reaching the end of an astrological period and there will be a great change in human life which may be either catastrophic, leading to a breakdown in civilisation or a rekindling of human life into a new world of brotherhood never known before. The latent forces in the world may bring us terror and destruction or an age of sensitivity and creativity.

At the physical level the world is dependent upon American money. America, under the sign of Mercury, is a new civilisation, uncultured, unstable, full of new ideas, goodwill, extreme lack of tact and diplomatic subtlety and generally immature. Its civilisation could swing in any direction. "Let us hope that great county is never led astray from its high ideals!"

Great Britain provides the world with an example in good government, diplomacy and security. She is a land of democracy but also deeply conservative, clinging to old ideas and romantic notions of her past imperialism. This is a country to be studied and for which the world should be grateful but from which leadership at the present time could not be expected.

Russia, under the cold malevolence of Saturn, is an unfeeling state, static, solid, rigid, inflexible, a repository of heartlessness.

India is a spiritual country suffering seriously from quarrels with Pakistan, internal poverty and nationalism. Yet India is also a storehouse of spiritual insight and feeling that can bring much hope to the world. India may stand as a peacemaker between opposing forces.

The only hope for the world lies in a renewal of spiritual feeling not from any specific religion, be it Hinduism, Christianity or Buddhism, but a resurgence of a psychological empathy for one's neighbours, be they of the same race or different, and a contemplative ethos directed towards life itself.

Ahimsa, the doctrine of non-harming, provides the clue which should be applied in all the affairs of people. Only this spiritual insight and love for humanity without regard for doctrine and ideology can bring about a brotherhood of all. Acts and ideas that increase the divisions between mankind need to be rooted out and replaced by kindliness.

Although many people express a desire for peace, their nature remains warlike. The policies of such people spread the seeds of war. This is also true of each one of us individually. Examine yourselves to find those seeds and destroy them. *Ahimsa*, hurt nothing, fill your life with love for humanity and contemplation of this wondrous world.

All very well, I thought, as I walked back through the refugee-crowded streets with their brothels and petty crime without which so many could not live. A little too easy, maybe, too global a prescription. The world was a trickier place than perhaps the yogi knew.

Chapter Seventeen

Fate or Karma

I have seen more of Yannang and through him gained deeper insight into the struggle of Hong Kong life. He has no teacher to advise him for there are so many students that individual tuition is rarely possible. One evening he said to me,

"Sometimes I feel so small. The world is so vast a place and my own life such a fragmentary part of it, so transitory. What would be the use of becoming a merchant like my uncle? It does not seem to lead anywhere. The father of one of my friends was once a scholar but now he gambles all day. I do not want to be a rich man but I do so want to understand."

Yannang loves literature and the fine arts, yet in Hong Kong there is little opportunity for a personal culture which needs leisure and peace of mind for creative thought. Very few young Chinese today are interested in their country's history or the great philosophic tradition to which they are heirs. The jazz and dance hall mania has swept in from the West to supplant all that. Most youngsters want to be more Western than they can understand. Such is the fashion, such the craze.

Standing on the hillside with Yannang, gazing down through swirling mists upon the roaring, noisy city, the neon signs already blazing in the early dusk, I felt how terrible was fate – that great, impersonal tide that dominates our lives sweeping us where we would not. As the harsh reality of modern Hong Kong becomes clear, the old fateful forces return to press down upon me. Where there is mystery and a poetry in the unknown there is romance, which gives rise to inspiration but, lacking substantiality, this in time gives way to disillusionment.

Yannang works hard with little advice, no father to talk to, the perpetual pain of separation, of exile and insecurity, the nagging fear of poverty. These things are real for him, as they have never been for me in my sheltered life. It is easy for me to talk about ancient history, folklore and philosophy, yet I wonder if, at the back of his mind he may not perceive the futility of such studies in a life oppressed by hunger and circumstances. His courage is great and his devotion to learning is one of the most wonderful things I have known. At nineteen he has thrown off the usual fallacies of wealth and others' esteem and has developed the critical power of a strong, sensitive mind. To him successes and failures are no game but a battle. This is true diligence – a word the Chinese use a great deal and with high praise.

One evening, when Roger and I met Yannang and a friend, the latter enquired with great seriousness into our beliefs. Addressing himself to Roger, he asked, "And what is your philosophy of life?" Poor Roger, I saw his eyebrows soar skywards as he rapidly thought through the public school code.

At times Hong Kong now seems to me to be a place of high tragedy. There are few who believe that the colony could be held against a Chinese assault for long. The community here thrives because the People's Government has not yet seen fit to attack us. There would of course be an almighty battle and I dare not think what would follow.

The local Chinese would be in a fix if such an event were to occur. A passive people in a crisis sits still. Yannang has faith in the good government which the British supply but he is, after all, Chinese; he belongs to the people over the mountains. If the communists were to come, young idealists would simply cover up, becoming impassive, blank to all influences, helping no one, daring little courageously but rather turning back perhaps to a country life, where at least the mind could find some freedom. Yet, perhaps I am unfair. Quiet courage may go deeper than I suppose. Western films about heroism rarely portray the bravery of those who try to live their own lives in conditions far from freedom.

After one evening together, Yannang wrote me a long letter sharing our ideas over again. I wrote back to him:

"I, too, returned to camp with a full heart that night. I think maybe we understand the true sympathy of friendship. I sincerely hope so for both our sakes. Like you, I have written a long diary in my letters home, in which I have recalled whole passages of our conversations as if we were still talking together.

You ask me to correct the thoughts you express. Oh Yannang, I wish I could. What you say is pure and graceful in expression and the sorrow of homelessness runs like an arrow through my heart also, as I read what you have written.

Indeed my home in England waits for me, my mother anxiously looking forward to the return of her travelled son. There will be celebrations, talk and family love. When I think of your predicament I find the comparison painful. Yet we must address these problems together when we meet, talk about it, not hide from it. This has happened to you and you cannot forget or put it aside. You will live on, Yannang, after I have left Hong Kong. There will continue to be good wishes and friendship and love. There is as much kindness in the world as there is terror and despair. I believe love wins through. Despair in the world is no new thing and neither is love. We need a faith in the beauty of nature and the kind heart of man for all must in the end be well. At least, thinking so, the sorrowful moment will be easier to bear." And I quoted to him the psalmist David's writings on despair and the manner in which, taking courage, he walked on. "In you I can see both sorrow and courage and I know you will come to understand both. I love you for that."

*

The Buddha statue

The professor seemed pleased to see me and ushered me into his flat. It was a spacious apartment, two sides of it window and a group of rooms leading off the main hall. There was a highly polished wood-block floor without mats and modern furniture, tasteful tables, chairs and stools.

After a brief exchange of pleasantries, he retired for his Sunday morning shave while I conned the morning paper. It was nearly half past eleven. As usual the news was unutterably depressing yet after a while I became aware of the music floating through the room from a little wireless. I had not noticed it when I had arrived. It was Bach's *St John's Passion*. It soared and roamed, tilted and slid into a long cascade of sound. My world steadied, became quiet, the view of the harbour beyond the window seemed to stretch further and further. Below lay the hillside park and scattered houses of the university compound and beyond that the city sprawled along the slopes of the hill leading down to the harbour with its liners, cargo boats, lighters, sampans, junks and ferries, and, beyond that, Kowloon and the hills leading towards China.

I heard a little bell ringing and, looking up, saw a small porcelain bell hanging before the open window. Below the tiny clapper a piece of paper was being blown by the slight breeze. As the professor returned I pointed to the bell.

"Ah yes – it represents one of the temple wind bells of Japan. Every time it rings it says a prayer. Look, it has Kyoto written upon it. That is where it comes from."

Professor Kirby holds the Chair of Economics at Hong Kong University. I had met him at a private dinner party given by Mr A.C. Scott, an expert on Japan. Kirby was educated in Japan and speaks both Japanese and Mandarin fluently. During the war he held a kind of roving commission with the Chinese army in Chung King and at various war fronts. When Hong Kong was recaptured he acted as interpreter on HMS *King George V*. He is a strange old boy, very much a professor and correspondingly vague. He writes many papers and has a book on China in press.

We strolled together through a maze of streets and down Ladder Street, a long flight of steps leading down the steep hillside, flattening out every time it met a cross-roads. In Upper Lascar Row, also known as Cat Street, we began exploring the numerous shops. Everything seemed to be on sale from ancient sewing machines to old tin cans. Open to the street and stuffed to the ceilings, antique shops were filled with ivory carvings, work in bone, wooden Buddhist altar pieces, paintings, scrolls, trinkets, scent bottles, ancestor portraits, incense burners, innumerable ancient coins, implements and vases of all sorts and dimensions. The professor, something of an expert, told me there were three price ranges, one for the Chinese, one for the British and one for Americans. So one has to be decidedly British and pose as an expert, muttering about the Sung and Ming dynasties and expressing doubt when the dealer dates a piece absurdly early. Everything is to be minutely examined while one expresses extreme poverty and inability to spend even a penny.

Kirby was a well-known and welcome guest at all the shops and, after a quarter of an hour, speaking Chinese, he clinched a deal which had been debated for weeks. He came away with two enormous scrolls. They were ancestor portraits which interested him. Within the last fifty or so years a tradition had become established whereby the photograph of a deceased was copied exactly and a set of gorgeous robes of a bygone dynasty painted around the figure.

At the back of one little shop I spotted a small, throned Buddha image in gilded wood. It seemed a lovely little piece with a wonderfully serene expression, quite unlike the worldly, laughing Buddhas of which there are many in the shops. The professor dated it as mid-eighteenth century while the dealer put it earlier. It glowed gold with a rare quality that touched me. I asked how much. $220 I was told. I offered $100. At the time I really had no intention of buying it but the more I examined it the more I felt it was really worth having. The professor remarked that if I did not buy it, he would. That decided the issue. I was not to know this little figure would be of great importance to me and to others long into the future.

*

Unwanted promotion

For the last month I have been truly happy. My conversations with Yannang, my expeditions into the city and plans for a short holiday in Japan have all been juice for the spirit. One of the secret ingredients has lain in Brickhill itself. Often in the evenings I would climb up the hill beyond the perimeter wire to the very top. I would sit there watching the changes of light and shadow as the sun set.

I cannot claim to know anything of Eastern meditation but, somehow, perched up there on my rock, my mind became empty of troubles, becoming absorbed by the beauty of the world. I found an inner quietude and certainty I have never known before. This was not something mystical but a form of reflection; the view became mine while the details of a flower I picked focused my attention. Then, letting my eyes drift over the curves and slopes of the hills, the forms of rocks and trees, it seemed as if I was gliding my hands over them so close did they feel. I would come down to the mess for our evening meal, as refreshed as the earth after a cooling shower and as quiet in my mind as an unruffled pool. I believe these moments to have been among the happiest I have known because at such times there was no wish for anything else, no desire, no thinking, no looking for anything outside my vision.

But now my mood is as grey as the sombre sky.

Suddenly, without warning, I am told that next week I will take over the Regimental Headquarters Troop in Stanley as Troop Commander and that, as a result, my proposal for leave in Japan is cancelled. One is never allowed to be happy for long. All day I have felt caged, trapped in a world of regretted circumstances, near to despair for I was so looking forward to leave. I blasted all those military deities who push people around as if they were toys; those fools of officers with their petty pomp, their self-opinionated airs and graces, small minds and absurd idiosyncrasies. My inherent loathing of the whole system sprang up like a rampant dragon and I was hardly in control of my resentful thoughts.

I went to the adjutant, said I was really happy at Brickhill, that my passage to Japan was booked, that I only had three and a half months of service left to do. A reasonable man, he listened reasonably. He went to talk it over with the CO and told me he had done all he could. The CO had said, "Hard bloody luck!"[*]

The adjutant did his best to help. I had been chosen, he said, for my 'maturity' to do a responsible job that needed some innate cunning and tact. He poured it all on – useful job, usually only staffed by regulars of the rank of captain, an interesting opportunity, a free command. As for my leave – well national service officers were only here for a year so they didn't really need any! He hoped I would not bear a grievance.

I raged around suddenly realising how attached I was to Brickhill. I loved the odd little place. Two bombadiers came running up to me after a shooting match, "We've won, Sir – we've won!" Faces as radiant as school kids. I could have cried. I seemed to have grown up with these men and to have a bond of companionship with them. They seemed to respect me as a friend rather than as an officer. And I certainly felt towards them as friends rather than "the men".

Stanley, the Regimental Headquarters, is a vast sprawling camp. It is difficult to get to know anyone there. There is saluting all the

---

[*] Right at the end of my service he relented and Chris and I had two weeks sailing to Japan and back; a wonderful journey.

time, rigid etiquette and an officious military atmosphere. And I had the impression that the subalterns there were a dull, unimaginative lot who never seemed to use their time in HK in any creative way.

On and on I moaned. The happier one is capable of being the more miserable the world appears, I muttered to myself. I opened newspapers only to read about H-bombs, the ruin of continents, human power rivalling that of the sun – the air full of war and rumours of war. I realised how strong is the fear of war, the sense of fateful destiny. I was angry with the CO for not giving me a better time after all my hard work. Poor me. It is given to some men to snuff out candles – one day they will do it on either side of the altar of hope. Grrrrrrrrr...

Yet, I reflected, Yannang and I have spoken so much about accepting life that it now appears to be my turn to swallow a bitter pill. I realised more and more how I depended either on solitude or my few dear friends for spiritual comfort. Yannang has filled a well of loneliness into which I seemed to have fallen since leaving school. I sensed myself to have an odd character, feeling and thinking about things differently from most. "There is," I wrote home, "perhaps a quality of contemplative thinking and a need for freedom which I hold very dear. But I must not be so introspective. It's not polite!"

Turning over the new job in my mind I could see it would be a challenging one. My duties would include attending to the welfare and discipline of a wide assortment of men, functioning as drivers, mechanics, cooks, clerks, dutymen of various kinds, and arranging the pay of the Chinese labourers and civilian staff. I would have to deal with truculent senior NCOs of many years service and, at times, send orders from HQ to regular officers commanding the various regimental sites around the colony. Innate cunning and tact – a free command! Indeed. I do not suffer those whom I consider fools gladly and was afraid of losing my newly-established inner calm in a series of irritating incidents.

Even so, I consoled myself, the job did indeed offer an opportunity to experience responsibilities usually only given to regular officers of much higher rank. It would be, indeed, a sole and free command of a lot of men functioning at the heart of the regimental HQ. I was, I realised, pleased to have been chosen and had an opportunity to learn much about the problems of effective administration. I would miss the radar and the gunsite. Oh well, I would have to get on with it. When there is no choice – act.

Chapter Eighteen

Troop Commander

The mood of HQ

Compared with the facilities at Brickhill, the officers' mess at Stanley comprised a palatial residence set among lawns with pleasing views out to sea. I had a large, upstairs room, airy and bright, which shared a wide balcony with other rooms on the same floor. I could saunter along it or around the whole building or take a chair of an evening and view the scenery with a regal air and usually in solitude, since the other officers on my floor spent much of their time socialising below.

I had suffered a complete change of company. Roger of Brickhill had finished his tour of duty and was *en route* to Blighty. The new faces in the mess were pleasant, affable but, so far, uninspiring. A sprinkling of ancient majors tended to keep the level of conversation as dull as possible.

I wrote home at this time: "A lot of the joy I had found on Brickhill has been lost at Stanley. In the mess I am rather an odd man out for there is no one at present with even the remotest similarity of interest. I find little humour or jollity here. Everyone is horribly 'regular', Sandhurst products, an ancient major or two, or boys barely weaned from school. One subaltern has never been further afield in Hong Kong than the Royal Yacht Club. Such an attitude is broadly accepted. These are all good lads, easy enough to get on with but, dare I say it, ineffably boring. Sorry!"

*

The new task

My task increases in interest as the days pass. It is entirely administrative. No more am I directly concerned with the guns, the radar or gunnery as such. My office, just down the road from the mess and within the headquarters building, lies next to those of the CO and the Second in Command. It is well equipped with comfortable chairs, a spacious desk and innumerable filing cabinets, regimental index systems, covering almost all aspects of regimental life and the individual details of both officers and men, and a hefty wall safe for cash and regimental secrets. I share the office with my Troop Sergeant Major and two bright clerks.

HQ Troop carries out all the multitude of administrative duties essential to a large regimental headquarters. Clerks, drivers and orderlies of countless description make up my unit, together with a large REME detachment, officered technically by their own REME Captain and his sergeant major. I have under my command one hundred and ninety-three men grading from the Regimental Sergeant Major down to the greasiest of sanitary orderlies. Their personal documents, carefully numbered and filed, fill a locked cupboard. I hold the qualification record cards, dental histories, regimental and battery conduct sheets and education certificates, as well as numerous other collections of facts and figures. One of the more difficult and time consuming activities of the clerks is keeping all this information up to date. On inspection much of it turned out to be incorrect or unamended for many months.

From time to time I have to take 'Orders', which means I have to try a case of indiscipline by some member of my troop under the penalty system laid down under military law. I hold the immediate fate of these miscreants in my hands!

One of my titles is 'Officer in charge of Civilian Labour'. I have to employ and discharge Chinese workers according to a complex set of War Office regulations. Engaging an amah for a sergeant's wife is an entertaining activity.

Once a week, I handle a large pay parade for the troops, in which more than a thousand pounds runs through my hands in the course of an afternoon. Once a month, there is the civilian pay parade in which all the civilian employees of the regimental headquarters, coolies, amahs, cooks, Chinese waiters, Chinese clerks and dhobies (washermen) receive their dues: again a large sum flows over my table under the watchful and wily scrutiny of a Chinese accountant.

This mountain of work is eased by the varying contributions of my immediate office staff. We manage the allocations of leave, arrangements for courses in driving, education, water duties, physical training and various sports as well as keeping score of personal attainments under the 'Star Qualification Scheme' which has a bearing on the men's pay. We keep the details of all regimental equipment, its efficiency, redundancy, need for repair replacement and so on. In the pay office I have a pay sergeant, a clerk bombadier and a learner clerk, and, for the civilians, my astute Chinese gentleman accountant. Further staff deal with POL, that is petrol, oil and lubricants for the numerous vehicles of the regiment, and with accommodation details such as barrack room management and personal kit. I am also in charge of a considerable small arms armoury and a signals unit equipped with radios, spare parts and other stores. The signals unit is the 'control' for the regimental radio net, for which I am also responsible.

My desk is the hub of all this activity and all the 'business' that the various offices do passes through my trays and all their documents have to receive my signature. Yet, my greatest responsibility and the one in which I take the greatest interest, is to ensure the welfare, hygiene, turnout and discipline of the men.

The major contrast with Brickhill is that, after morning parade, all these men spend the working day distributed around numerous offices and other locations on a very large site working under their respective departmental heads who are often majors. Liaison with these often opinionated and relatively 'elderly' characters is by no means simple. Frequent little tiffs occur.

One morning the DO (Director of Ordnance) rang up wanting to know why the armoury was in the charge of somebody who was no longer in the regiment! As I had only just taken over command I had no idea. He was very acid about this but it soon turned out that the fault lay with his own sergeant. Three days later I put one of his men on an education course for which he was due. At this I received a very apologetic phone call beseeching me to return him as soon as possible. I decided to be as magnanimous as possible, gradually learning the power of a skilled use of the telephone in such matters!

Various pay returns have to be in my office on certain dates each month, so that we can collate them and forward them to HQ Landforces, Hong Kong. One battery commander never gets his return in on time. I had repeatedly to ring him up and ask for it. One day he blustered and fumed down the telephone – there had been no changes since last month – some orders said this and others said that – I was politely unconcerned by his excuses. All I needed was his return on the following day.

"I have to make my report tomorrow and I shall expect your return by lunch time!" I put the receiver down.

Apparently he went roaring about camp all day muttering imprecations against "that young pup at RHQ." Nevertheless, I had my return in on time. To back me up I could always get the Second in Command to send a demand note. Since this would amount to a reprimand, even regular officers, technically senior to me, avoid the risk.

My immediate senior is one of the top-ranking officers in the regiment. I am answerable to no one lower in the hierarchy. Sadly, this man suffers from the mental impediment of an extreme tautology of speech and a conceptual vagueness that amounts to idiocy. I have stood for hours in his office while he waffles to someone else when my urgent request would take a few seconds. I have found the answer to this. The telephone again! Even though his office is more or less next door, I ring him up whenever I want something, for he finds the jangling instrument impossible to ignore.

Some of the charges I deal with need to be remanded to him for a disciplinary decision. This is a terrible affair. He seems not to know the tight military law and usually administers a mild admonishment. The miscreant comes out grinning.

A man persistently late on parade was asked,

"Haven't you got a watch?"

"Sah – No Sah!"

"Well – never you mind that – there is a perfectly good watch on the church tower. Just keep a watch on the church watch next time."

"Sah!"

To hear him lecturing a confirmed lecher on a VD charge, like a kind father talking to a twelve year old, is not funny. It is pathetic. Such a case merits twenty-eight days detention – he gave three. I have taken to suggesting the appropriate punishment and I have begun to deal with a wider range of cases. One man was brought before me for failing to appear on parade. I gave two days CB – Confinement to Barracks. I think he thought me far too strict.

The truth is that RHQ standards of turnout and discipline are lamentable – far below those obtained on Brickhill, in spite of our relaxed regime there. I felt that at RHQ we should be better than outlying sites and set an example. I began a series of vigorous inspections both during parades in the mornings and in visits to the barrack rooms. I discovered:

- Three battledresses covered with mildew.
- Several pairs of boots rotting with fungus.
- Greatcoats left in the dhobie since the previous year.
- Lockers smelling like Chinese latrines.
- One man had four uniforms screwed up in the bottom of his locker, all filthy. He was wearing overalls all day!
- One mosquito net sodden with rain from being left hanging over a balcony for a week.
- Barrack room blankets apparently never changed nor fumigated for as long as anyone could remember.
- Boots left in the cobbler's for six months – thus allowing the man not to polish them for inspections.
- A Chinese laundry with so much faulty wiring that it might have gone up in smoke any minute.
- Bed bugs in the telephone exchange.

As a result of this shake up, I have had four applications for transfer to Malaya!

In this good work I am more than aided by my energetic and forceful sergeant major. He was a sergeant at Oswestry, when I was a gunner in training there, and he comes from Newport, Isle of Wight. Only recently promoted from sergeant, TSM Jeffs is aiming high. Harsh yet humorous, strict yet understanding, full of drive and knowledgeable about all the many things I am ignorant about, the TSM is a first-rate soldier and an immense support. He makes up for all the uncertainties that a national service trained subaltern cannot avoid. Jeffs is a great egoist – "I did this" "I did that" and there is precious little it seems that he has not done. Certainly everything he does is done very well and he ensures that everyone notices it. He is aiming for a quartermaster's commission before he finishes. Within the troop he is rapidly becoming a legend. I like to think we make a good pair.

Even so all is not well. The morale in RHQ is bad. One bombadier remarked to me, "This is an unhappy regiment." I was sorry to hear it. Some senior NCOs are openly critical of the CO. "All he cares about is training, he does not care about the welfare of his men!"

The Colonel is indeed very keen on sustaining military training, believing perhaps that this alone can sustain morale. His 'regimental policy' fails to emphasise welfare. As a national serviceman I cannot help finding this amusing. After all, the Chinese have Russian planes that can fly so fast that our ancient radar sets cannot keep up with them. Such ardent military preparation seems a little misplaced when the equipment is really too old to do its job. Yet there is no doubt the efficiency of the regiment has increased greatly under his command. In any case what else should one expect from a CO!

Coming from Brickhill I had been surprised by this deep-rooted discontent. I said to the pay bombadier that I had not encountered anything like it at Brickhill. "Well," he said, "Brickhill is known to be the happiest site in the colony!" I was overjoyed to hear this for I felt that our style of command at Brickhill had had much to do with it.

I pondered the contrasts between Brickhill and Stanley and found that the difference in feeling must have been due to situational factors as well as the attitudes of us officers.

Brickhill had been isolated and self-contained. By contrast RHQ is the hub of the regiment loaded with high-ranking officers and only a part of a very large garrison.

The isolation on Brickhill had allowed a great sense of loyalty and mutual feeling to grow up there. A team spirit was manifest in everything that happened. Such feeling did not exist at RHQ.

Our careful man management had produced an unusual atmosphere of informality on Brickhill. Officers, NCOs and men had no marked social barriers between them. All our duties interlocked, were mutually understood and supported. The loyalty between ranks operated both upwards and downwards.

Captain Robin Chandler, the TC on Brickhill, was personally not good at managing men. He had left most of that to us national service subalterns. Yet he was technically brilliant and provided an enthusiastic if occasionally rather overanxious drive behind our gunnery and radar training. The CO, in his bluff way, had several times complimented us on our site efficiency and we considered ourselves the best-trained unit in the regiment. The results of the January firing camp and the night exercise had confirmed that for us. Both officers and men felt that the site was good militarily and that our activities were worthwhile. This bred both confidence and enthusiasm, so that when failures did occur we were quick to try and mend them.

In RHQ there is a strict regimentalism; officers and many NCOs tend to have their accommodation well away from that of the men. Barriers between ranks are clear-cut and sustained. Formality reigns in all dealings between the ranks. All jobs are specialised and often highly focused on individual practitioners. The men are widely dispersed and work in separate offices with little contact with others. There is no sense of working together towards a common objective nor, therefore, a feeling that the troop must stand or fall by team work above all else. Little team spirit operates in the activities of RHQ.

On Brickhill, officers and NCOs lived cheek by jowl so that supervision of work was easily achieved. We did not need 'bullshit' to sustain our standards. At RHQ, supervision cannot be that close and standards of turnout, discipline and hygiene fall easily. The Sergeant Major and I have to keep a constant watch on these matters. If they fall below standard, both health and contentment become jaded.

On Brickhill I knew every man individually and often his whole life history as well; parents, girlfriends at home, popsies in HK. Personal troubles, many of them seemingly quite simple to those of us with wider education, often appeared as mountains to the men. A few words of consolation or advice often cleared things up. Several times, by talk alone, I had been able to prevent a man going AWOL (Absent without Leave) just because he was 'fed up'.

In RHQ there were so many men that I did not even know most of their names. Rarely did I hear of personal troubles until they became very difficult or surfaced when a man was charged with some offence. The men tended to keep themselves to themselves, avoiding contact with those above them in the military hierarchy. The phrase 'bloody orfficers' was often muttered at Stanley in a way it never was on Brickhill. It is easier to get into the city from Stanley and correspondingly easier for men to get into trouble. Many more disciplinary charges had to be made at RHQ than was the case on Brickhill.

It seemed to me that efficiency and contentment in a troop depended entirely on the right relationship being established between officers, NCOs and men. RHQ runs on discipline when it runs at all. Brickhill tended to run on a sort of mutual understanding. The informality of Brickhill was a great asset. By informality I do not mean a familiarity which could erode the respect that sustains discipline, but rather a two-way friendliness between the ranks, based partly on humour yet also on a respect for the contrasting capacities and roles of each rank. This seems entirely lacking at RHQ.

The main troubles at RHQ are the large number of men, the lack of a commonly perceived objective, the absence of an isolation that encourages fellow feeling and the deliberately disciplined separateness of ranks.

I therefore set myself and my sergeant major two main objectives: firstly, to improve standards of turnout, discipline and hygienic training, even when this required the severity of a reforming approach; secondly to get to know men on a more individual basis, to encourage their wider interests and to facilitate recreational activities other than the cinema, the beer halls and the brothels. We felt that a feeling of troop loyalty and fellow feeling among the men might be germinated in this way. The rudiments were present. We sought to make them grow.

*

On trying to get things done! June 2nd 1954

I am like a man who has been given a complex machine to work. For a few days he looks at all the bits and pieces and sees how they work. After that he just sits and watches it, oiling it occasionally and carrying the can when anything goes wrong. The complicated administration of RHQ Troop has boiled down to a matter of seeing that my clerks do not make mistakes. There are few opportunities for real leadership, since all my men are employed as drivers or office workers. I function in liaison between higher-ranking officers who drive me round the bend with their pomposity, verbal diarrhoea and stupidity. As I said before, my immediate superior is the talk of the regiment – no exaggeration. During Officer's Days he attempts to stand in for the CO who is in England on compassionate leave. Everyone, from the newest subaltern to the battery commanders, sits there wringing his hands in boredom and amazement at his absurd statements, his utter lack of logic and the smokescreen of hot air he produces. Sadly, the man is a fool. Last week he ordered me to cut down some of my men's pay since they had just spent a little of their savings. This is actually illegal for no one can tamper with a man's pay except under very special conditions. I remonstrated without avail. The pay sergeant, my sergeant major, the pay clerks were all furious as, of course, were the men involved. Another troop commander was treated the same way and erupted in fury. I ask myself how can I maintain my own morale let alone that of my men with a fool like this in charge.

In spite of these frustrations I am accomplishing some improvements. To interest the men and divert them from the bars and brothels as the only outlet for amusement, I have started a series of organised visits to places of interest in the colony such as factories, print works and, yes, even monasteries! I am getting much support from Sergeant Major Jeffs who continues to embarrass everyone by his efficiency!

One weekend I led a party of nine on a long hike in Lantao Island, stopping overnight at the Po Lin monastery. I was amazed to see how these bored clerks and REME fitters responded. Their jollity and enthusiasm was terrific, morale at its highest. The monastery, where I am now considered to be a friend, treated us royally and two of the more intelligent NCOs watched the morning ritual with great interest. Everyone seemed captivated by the beauty of the open countryside and the spacious hills.

On arrival we were served a marvellous Chinese dinner. The men were surprised when what appeared to be mammoth steaks arrived. When they learnt this was a meal of fungus they were horrified. One of them thought he would soon be sick. I gently encouraged them, hogging my own dish, and soon everyone was tucking in and enjoying the novelty. One of my NCOs now goes back there quite frequently, mainly for sketching.

Another party visited a printing press and another the Coca Cola factory. Two small parties are scheduled for the Leprosarium. I have also applied for a regimental beach hut! Of course it was refused as if

I were quite out of my senses but it would be an asset. Some of the officers consider me a little daft to be so concerned about what my men do in their free time but gradually the idea is becoming respected. Some senior battery officers have asked me for details of the trips I have arranged. I am also considered to be the regimental expert on the Chinese! If I had greater rank I believe I could eventually influence regimental policy towards a more considered understanding of the men's welfare.

One day, on some important annual holiday, we had a major regimental parade during which RHQ troop had to march past the CO, standing on a saluting platform. We trained and marched around the parade ground until I felt we had the matter reasonably on hand. The day came, not without embarrassment, however. Launching into the march past, I found to my surprise that my pace was much longer than that of the men so that I was steadily drawing ahead of them, so much so that, as I was approaching the saluting base, I was virtually alone. Worse still my command, "Eyes right", could not be heard by the ranks so far behind me. Shambles! I had to put up with a good ragging that evening. Much later, talking with a major, he told me he had the opposite trouble – being a shortie he was virtually trampled upon by his men whenever such a parade was held. How one gets this right remains beyond me still! Anyway, it is only a few weeks before I shall be well out of it all.

Chapter Nineteen

Dragon Boats

The Rains arrive, May 26th 1954

Last week the emergency began. For weeks on end the weather had been dry and dusty and the early spring rains had failed. Only a few feet of water remained in the reservoirs and the city water supply had been restricted to two hours in the morning and two in the evening. Old water buckets, basins, bowls stood everywhere storing the daily ration. The large restaurants were surviving well but, in the overcrowded tenements, the shortage of water had become acute. In camp, all water to lavatories and baths was cut off. Special washing parades were held on the sea beaches, where the lads were able to remove the worst of the daily grime and to cool off. It had been a sweaty fortnight, dust everywhere and no sign of rain.

Last night, at last, the monsoon began, first a shower, then another, and today a steady downpour. I was riding in a bus when the first drops fell. The coolies in the streets put down their burdens and stood smiling at the sky, old women peered out from the arcades, lifting their hands to the sluicing rain. Soon the gutters were swirling with dirty, frothing water washed off the roofs and down the clogged drains of countless tenements. Where clearer water flowed, little shoeshine boys ran along, splashing their bare feet in the gutters laughing and teasing one another. The gross Indian gentlemen, who recline in rattan chairs outside the doors of banks and jewellers shops nursing their rifles on their knees and looking far from protective, grinned expansively as the rain blew into the arcades upon them. The bus conductor shot up the window and laughed; "Ah – a good thing this, eh?" People, like etiolated flowers, were taking on a new lease of life. There was something organic about their joy – and something

very inadequate in my own reaction. I was annoyed because I had left
my mac behind!

*

The festival, June 5th 1954

The calm of the evening was disturbed. At first I could not
perceive why, then it dawned on me, the strange sound of a distant
drum and a light danging of metal on sounding brass hung in the air.
Following the evocative sound I went out on to the balcony outside my
room. Out in the bay beyond Stanley village lay a long, cigar-shaped
craft. As the drum beat, so the long, thin ship went gliding across the
water, a dragon boat at practice. Above its prow the dragon raised its
proud head while, along its length, gay pennants fluttered in the
breeze. In the centre stood the drummer behind his drum and the
crew paddled to his rhythm.

Chinese native craft are among the most beautiful small boats I
have seen. Whether it be a great junk with ribbed lateen sail, full
spread like a great bat's wing, its shadow spread before the sun on
silver waters; a sampan bobbing along with the big-hatted oarsman
sculling away side to side over the stern; or this mysterious ship
gliding along like an alligator head held high and tapering tail raised
above the water; all these boats seem closer to nature than any other.
It is as if the builders have for centuries striven to mould their ships to
the landscape, not taking advantage of nature as we do in our glossy,
streamlined yachts, but simply conforming to her way – the Tao of
ships merging with the Tao of sea, bay, and mountain.

Down in the city the town had that air of gaiety about it peculiar to
festival time. Tables were set in shop entrances, loaded with food and
drink offerings to the gods. The black-clothed women were burning
candles and joss sticks before the Door God shrines and others were
carrying paper dragon boats to be burnt as an offering to an ancestor.
Yet the festival actually commemorates a sorrowful story which
Yannang related to me on the top of a tram.

Chu Yuan was a virtuous minister in the state of Chu (400 BC)
who, as a result of court intrigue, had been exiled to a country area,
remote from the capital. From this distant perch, he observed the
political manoeuvres of the various neighbouring states and he could

see that the powerful Chin, under a pretence of friendship, were preparing the overthrow of his homeland. Chu Yuan was also a great writer, the founder of a school of prose poetry but, for all his eloquence and wisdom, he had no control over the unrolling of affairs. He poured out his grief in a book, *A Conversation with a Fisherman,* which was to become a classic. One day, walking beside a river, he saw his reflection in the water. How worried, how tired he looked, how useless his life had become. He leapt into the stream and drowned. The villagers, who loved him well, raced their boats to the spot but to no avail. Although they sprinkled food upon the water to keep the fish from eating his body, he was gone forever. On this day of commemoration, boats are still raced and food is spread on the water, in appreciation of his undying spirit.

The rite is in origin more ancient still. It began as a cult of water deities who ruled the lives of fish and fishermen alike. The scattering of rice on the waters propitiated the spirits of the drowned who, having no graves, had become wandering and malevolent ghosts. Since dragons are the controllers of water and rain, the boats are shaped like dragons to ensure the arrival of the rains. The races symbolise the dragons' contest in the skies manifest by the vast clouds, thunder and downpours that characterise this time of year.

The dragons were certainly doing their stuff. For three days rain had poured continuously on the colony and the races themselves were held in a downpour. So much so that, after the races, the ever practical Chinese decided that it was unnecessary to scatter any rice at all this year!

Dragon boat races take place in many parts of southern China and the festival is one of which the communists approve. In Hong Kong there are races at Aberdeen, Cheung Chau Island, Kennedy Town, Tsun Wan and Tai Po. Yannang and I went to the races in Kennedy Town where the best boats of the colony competed under the gaze of the Governor and Lady Grantham, who afterwards distributed the prizes.

I had not seen Yannang for a fortnight as he had been working hard for his exams which fall at the end of next month. On seeing him, the rains began to work their magic on me also. The arid days at Stanley, the boring company in the mess, the men's troubles, a bombadier's divorce, were suddenly all behind me. Yet it was not as if we talked of anything of consequence. Wandering through the streets, dodging the showers, the pleasure of his company was sufficient.

We arrived early, understanding that the races would begin at two o'clock. They began at four. "Oh well," said Yannang. "The Chinese sense of time is not always very exact!" However, there was never a dull moment. The finishing line lay between the two bamboo piers of the Chinese swimming sheds in Kennedy Town and the framework of each pier was already crowded with people, mostly wearing swimming costumes. The front row was in continuous turmoil as those behind pressed forward pushing those in front of them into the water. At the ends of the piers firecrackers were exploding with flashes and plumes of smoke and, beyond them, a motley collection of junks, sampans, launches and wallah wallah boats were drawn up, all flying great banners and streamers of bunting. As one large junk arrived 'dressed over all' firecrackers were being thrown from it in all directions.

The first of the long, narrow dragon boats arrived, forty barrel-chested Chinamen flaying the water with small paddles, each man plunging his instrument deeply into the water in dynamic movement. With twenty paddles to a side moving in perfect unison, the boat looked just like a great seaworm swimming. The illusion was even stronger when there was a slight inaccuracy in the timing and a wave of paddling passed down one side of the boat.

The dragon boat paraded gently across the front of the course and then, with the drummer beating a wild rhythm, it turned and dashed in towards the stands, the dragon's head reaching out with gaping jaws like a voracious animal in pursuit of its prey. A fine spray flew out on either side and, lashed by the rain, it charged down the course half hidden in the smoke of a thousand firecrackers. Suddenly all the paddles were jammed into the water and, braking violently, the boat came to a halt, with the dragon head almost rammed within the bamboo frames of the sheds. One after another the boats arrived, each presenting itself with bravado in a charge along the course. In some of the boats the drummer stood in the prow rather than in the centre. Eventually all six boats were present.

The Chinese people are generally thought by Westerners to be silently inscrutable. Indeed, at British ceremonies in the colony, Royal birthday parades and so on, even though they turn up in crowds to watch the fun, they show little excitement or enthusiasm. And, indeed, what do these essentially British events have to do with them? But here the cheering and waving, the tumultuous firecracking, the atmosphere of mirth and frivolity brought with it a great sense of holiday.

The Governor arrived, the first bar of the National Anthem was played, the rain poured down, the nearly naked youths kept falling into and scrambling out of the waters and then, amid deafening explosions, the first race was on. The crowd cheered madly. The voice of the commentator became quite inaudible; his friends were cheering into his microphone. The smoke was so dense only the last quarter of the course was visible. Six boats came dashing through the spray, drummers gesticulating wildly, the crews flaying the water, each dragon head ferociously reaching out for victory. Amidst huge applause they jammed on the brakes, coming to a halt in a welter of churning water, sea snakes from an ancient time.

By now it was raining very heavily indeed and the stands were bobbing with hundreds of the black umbrellas the Chinese use against either rain or sun. Naturally those behind could see nothing so a great cry went up as one by one the brollies were grasped from behind and extinguished.

When it was all over, there was a typically Chinese chaos which everyone enjoyed hugely. The management had planned carefully so that everyone could get in but, at the end, because the Governor had to leave first, the exit became totally blocked. Governor or no governor, once a Chinese crowd moves there is no stopping it, so it began to flow around the side of the entrance to come face to face with barbed wire.

Among a people other than the Chinese this might have produced a catastrophe but, here, everyone roared with laughter and, in great good humour, came to a standstill and just looked at it. In a typically Chinese solution, the police promptly cut a hole through the wire and everyone poured through. By this time of course the Governor was on his way to tea and the entrance was free. Watching all this in heavy rain with my mac over my head, I found that two small boys had appropriated my sleeves and were using them as hats, grinning about in delight.

Back in camp I saw the dragon boat of Stanley return to the bay. Rolling on the swells of the Pacific the craft looked even more magnificent, the dragon head rising and falling on the waves, paddles working the dull, rain-smashed sea, dark green hills behind a glistening shore. The boat again seemed imbued with the poise and ferocity of a strange sea animal, manifesting the beauty and terror of the ocean.

Chapter Twenty
Leprosarium

Active Christianity, June 26th 1954

Today I witnessed some of the finest Christian work done in the colony, work which showed that love and charity is best expressed in something practical and not too sublime. I visited a leper colony.

The Hong Kong Mission to Lepers has, in three busy years, constructed a new leprosarium on a small island lying between Lantao and Hong Kong. Many lepers have been collected here from all over Kwantung. Many are from the colony itself, while some of them are inmates of a previous establishment in China simply pushed over the border by the communists. The island has been renamed Hai Ling Chou meaning 'the island of happy healing'. Indeed it seems to be so, for I saw European and Chinese doctors and staff working together in a common cause and showing a real compassion for their unfortunate patients. This struck me as true Christianity, so different from the platitudinous milk and water attitudes I find in middle-class England today. Most important, nobody here mentioned God, Christ or even religion, the 'work' took first place, a work steeped in human kindness. "By their deeds shall ye know them!"

After a choppy passage, we were glad to land at a little beach sheltered from the strong winds. Just beyond the shore and in the centre of the bay stood an elongated Chinese building, white with a red-tiled roof, set among green lawns. A moon gate led to it and on it was the character for happiness painted in gold. On the pillars, further characters told of the spirit of compassion that is invoked here.

We were met by Dr Smily and Miss Moore, the matron, a motherly Canadian woman speaking fluent Cantonese. Dr Smily is a tiny little man, over seventy years in age, I guessed, with a slightly humped back, impeccably dressed in a fresh, clean shirt, hair parted as neatly as could be and wearing a hearing aid. The chief doctor on the island, he has spent nearly the whole of his life among lepers, at first in south China, then in Peking and now in his last post in Hong Kong. I was aware at once of a remarkable man, tenacious, methodical, kindly, patient, with a sort of brilliance that stamped him as a truly great personality. He took us first to the staff house, a superbly designed Chinese building with moon doors and octagonal windows, where we were treated to a strange alcoholic beverage made on the island from fermented sugar and tea.

Dr Smily led us round. Beyond a slight rise from the landing beach, a collection of grey stone dwellings, in Chinese style, houses the patients. The main hospital – the Maxwell Medical Centre – stands among them as a brand new institution. One of the assistants showed us how a skin smear is taken from a patient – a submissive girl of twenty-nine who was getting on well. Dr Smily explained the disease to us and because our party contained several young doctors, he was evidently more forthcoming than usual. He was careful to see we did not touch any possibly contaminated material and, on entering the accommodation of the most afflicted patients, told us to touch nothing, including walls and doors. A young American, who put his hand on the railings, was ordered to the wash house to scrub his hands.

The worst cases were terrible to see, swollen faces with scarlet patches, some with sores, twisted limbs, decaying feet, fingers rotted away, toes gone. Paralysis of limb and face muscles gave some of the patients a grotesque and horrible appearance. Dr Smily, the matron and the assistants walked among them, a kind word here, a greeting there, a swift enquiry, on the spot examinations of some of the worst conditions. Dr Smily spoke to the patients with infinite gentleness and assurance. The young doctors in our party were visibly awed. So was I.

Children were playing down the hill from the hospital. A gang of little boys came running to the matron. "Oh, they've found a rat hole," she said, chattering away to them as if she was one of them herself. The kids looked happy and jolly enough but all of them had the disease and it would take many months to cure.

Set in the little valley were a number of small fields where vegetables were being grown and a promising grove of papaya had been planted. There was a pigsty and a little brown bull and a cow, the gifts of my banking friends on the Peak. The teenagers' house, at the end of the valley, was where the bigger boys lived separately from their elders and among a group of fields and trees of their own. Nearby, a pond was overflowing to create a flooded marsh where there were lotuses in full bloom, symbols of purity spotless in the mud. They seemed poignant here, where these poor sufferers received such touching care and security.

Back at the house we all had a thorough wash and a drink. I bought some towels embroidered with the Nestorian cross worked on them by the lepers. Our party departed in thoughtful mood. A friend, one of the subalterns from the regiment, remarked to me, "How wonderful to be a doctor. I wish I had known about it earlier." I was thinking the same.

*

A difficult correspondence

My letters home were read by my parents with close attention. They found it difficult to understand my fascination with the Chinese religious world although they were otherwise very sympathetic and interested in my explorations of an environment so new to me. They felt that my enthusiasm for Buddhism was getting a little out of hand and began expressing their worries.

Both my parents were Anglican Christians dedicated to the work of the church but they were far from being fanatical about it. Indeed my father, an engineer originally by profession, had once made it clear to me that faith sometimes coexisted with doubt. In church and doubtless hearing the faltering manner in which I was muttering the Creed, he added the words – "in so far as it can be believed" at the end of his own recitation. I was touched and reassured by this tolerance.

I was concerned not to hurt my parents but I could not gainsay my excitement at my cross-cultural discoveries. I tried to write home about this. In the course of time my parents came to accept my interest in Buddhism as being better than atheism but I feel they always wondered how they had gone wrong in failing to instil a deeper faith in me.

"I noticed with some misgiving, Mummy, your somewhat stringent criticism of my apparent disloyalty to what you call the 'faith of my fathers'. I feel that in any man's search for truth the very idea of disloyalty cannot enter, since to be loyal to what is seen as a partial truth is to defeat the high ideal of the search. Truth lies beyond the tales of gods and creeds and in a sphere of thinking where an impartial light, so to speak, shines. Where there is an impartial view, there can be no loyalty or disloyalty but simply faith and love for that light, whencesoever it comes. In any case, I find something stultifying in conviction. Keeping an open mind is the key to ever renewable novelty and joy.

"Actually in my conversations with Yannang we often talk about Christianity and it has been valuable to hear his perspective upon it. The Chinese throughout history never believed in a single personal god. The one philosophical movement which did introduce such an idea, together with an emphasis on the importance of individual love and freedom as opposed to the focus on family values and social harmony stressed by Confucius, failed within a century of its origin. Motse, the philosopher who introduced the idea, became almost forgotten until recently. Likewise the early Nestorian Church in China did not last for more than a century or so. Long before "Mohism" and before Christianity reached China, the Chinese had well-established systems of religion and ethics in Taoism and Confucianism.

"Yannang, in spite of his Western education, remains very true to his Chinese traditions. The central Christian idea of a personal God in the heavens is thus lost on him, as, indeed, it was to me as I came to study science in depth at university. Yet perhaps the idea of a personal God is not the most vital of Christian ideas. The self-sacrifice of Christ seems altogether more central. Christ's compassion rather than God's will occupies the pivotal place. Here we find some empathy with Buddhism because, to the Buddhist, compassion is the highest virtue together with *prajna* or insight into one's own nature. So, when we talk of a Christian 'love of all things', Yannang understands this very well.

"Sometimes we have read the Bible together. Unfortunately the first book he opened by himself was the Song of Solomon and this took some explaining. Quite what the 'scented breasts' of the song had to do with Christianity he couldn't make out! The first problem was indeed the continual reference to 'God'. God, as a being directing the world from on high, is nonsense to Yannang. We explored a better meaning for the word and came up with 'that idea which brings meaning and wonder, joy, happiness and peace into one's life.' Yannang concluded that God was the 'idea of the love of Nature and compassion for man.' Reading through the twenty-third Psalm in this light together seemed to add power and grandeur to it.

"To some, the Christian God may be viewed as a 'personalised idea' and to use the word with this sense may not be so illogical after all. By personalising the idea it becomes easier to draw strength from it and, in emotional stress, even to pray in such a way as to invoke power and renewed faith in it. Believing in this way allows the Biblical stories to be read through in their full grandeur even by a person who may not admit the objective reality of God.

"Even so, Yannang and I hit upon a more ultimate question upon which both Buddha and Confucius maintained a noble silence, namely 'If God is in the mind as an idea, what then made the mind?' The quick and thoughtless answer of course is God. But to what does this question point? Both of us felt that theology cannot answer such a question. Whereas Christian charity and good works set an exemplary standard in ethical life, theology often seems mere sophistry. Even so, there is an approach to an answer in the Bible. The word Jehovah means 'I am that I am', an expression resembling in a most remarkable way the Buddhist notion of 'suchness'. The earth *is*, I *am*, we *are*, it is *such*. The universe is such as it is and both we and all manifestations of life are aspects or expressions of that 'suchness'. Suchness is a word for the unknown basis of *being* whether material, biological or spiritual. In suchness is both the beginning and the ending. 'I am Alpha and Omega – the beginning and the end'. In Taoism, Lao Tse began his great work, the *Tao te Ching*, with 'The Tao that can be expressed is not the eternal Tao.' Suchness remains a mystery – like God.

"I find the great difference between the Christian tradition I have known and religion in China to lie in what the adherent does. At home, we have an emphasis on petitionary prayer, worship of something beyond, out there. In China, such perspectives are replaced by meditation, yogic exercises and mysticism, set within a form of worship that returns reflexively to one's own mind after an outward excursion. Prayer and petition in the West move outwards towards something else. This is not so in a mystical religious life, whether Western or Eastern.

"I am trying to express myself as I see things now for I cannot and will not pretend to be other than I am nor to believe other than as I do. The only difference between us may be the contrasting expression of religious feeling in two generations. I believe and hope there is no actual conflict."

Chapter Twenty-One

Flashback

Dear M and D, *(12. 3. 54 from Brickhill)*

I am not in the least bored by your letters. The peaceful and tolerant nature of my family background is an inspiration. Your descriptions of home life are a real joy to me and keep me in touch with you all. So, too, do I value your news of local events, parish affairs and so on. If I do not always refer to these in my letters, it is simply that so much happens here that I feel I must write to you about it. In many ways my letters to you are my diary.

In showing concern for where I stand and in voicing those concerns, you make me think and attempt to relate my new experiences out here to my earlier life. So I will try to define my viewpoint. I can begin by looking at my personal history and, since I doubt if we have ever really discussed this at home for we are quite reticent about such things, this may be a good way to begin. In any case it helps me make a sort of assessment of where I am.

The whole trend of my thinking and feeling since the age of fourteen or so seems, now I look back on it, to have followed an almost inevitable path; the coming to the surface of my own psyche, a feeling of my soul moving deeply within me to disclose itself. For a long time this movement was fettered by circumstances, which partly succeeded in conditioning my life as I grew up. Firstly, there was public school pride and snobbery, which some of my friends at university helped me to understand without knowing that they did it. Secondly, there was materialist thought which, while studying science at school and university, I found a prerequisite for an objective scientific approach. The part of me that refused this materialist view led my supervisor at university eventually to realise that my mentality would, perhaps, never be strictly or wholly scientific as he saw it. Materialism and an extreme dedication to intellect eventually squashes the soul. The thinking mind is only part of the personality, a flighty and capricious part, and its over-use leads to a blunting of subtler feelings and that awareness of beauty in life that is ultimately focused within rather than without.

I shall never forget the joy and wonder that seized me after my finals, when I went to Switzerland on my first continental holiday and found it no longer necessary to think logically and scientifically all the time. There was great peace as my mind relaxed to allow deeper feeling to arise. I thought as a 'whole', rather than as an objectifying intellect. It is this totality in thought that seems to characterise traditional Eastern thinking and to be its essential difference from modern Western philosophy. While the latter has produced marvels as well as horrors, the Eastern man of character appears to think more with his heart than with his mind. Indeed the Chinese word for mind is often better translated as heart. It is exactly this 'heart' that has been seeking expression within myself since I was a boy.

You remember when I was fourteen I spent a whole Easter term convalescing at home. As I grew stronger, I spent much time walking in the forest,* long walks alone on the moors and through the woods experiencing the opening of springtime leaves and birds singing in reborn trees. On those walks, I had one or two experiences which at the time seemed quite natural (as indeed they are) and about which I thought little until I began to question the materialist outlook I was picking up through studying science at school. My memory is vague now but I can still see the moss on which I sat, the great, bare beech branches tapering upwards like cathedral tracery and the thin flecks of green emerging upon the twigs. It seemed as if my whole being swelled out of itself, embracing the ground I lay upon, the trees around me, the birds and squirrels that moved against the sky, the soft murmur of the breeze in the twigs. I became these things and was no longer the observer; the trees were within me and I within them. I had experienced a feeling of all-pervading oneness – there was no separation for everything seemed to possess the same quality – the essence of mind and being. I remember praying passionately and with such thankfulness to Jesus, who seemed to represent this force – not as something separate but included within it – yet who was somehow the donor of my vision.

---

* The New Forest.

It was this 'insight' that sustained me when my scientific training caused me to abandon a living faith in the Christian conception of God. God then became to me not a distant father but an intrinsic quality inherent in mind and matter alike. Yet that early experience has never come again. It was as if the development of intellect prevented it. The same happened to Wordsworth. However much I have sought, I have never felt so wonderful a thing as that again. In every serious contemplation my whole being craves for that experience of direct insight into peace, beauty, all-embracing love. Sometimes I feel I am near it – then my mind surges in, asking why and how – and the pure exaltation never comes.[*]

World and life are to me wondrous, beautiful, full of loveliness but sometimes that feeling fades and all is jaded, tired, without value; then, once more, through some place or some person, that essential faith in living is reborn and I hope again. Plato writes in the *Symposium* about the spirit of man ascending though a knowledge of beautiful things to beautiful forms, persons and ideas until at the last the absolute beauty is understood and the soul merges into it for that is God.

This way of thinking, you will agree, is not Christian in the strict sense for it takes no account of God the Father, God the Son and God the Holy Ghost nor of Christ, the redeeming son. God is not here a cause and the Universe an effect. Here God and World are one and the same as root and tree are united. We speak here of the absolute, the essence, the unknown, the indefinable quality that lies within everything spiritual and material in every man as well as every animal, in every race and behind every idea however rejected.

I never forgot that experience in the beechwood. I could take you to the exact place, if not the exact tree, right now. From it I built up a view of how things are. My only guide was Plato, my love of nature and the profound platonic love I had for a boy at school who seemed sublimely beautiful to me. He existed, however, only in my mind and the image was not projectable on to the real for the actual person was quite different, simple and not complex like my fantasies.

Here in Hong Kong I find these fundamental ideas reflected in countless varying ways and especially in Ch'an Buddhism. This is the

---

[*] Later in life I recovered this original freshness from time to time not by effort but as a result of 'grace'. It is the root of Zen meditative experience however rarely come by.

reason for my interest in these things for I sense some fulfilment here. In the West, Buddhism is often described as selfish and pessimistic. In his introductory book, Christmas Humphreys, the eminent crown prosecutor, argues that this is deeply mistaken. The literature often talks about the Void. The real meaning of this term, at least in Chinese Buddhism, is not nothingness. All life is bound up in a vast unity by some common denominator, a quality which is not material yet subsumes all material and mind qualities. It is a substratum. It implies great brotherhood for each person is, at root, identical in spiritual constitution. Since the same quality underlies the universe, all forms however diverse are intrinsically related. This all is nothing yet the no-thing-ness is full. A bowl at the bottom of a pond is empty yet also full of water.*

Motive is more important than deed. Altruism is part of the way, the giving of self for others because one knows that all, at root, are connected. Here we have the 'we consciousness' mentioned by such writers as Jung, Schweitzer and Buber, which seems vital in the present world situation. There are many religions but only one religious sense. It is this quality that interests me rather than the specifics of a religious creed. I seem to have found something that points to a still centre.

Eastern thought turns ever inwards towards the common material of life. Western thought begins with simple things and then builds a complex system, hierarchically organised, linear and projected outward on the world. Westerners make fine logicians and scientists. An Easterner, by plunging directly to the depths of things in experience, has developed greater insight into self. The logic is intuitive and goes with a relative indifference to things that happen outside the personal. Intellect is a prize goose that lays golden eggs in the West. In the East the heart brings forth a golden flower.

In your letters I have noted some remarks of regret, as if you feel you should have made me more orthodox by teaching me better Christianity. You have nothing to regret and you have failed in

---

* The letter contains a lengthy description of the Buddhist ideas I had acquired by that time. Some of them were mistaken and veering towards Upanishadic Indian notions. I had not yet read enough to have the various teachings clear in my head. Nonetheless, I had well grasped the main theme. In order not to present an erroneous account of Buddhism I limit this edited text to the essential thrust of my thought at the time.

nothing. I am conscious often of a gratitude to you both for the security and freedom of expression I have enjoyed. I have been able to learn in a family atmosphere that did nothing to hinder and the freedom you allowed me has prevented any addiction to a way of life centred on playing bridge or drinking cocktails. You say you are ordinary but I do not think so. You are more discerning than most and make me sit up and think when you write letters like the last two I have received from you both. Most parents do not have the interest to do that and are too conventional to understand. A quiet life does not mean a dull life. It may be very full and much richer than a life devoted to social exhibitionism and exclusiveness. I hold you both in high esteem.

With love J.

Chapter Twenty-Two

Return to Macao

The evening sun gave a ruddy tint to the waters already yellow with Pearl River silt and, here and there, flecked white by the wind. The Macao ferry churned along. Behind us the peak of Lantao, for once free of cloud, rose against a pastel sky, green merging into mauve on the higher slopes. Around us, large brown-sailed junks tacked to and fro, their nets dragging deep into the water. Nearer shore, where the rich mud was stirred by our propellers, we passed shallow draft boats with long fishing rods from which scoop nets were suspended, all, like ourselves, headed for the harbour.

As we arrived, sunlight glittered on the scarlet, green or blue tiles of the gay Portuguese villas set beyond a seaside boulevard lined with shade-giving trees. The spire of the bishop's palace, the lighthouse tower and the gaunt facade of the ruined San Paolo church were silhouetted against the sky, from time to time, caught, as it were, "in a noose of light" like the sultan's turrets of old.

The Bella Vista Hotel was quiet and comfortable. Yannang and I were given every courtesy and a twin-bedded room which, even though still very hot, had a passable view and a fan. We took dinner on the balcony. Just below us lay a dance floor illuminated by glowing Chinese lanterns, a stage set fit for ballet. The late evening cast a salmon-coloured light upon the scene beyond which the yellow waters, patchily blue here and rose pink there, stretched away towards the growing haze before Lantao mountain. A dark cloud lay long fingers along the horizon and, from behind it, rose the pale disc of the moon and a timorous track of silver petals decorated the sea.

I ordered a bottle of Friesca, a light *vino bianca* of enjoyable flavour and we lifted glasses to one another and to the moon, which, for a moment, was poised above them before sliding down, drowning in the golden aura of the wine, a coin now glowing dully at the bottom of our glasses. For a long time, as has become our habit together, we sat watching the colours fade and the moonlight taking their place. The full moon soon spread its splendour over land and water. Becalmed junks at sea beyond the harbour entrance became tall, black towers, mysterious and beautiful.

Yannang broke the silence, "This is like one of Li Po's poems. He loved wine under the moon and, in almost all of his poems, one or other of them and often both appeared. In one poem he sits alone drinking with his shadow. We are luckier than Li Po for we do not need our shadows!"

I knew the poem from Arthur Waley's translation and I told Yannang about old Khayyam of Persia who, in his wistful way, also loved moon and wine. "And when thou with shining foot shall pass..." The warm wine filled our veins with romance. Time stood still. We went out into the town.

Compared with Hong Kong, Macao is a quiet place; little cobbled squares and steep sea-glancing lanes give the place a Mediterranean air. The bright coloured buildings, towers and spires, the sound of church and monastery bell, dark-robed roman priests walking the streets, are all unmistakably south European. Even the Chinese, with their dark eyes and black hair, seem not out of place against such a backcloth and it is only when one turns a corner into a narrower street, pungent with the smells of cooking and burning joss sticks, that one finds oneself again in China.

We noted how friendly were the Portuguese police and the Chinese people, how the African soldiers lounged about in the shops. The Portuguese seem to 'fraternise' very easily with indigenous people and many of the 'fan kwai' could speak Cantonese. Yannang remarked how the Cantonese seemed less careworn than in HK, less worried, more friendly and not so talkative. It was all very relaxing and I found, too, that my companionship with Yannang and my presence in a Chinese crowd drew barely a glance. In Hong Kong, I am often an object of attention whenever I mingle with the Chinese with or without a Chinese companion. Yannang said it seemed as if tension between the different sorts of Chinese people was also more relaxed here and that Europeans and Chinese accepted each other more easily. Although the British administration is reputedly more efficient and less corrupt than the Portuguese, it has never quite mastered the art of informal interracial friendship. Britishers love their cliques, their select clubs, their homes as their castles to themselves and the Chinese have never bothered to penetrate such exclusive preserves, being content with their own sense of private superiority. The small size and almost rural atmosphere of Macao is easygoing by comparison and business rivalry and cut-throat competition less marked.

In the Piscina night-club we found the bath full of swimmers, a magic show with an attentive audience and, on the roof, a dance floor well covered by Chinese couples.

"How stiff they look!" remarked Yannang, as we sat sipping an iced coffee apiece. "Are they really enjoying themselves? They look almost unhappy!"

To my surprise I realised that Yannang had never seen Western dancing before. I tried to explain that dancing is often expression in movement alone and that to show one's feelings amongst so many might be felt embarrassing.

"It all looks rather carnal," he said, watching the narrow-slitted dresses of the girls sliding up their legs. "What is it like holding a girl so close when you dance? And which is more important, the girl in your arms or the rhythm of the dance?"

"I am afraid that can only depend on the dancer," I replied. "Certainly the two essential drives behind dancing are sex and the sheer bodily delight in rhythmical movement but when the whole atmosphere of the dance is put together it creates something beyond either. When one is dancing well it is like flying and to fly well one needs a good partner. If she is beautiful and moves with grace, the flight is romantic, like that of butterflies in the sun."

I had to admit that the stiff, expressionless dancing of the Chinese was dull to watch. Their rhythm was poor and few of them were giving themselves freely to the music; the long expanses of hesitant leg and wobbling, female buttocks were barely aesthetic. Ballroom dancing needs flowing dresses that hiss through the air on a spin turn. Back at the Bella Vista, we watched Portuguese couples dancing to Latin American rhythms beneath the light of the lanterns. They swirled around with grace, abandon and mirth and Yannang then understood what I had told him.

We sat on the seawall; the air was still; Chinese voices murmured in quiet conversation nearby; occasionally a vendor would add a shriller cry; the waters lapped on the stones a few feet below us. We clasped our knees in our arms and gazed at the moonlight flickering on the sea, wriggling and twisting like a mass of little seaworms shining with iridescence and dancing blissfully on the surface. I told Yannang about the palolo worm which, at certain states of the moon, rises to the surface and dances its fertility rites there.

"Really, I prefer this silence to the gaiety of the dance halls," said Yannang.

I agreed. "There are those whose chief delight lies in soft lights and sweet music but you and I belong to that other group, the lovers of new-mown hay and stars. Here too we can watch the moon worms dance! Life is a poem, you see."

"At this moment – yes," said Yannang thoughtfully.

Once more we sat on the balcony sipping wine in silence. The last few couples were lingering on the dance floor and, although I knew this was one of the last times we would be together, I was not troubled by the thought. In the wonder and beauty of the night our companionship was perfect, the moment ethereal and untarnished, the moonlight holding us in thrall.

The last dancers bade each other farewell; the band packed up and went; earth fell silent. Around three o'clock the moonlight faded and we retired to bed. At Yannang's request I read a poem for him before we slept.

Chapter Twenty-Three

Buddha Light – Lunar Light

Moonlight floods the ocean waters
with a river wide as Amazon;
one small junk, silhouetted,
black and cowled like an ancient spectre
creeps unheeded on the dazzling sea;
rising to the lambent moon
my eyes fix in a kind of ecstasy
which swells and beats
with the grasshopper's song
and the wavelets sounding
a thousand feet below.

In camp

The worst of the rain is over. For hours it has fallen steadily from a laden sky but now, the clouds rising to a greater height and clearing the tops of the hills, only an occasional large drop spatters the road. Thick blankets of fine mist are rolling in from the sea, blanketing the valleys below the camp, filling them up and brimming over the saddles and crests into the hollows beyond.

Around the officers' mess the mists part for a moment to give us a vista of unparalleled grandeur and strangeness. Everything drips in the saturated air, leaves, eaves, branches, railings. A light breeze from the East, laden with moisture, fans the hills of the islands and, as it rises and cools, the vapours condense, forming shadowy pennants flying from the crests. At sea, the vapour clears now and again to reveal the moving waters; sometimes the tops of a junk's masts stick up above the mist. Around the waists of mainland mountains clouds form white girdles and plumes of vapour cling to their summits, as if afraid to float away.

*

In the city

Once more the students of Zen assembled in Dr Ronald Ching's consulting room taking Chinese tea together. Mr Yen dived immediately into his topic.

"It has been said that Buddhism is a belief based on the idea of 'Mind Only'. Let us see if that is really so and what it might mean. What do you think the mind is? Let us not confuse it with the 'grey matter' important for our behaviour though that is. The word 'mind' implies experience and is not to do with the material basis at all. Is mind the same as the sense of self? Is it the 'I' quality that underlies almost everything we do and every thought we have? Can you find the mind? If you go in search of it directly, much as you might go looking for a goldfish in a goldfish bowl, what do you find? What sort of fish is this? This question 'What is my mind?' opens up the whole story of Ch'an, of Zen.

"I will tell you a story," Mr Yen continued. "When Bodhidharma first brought Zen to China he taught for a while, had that unsatisfactory encounter with the emperor and then went off into the mountains meditating, facing a wall for nine years. He was waiting for his successor to put in an appearance. Eventually a young man came and knelt beside him. After a time Bodhidharma, looking sideways, asked him, 'And who might you be?'

"'I seek the dharma,' was the reply.

"'O ho!' said Bodhidharma, 'And I suppose you think that's the right way to go about it. Just coming and asking for it. What can you learn that way? Other men have given blood, their lives, their pith and marrow for the dharma. Do you think you can find it merely by supplication?' and he turned back to the wall and fell silent.

"The young monk was in distress for he had been seeking for a long time and knew Bodhidharma was his last hope. He drew out his knife and cut off his arm. Holding it out with his intact hand, he pushed it towards the sage.

"At length Bodhidharma eyed it 'O ho – that is something!' he said and looked at the young man with fresh interest. 'What can I do for you then?' he asked.

"'My mind is weary, worried, uneasy. I have sought for peace everywhere but have never found it. Please, make my mind tranquil.'

"'Ah, but first you must show me your mind,' said Bodhidharma. 'How can I make it tranquil unless you can show it me? Can you do that? It is the first step.'

"The young man pondered for a long time.

"'But I cannot do that. I cannot even find it.'

"'There then, it is now tranquil,' said Bodhidharma.

"And suddenly the young man understood what he was being shown.

"Unless you can see it too, such a story needs some decoding. The young man went into himself to find himself and however deeply he searched he could not locate his mind. He thought there must be something there but, again and again, he came upon empty space. He had not realised that it was possible to set aside all his worries, thoughts and attachments and perceive that which remained when he had done so. All such matters were mere thoughts and emotions floating in the space he could now see for himself. Bodhidharma's remark jerked him into this realisation. The emptiness in which he had been searching for himself was himself and he had never known it. There was no thing there yet he now knew what 'no mind' was. It suddenly became for him the presence of freedom.

"This is an aspect of experience we cover over with all the noise of thought, so that we too rarely recognise it. It is in fact the bowl in which thoughts swim. We sometimes call it the 'unborn' because it is that in which thoughts get created. It is prior to thought.

"There is nothing special about this. It seems odd simply because, being so attached to thoughts and feelings, we so rarely recognise it. Yet, when we watch our mental processes closely enough, we can see they are no more than a muddle of ideas or regrets from the past mingled with hopes and desires for the future. So long as we remain in this muddle we cannot come near the timeless truth and realise that all experience floats in experienceable space.

"The truth of this 'unborn' spaciousness of mind exists apart from the worldliness of our day-to-day affairs. It pervades them, of course, but, when we are enmeshed by them, we do not see it. We have to withdraw somewhat and watch the process, our reactions in our work and our play, the very mind games that preserve our sense of identity. We have to understand what our minds keep going on about before we can see our root nature. And this root nature is the truth in the sense that it is basic to all and all-sufficient. Anyone who has found it affirms the same insight and, oddly, their stories end at this point for there is nothing else to say.

"And we can say that this 'unborn', which is the basis of mind, is also the basis or true nature of everything. It is as much in this table, these walls or the sky as it is in each one of us. Only by standing back, watching and waiting can it be perceived.

"This is the 'mind only' of the texts and not the chattering mind of thought. We may say that, when the mind falls into such peace, it begins knowing something of the 'unborn' nature so that eventually it may become fully an expression of Buddha nature itself. The world goes on as before and you, too, with it but you have seen the basis. You remain engaged with the world, doing your job, studying, writing, making money, whatever, yet you are also beyond all that because you are aware of the full perspective, the untarnished truth."

How Mr Yen's eyes shine when he speaks of these things! His English becomes more fluent, his voice powerful and compelling. I almost believe he knows the state about which he speaks. I feel myself sometimes a doubting Thomas at his feast.

I questioned him about the contrasts between Christianity and Buddhism.*

"In both Christianity and Buddhism something is renounced or abandoned," I said. "In Christianity the self is sacrificed in the love for others. In Buddhism the self is to be raised to enlightenment and that enlightenment then spreads a spirit of unifying love among all men. The Buddhist, by his striving for enlightenment, raises the tone of thought, altruism and feeling in all who know him. It works by subtle influence. The Christian, by working for others, achieves immediate practical aims in medicine, nursing and so on and this is his expression of love. Perhaps the Christian gives his soul for others

---

* In shifting the conversation away on to my own concern at the time I missed the full import of what Mr Yen had been saying even though I was able to report it accurately. Sometimes it takes years to fully experience the meaning of words in the hearing of Zen teaching.

while the Buddhist tries to lose it in an universal love. Which of these is of the greater value?"

Mr Yen thought before replying, "I have much admiration for the positive good in Christianity and you must not think that I deride it in any way. Yet, it seems to me, that in giving the soul for others the Christian is thinking in terms of purposes and achievements and this can only alter material conditions. However good such changes may be they do not lead to tranquillity of mind but only to further search for self-sacrifice. At the back of the mind there is always the idea of a personal salvation in attaining some heaven where all is at peace or at least engaged in some sort of permanent hymn singing. It is necessary to follow the laws of God that are outside oneself."

"I ask you to what have such practices led? Look at history, the crusades, the inquisition, the many wars of religious intolerance between Christians themselves and missionary aggression, if I may call it that, against other cultures. We have not seen that wanting in China, I have to tell you. Whatever errors may happen between Buddhists such traumatic events do not mar Buddhist history for Buddhists do not think in terms of worldly purposes. The very notions of 'you' and 'me', 'mine' and 'yours', 'ours' and 'theirs', 'we' and 'they', Christian and pagan is foreign to true Buddhism. In Buddhism a man or woman is simply such, whatever his good or bad qualities."

"Yes", I said, "But to return to the practical world of today. We see the sleepers in the streets outside this building and the poverty in the shantytowns. It is perhaps only the purposive, directional love of the Christian variety that can bring about changes in the lives of these people."

"In the long run, you must know, it is not material comfort so much as peace of mind that is the vital ingredient in human happiness," continued Mr Yen. "By all means change your houses, set up hospitals and schools, missionary educational centres and so on. They do indeed do much good but it is the mind of the individual which counts rather than mechanical conversion of the masses. You see – if the mind is at peace and a resource unto itself then conditions do not matter so much. Again, even if conditions for the collective are altered, the same personal troubles and neuroses persist because the root of the mind has not been touched. Buddhist love is boundless and not limited by charitable ideals. When rightly understood it embraces all sentient beings."

"But, surely," I persisted, "boundless love means a love without direction or goal. Love must be purposive if it is to achieve anything. Simply wishing that love embrace all sentient beings will not help the man in the street very much. It is too abstract to touch him."

"I am not so sure," Mr Yen responded. "A coolie can understand and from him it can spread from mind to mind irrespective of education. We are speaking of a surging awareness of a possibility, the peace of mind obtained by knowing the mind. Awareness is a property of the individual, not of a group striving after ideals and good deeds. Awareness is dispassionate and spreads love boundlessly. Directional altruism is good but cannot move the mind to spirituality for it works within the narrower field of emotion. No spiritual person could sing 'Onward Christian soldiers marching as to war' with an easy mind. This is the fruit and cause of emotional fervour, the same enthusiasm that produces intolerance, crusades and, maybe, concentration camps!"

Back in camp I fell to musing on our discussion. It seemed to me that the altruism of the Christian and the universal awareness of the Buddhist can both be found in varying degrees in all peoples and races. They are universal possibilities of the expression of human spirit. Yet it is true that the 'we consciousness' that Jung feels lies at the base of altruism is indeed on a different level from the pure spirit of Buddhist thought. It is more emotional, less aware, lacks the insight. Spirituality is the time when a man stands utterly alone facing the forces about him and asking who and what he is and how to find peace and happiness. It is a thing of solitude, of hills and monasteries, of the blissful mountains some find within their own minds. And there are also those who have found it in hell itself, prisons or concentration camps.

In the world of practical affairs the drive and purposiveness of Christian goodwill is of paramount importance. This is a material religion of mind rather than soul. In the inmost self it is Buddhism that helps more because it understands so much more, goes so much deeper. Today, peace of mind cannot be found by many in Christianity because the root ideas have become lost, out of favour in a scientific age. New words with which to reinvent the old inspiration seem essential.

In Buddhism ideas of mind and universe relate more easily to those of science. I think a more perfectly understood religion will arise ahead of us in which faith, love and altruism will express themselves through a renewal of spirituality in the West, emanating essentially from the traditions of the East. The heights of such spirituality may be scaled only by the few, yet these few may be of any origin. This is psychology but it passes beyond all words to the infinite experience of being itself.

*

The moonlit hour

I was awoken by the light and at first I did not understand the reason for my restlessness. I tossed, turned, squirmed into a ball, lay flat on my back and opened my eyes. A silvery light poured through my windows, casting a long shining beam across the floor, over the table, the armchair and up the wall. The door out on to the wide balcony, which ran all around the building, was open and through it too the brightness poured in cascades of light and shadow across the ridges of my wardrobe doors.

I went outside and leaned on the balustrade. In daylight, with clear sky and good visibility, it is possible to see out beyond Lama Island to Lantao and beyond Lema to the furthest Communist-controlled islands, mere shadows on the horizon off the mouth of the Pearl River. Even on the clearest day it was rare to see so far and, at night, the outlines of Lama and Lema were only marked by the ring of fishermen's lamps around their coasts. Yet now every detail of the whole, great seascape lay before me, bare and shining in an unearthly pattern of lunar silver and black shadow. There was about it a curious quality of 'holding the breath', a waiting for something to happen, a pause on the edge of anticipated excitement. The crepuscular wonder of a slow dawning combined with the awe-filled mystery of early night, when the great shadows slink from their hiding places and cover the land.

The moon was huge, a shining disc difficult to look upon. Below it, a great spreading river of dancing light came cascading all the way from the horizon to the boulder-strewn shore below me. The air was still, with the silence of deep night, yet restless for it seemed that the power of that great orb held the landscape in thrall.

For a long time I stood in the silence gazing up at the moon's impassive face. I seemed to grow lighter as I watched, as if I had drunk deeply of a powerful and delicious wine. There was a heady tension in all around me. "What is it?" I asked the stars quite dimmed by the brilliance. "What is this unearthly quality that is stealing through this night?"

My whole being seemed on tiptoe, watchful, my eyes sweeping over every detail; moonlit waters; dark islands; the spectre of a great junk stretching its shadow along the track of the moonlit sea. I found I could not penetrate the mystery. I cursed myself. "What are you striving for?" I asked, "What do you expect to see or know? There is only rock and mountain, sea and sky and the eerie moonlight over all."

Yet the answer did not satisfy. There was a feeling of a great presence moving through the night, as if the moon had taken on some personified quality, as if a goddess herself was gliding between the sparse, enfolding clouds. "Maybe it is God," I heard myself saying to myself and the reply came, "All the world is God."

At once the striving ceased for I knew that in the awe and mystery of the night lay its own solution. All I could do was to watch. To try and understand would ruin the wonder of it.

Suddenly a bird, a mynah, cackled in the bushes below, another followed and for a minute or two they jumped about in the branches calling to one another, murmurously, as if sleepy. A shadow darted across the drive – some nocturnal animal. It was as if dawn were near and all creatures were shifting uneasily in the strength of the light.

I do not know how long I sat watching, perhaps for one hour but I believe it was more like two. All mental activity ceased and I thought of nothing, my mind suspended in a kind of awe and wonder. The uneasiness of the night remained about me.

At length I became aware of the moon slowly sinking towards the horizon. It became larger as it went but the light was less strong and changing in intensity. An orange hue was spreading within it becoming almost pink at the last, the moon track fading on the waters. It set in a ruddy orange glow, pulsating on the horizon beyond the furthest island, the mountainous shape of which cut great bites into it as it sank. A strange light hung about the horizon and then the night was dark, the stars shining out more brightly.

I felt a sudden relief as if the tension had left the air. There were no sounds now for all creatures slumbered. The presence had gone and I breathed the night air deeply into my lungs, easing the strain as it flooded out of me. All was solitude and peace. The goddess dreamed below the horizon and, after a while, I fell into a deep sleep upon my bed.

Chapter Twenty-Four

The Monk of Castle Peak

Lest the memory grow dim
Listen – listen –
The sea waves wrinkling moonshine
The acacia leaves rimmed white
All the air atremble with breathing night.

Lest the memory grow dim
I lift my pen to write
Few words, a voice, no more.
Ears tuned to paddy frogs croaking,
The converse of shivering silver leaves.

The hill sat brooding unamazed.

Lest the happiness grow dim
I lift my pen –
To write? To listen?
We sat there brooding unamazed
While the night talked.

Listen – listen –
Lest the memory grow dim.

All the cares of military life receded as Yannang and I boarded the crowded ferry and found ourselves seats. It seemed as if, once again, I had entered another world; for I seemed to be living a double life, freedom and happiness with Yannang, my Chinese and university friends and boredom, frustration and occasional rewards in the army. I was both "living and partly living" as Eliot puts it.

At Castle Peak we were rowed ashore in a sampan and set off briskly on our way. Finding a narrow flight of steps running up between large rocks in a grove of bamboo, we climbed to the top. We found ourselves in the forecourt of a well-kept temple. There were two halls, the hindmost on a higher level than the one fronting the court in which we stood. In it there were three large images, not of the gods we were used to seeing in the city but of the three great sages of Chinese wisdom. This was a temple to Confucius, the property of a society which cherished the old rites and customs. Members would congregate here from all over the colony for the official services dedicated to the sages of the old religion of Chinese empire.

The central figure represented Confucius and on his left and right stood Lao-tzu, the Taoist and Sakyamuni, the Buddha. Above them, on a board hanging from the roof, "The Throne of the Three" was written in bold characters. On either side of the altar and around the hall hung lovely drapings of scarlet silk work, covered with embroidered characters and symbolic designs. Grey stone pillars supported the roof some eighteen feet above us. The whole place had an airy cleanliness about it.

We reached the upper temple by a small flight of steps and found a complete pantheon of traditional deities. A hanging board read "The Throne of Enlightenment" and, below it, was the King of Heaven (Ya Wang Shang Ti), presiding over an extraordinary retinue, including Koon Yam (Kuan Yin, the female Avalokiteshvara), here personifying a goddess of Mercy, Dhamo (i.e. Bodhidhama), Sakyamuni himself, Ormitapha (i.e. Amitabha) the Buddha of the Western Heaven, a group of lawmakers and police, General Kang Wan and his two guards, 'All Seeing' and 'All Hearing', the protectors of the world and twenty-four successors of the Buddha. A separate altar to Koon Yam stood to the left and around them all were wooden screens of excellent carving and beautifully worked hanging tapestries. The tall, stone pillars were half-cased in red painted wood, upon which were many characters and symbols. The caretaker, a dear twinkly-eyed little old lady, came in and lit the evening joss sticks before the altars, whereupon a fine smoke coiled upwards to the roof, filling the halls with fragrance. She was most welcoming and asked us if we had a place for the night.

We walked on around the low-lying shores of the little estuary, where great fishing junks were drawn up on the sand with fires blazing around their hulls, the traditional method of killing shipworm and barnacles. Beyond the village, the path began winding up the hill through small pinewoods, past groups of pots containing the bones of the dead and on to a bare green hillside. Ahead of us, a cleft in the walls of steep rock comprising the ridge of the mountain was filled by a little stream where tall trees grew unblasted by sea winds. The buildings of the monastery were set back against the mountain, protected by the trees clinging to terraces carved from the hill. We passed under an arch bearing an inscription by Clementi, a former Governor, and into the shade of the trees and a strange, enclosing atmosphere.

The light wind was brushing the tree tops, birds fluttered here and there, giving occasional shrill cries and over everything there was a sudden intensification of silence. The pleasant, earthy odour of damp trunks, the respiration of many leaves and a general mossiness filled the place with unruffled calm. Before the gate we turned to look at the view. Below us, through the trees, the small fires were flickering about the hulls of the junks. I felt a kind of redemption, an escape from the worried frowns and threatening rumbles of the political world. Joyfully we stood alone amid the tall trunks hearing the sound of the breeze and scenting the air. At such times together we keep our silences.

Moving on up the path towards the first court of the monastery, we met one of the monks in his grey habit coming down the path. We were about to greet him when we noticed he did not appear to see us. He walked slowly by, eyes on the ground. We were amazed for, at Ngong Ping, the monks were always delighted to see us. Something seemed clearly amiss.

Up on a second terrace a large Buddha in *bas-relief* grinned at us from the wall, white-faced, yellow-robed, pot-bellied with an immense navel, the centre of his profundity. He seemed obese, if not lewd, with a horrid leer on his flabby face. Dramatic certainly, I felt, but worldly-wise and not in keeping with the surroundings. Climbing the steps we found no one about, a strolling dog came and sniffed us over. An eerie quietude lay about us in the fading light. Another two flights of steps led to a terraced, wooden temple, with a magnificently tiled roof curved up at the corners and embellished with rampant dragons. On either side stood two large buildings, evidently living quarters. At last a monk appeared and sat down in a chair by the door of one of the houses. We approached but he did not even look up until we almost shouted a greeting at him. He was solemn and evasive and we were clearly not at all welcome. Another small monk, with a bristly moustache, an unpleasantly aged, wrinkled face and cunning, little eyes flickering about unpleasantly in all directions, came up grinning. Yannang and he had a conversation and Yannang told me "They have no room and do not take visitors for the night."

We pressed the point saying we were students and very interested in the monastery. We only needed a place to lie down in, to wash in and perhaps a little food. The old man chattered on and I had the feeling he was telling us it would not be wise for us to stay. He showed us a room we might have had but added that only sick people ever used it. I had visions of leprosy and declined it. Day visitors were acceptable, he told us, but closer intrusion was clearly refused.

"Most strange!" said Yannang.

Two small boys came and stood giggling at us. Finally, we accepted some tea in the little café and, when the old man moved off, we questioned the boys and a young man who had been there for the afternoon. We gathered that the old man was rather eccentric and, although he sometimes permitted visitors, it was unusual for him to do so. He was the senior monk and had meditated for three years in one of the houses further up the hill. I felt that this might account for his inhospitality but said nothing. I was feeling peeved and the light was failing. Yannang, however, seemed not to mind in the slightest and the dismal prospect of tramping back down the hill in the dark through villages full of ferocious and possibly rabid dogs, a tedious head-aching bus journey back to Kowloon and a general loss of face evidently had not occurred to him. Afterwards he told me simply that, since we were not wanted, it would have been stupid to stay there as we could not have been happy. Anyway, perhaps the monks had a reason for wanting privacy. Yannang had simply forgotten about it. I wished I could do the same with my disappointments.

We set off down the hill again looking for a house where we might ask for a bed. I thought I had seen one away on the hillside to our right. Whether I really had done so or whether it was a kind of intuition I cannot tell but we turned off the main path. Twice we nearly gave up to descend the hill to a nearby nunnery when, on rounding a bend in the hill, we came upon a large house, almost a mansion. Most of the outhouses were derelict, the garden rank with weeds and the stonework pitted and worn by the winds of centuries. Passing a garden gate and into a small garden terrace, we found neither light nor sound anywhere and in five minutes it would be dark. We knocked on the door and the sound reverberated through the building. Ghosts of centuries seemed to be rising from their slumbers and the place appeared forgotten, abandoned and as forlorn as I was beginning to feel. There was no reply. We looked into the outhouses, no sign of life, and were halfway towards the little ratchet gate when I heard a sound.

"There is somebody here!" I said with great relief. Hurrying back to the door, we could hear a creaking on the stairs and the tapping of a stick on the floor. Bolts were shot back and the door opened to reveal the shaven head of a monk who was holding a great stick and looking out enquiringly. He said something. Yannang paused and spoke. They did not understand one another in Cantonese so he tried again in Mandarin. "Yes – we can stay here but he has no sheets!" I hastily assured him that visions of beds and mattresses had long gone from my mind. We went in to find a great image glinting down at us in the light of his guttering oil lamp. It was the weirdest image I had ever seen and might have given a child nightmares. A narrow-waisted figure with an inclined contemplative face was seated on a lotus and surrounded by rows and rows of arms, like the legs of some giant crab stretching up and out on either side. I remembered the cruel goddess Kali of India and wondered who this monk could be and what this crustacean image could represent. "Koon Yam of the Twenty-Four Arms," said Yannang. "The only one in the district." I was relieved – the goddess of mercy after all. For a moment the tall image in the flickering light had almost made me draw back a pace.

The monk and Yannang were now chattering like old friends and suddenly, interrupting my apprehensions over the image, Yannang turned to me with an expression of triumph and joy on his face.

"He is a real monk, a true one, the first I have met. He has studied a lot, visited India and Burma to buy images for a temple in Hankow but, finding his home town overrun by communists, he abandoned them and came to Hong Kong. I think we can learn from him for he is a true monk. This simplicity is a sign of it." He was delighted and clearly this discovery, if such it was to be, was going to mean much to him for the world is so full of charlatans.

The monk led the way up the creaking stairs, the banisters shifting dangerously as I put my weight upon them. His robes rustled on the steps and the little lamp he carried sent huge shadows galloping over the damp walls blotched by mildew. Upstairs a large room opened upon a balcony. A little lamp, merely a floating wick in a tumbler of peanut oil, hung from the ceiling. A row of images stood above an altar, Detsang Poussa, Sigamouni Bo and Koon Yam Poussa,[*] and, before them, lay the usual implements, a sounding bowl and a wooden fish. Opposite them, stood a military deity as a kind of guardian. The monk led us along a narrow passage, the floorboards bending down ominously as we passed and showed us our bedroom. Ah, mattresses I thought, never mind the sheets! But no – never have I seen so naked a room. It was totally empty, not a single item of anything adorned its simple space, four walls and two barred windows, all in their birthday suits. "Oh well, very nice!" I said, wondering how many mosquitoes lurked there; an ugly thought since we had no nets.

The monk was a cheery fellow becoming increasingly friendly. It was clear that he was immensely pleased to see us and that this was quite an event for him. We returned downstairs where, industriously, he began preparing a meal in a back room, where there was a huge pile of hay, two bricks for a grate and three long sticks which were fed gradually under a pot as they burnt. Grass was fed in to keep the pot boiling. Yannang was quite at home having cooked this way before.

While the monk was occupied, we explored. Not a single piece of furniture could we find anywhere, the altar table and images, a few pots, some cups and bowls, ancient chopsticks and a collection of books, heavily eaten by silverfish, made up the complete list of his belongings. We asked for the lavatory and were shown the back door. The monk rushed to fetch us some water for washing and produced some towels. For some reason I combed my hair and we were ready for dinner.

Tiny stools, standing about four inches off the floor, served as chairs set around a rickety little table, some two feet high. He served us himself with bowls of boiling hot rice and a dish of soya rind with vegetables. We were hungry and in spite of the splintery, old

---

[*]   Ksitigarbha Bodhisattva, Sakyamuni Buddha and Kuan Yin (Avalokitishvara) Bodhisattva.

chopsticks I fed eagerly. It was good. As we ate it began to rain and the sound of it sluicing past the paneless windows made me feel almost cosy. Bowl followed bowl while Yannang plied the monk with questions.

Apparently he was the present successor in the line of head monks of the Tien Tai sect and the thirty-third of that lineage. He had spent his early years studying at a Buddhist college and later in the famous Tien Tai mountains of northern China. During the war the Kuomintang had sent numbers of monks to India on goodwill missions. He produced two tattered old identity cards written in Chinese and English whereby I could read that his name was Mun Yiak (pronounced Moon Yea) and that his age would have been about fifty. Ageing seemed to have left no trace on him since his face was quite unlined. The certificates were dated 1942 and 1945 from Calcutta and Rangoon.

The rain stopped and, after the meal, Yannang and I went out on the upstairs balcony and sat upon the stonework. This was to be the night of the full moon and, although the sky was overcast, there were signs of it clearing and we hoped it would soon emerge.

Mun Yiak joined us with his little lamp which he placed on the stonework beside us. Conversation was not easy because Yannang rarely speaks Mandarin and Mun Yiak, being a native of Hupeh, had a marked accent. The solution was the writing of characters. We got a piece of paper and a pencil and by writing the characters for difficult words Yannang and he could understand one another. Although the pronunciations of words differ greatly throughout China, the written characters have a constant meaning, so that literary men of differing backgrounds can converse relatively easily through writing. The talk went on for hours, Yannang every now and then putting the substance of it into English for me.

Mun Yiak sat on the balcony with his legs crossed and his arms composed in the manner of a Buddhist image, his black robes and shaven head silhouetted sharply against the night sky. Yannang listened intently like a pupil before a master. The moon came out from behind the clouds, bathing with light the little estuary and the rolling ranges of desolate hills. On the waters a shaft of moonlight once more cut a rippling path of molten silver, ever-changing with the wind patterns, upon the surface and momentarily fading or re-appearing as slight mist drifted across the face of the moon. Three large fishing junks were easing their way out to sea, their lateen sails and steeply sloping hulls cutting sharp spectral outlines among the moonbeams. Around the house, crickets chirped and, in the rank herbage, a glow-worm or two lit their little phosphorescent lamps. Thousands of frogs in the valley below, intent upon conversation and doubtless much more besides, sent up a muted cacophony. Our magic casement was opening indeed "on perilous seas in fairylands forlorn."

Mun Yiak was telling us about Buddhism, his voice often rising as he emphasised one point or another. The doctrine of Tien Tai begins within the cycles of mortality and the troubles of life from which one must escape in order to reach the Pure Land of desireless delight. The endless circling through life after life takes a person into different levels of mortality, depending on the way he conducted himself in his previous existence. The future is thus in part determined by the present. It is not so much fate that determines inherited character but action undertaken during development and maturity. Moral choice is thus vital in the unrolling of karma. The highest beings are the Heavenly Ones among whom, surprisingly, the Evil One also lives. Men with peaceful natures rank second, men who like conflict third, then animals, starving ghosts and finally those incarcerated in hell. The gods of this heaven were once human beings, who, through good deeds, acquired special powers in combating the Evil One. Within these cycles everything is constrained by suffering borne upon the wings of desire. One's 'original face' is perpetually disturbed by the longing for something, however trivial or important.

Mun Yiak told us that one of the main pursuits of Tien Tai practitioners was the understanding of the causes and effects of all that happens. It is described in a book called the *Fat Fa Ching,* where the stated aim is eventual escape from perpetual cycling through existence after existence. Cause and effect represent the final duality which has to be understood and transcended. A practitioner has to study the books and practise a way of life that allows insight to develop. If one can understand the forces of Yin and Yang, accrued in past lives, it becomes possible to so direct one's present existence as to move towards the final goal. If one cannot perceive these forces, there is a slipping back and a falling away from the path. Everything one does affects in some way one's future, if not in this life then in the next. The intricate web of Yin Yuen (karma) pulsates down the ages determining the course of human history.

"What is the final goal?" we asked him.

"Great emptiness."

"What is great emptiness?"

"The result of right action. It works like this. The mind is related to the whole as my shoe is to the air around it. If I cover over my shoe with my hand the air inside is cut off and separated from that outside of it. I can seal it in and do things with my shoe which prevent the inside air ever knowing its parent outside. Yet, if, for one moment, I remove my hand, the great sky itself is linked with the fetid air within the shoe. So it is when the self-restricting mind is opened to the spaciousness of emptiness."

As Mun Yiak spoke he was demonstrating with his shoe and I caught the meaning even before Yannang translated. To achieve a final escape a person must have six qualities; the eyes of Heaven; the ears of Heaven; perception of other men's thoughts; an understanding of the past, the present and the future; be able to will the mind to reach anywhere and become empty of all desire.

"And how is this done?" we asked, not at all unreasonably I felt. But the light breeze blew out the lamp, so we went indoors and continued scribbling characters on the altar table. In the flickering light the gilt images in shadowy splendour gleamed down at us.

"There is a relatively quick way and a slower way," said Mun Yiak. "The quick way is meditation, the complete emptying of the mind of all external influences, of thought itself. This requires the most thorough mental concentration and the utmost care. It can be a dangerous method resulting in madness or even suicide. It is very difficult to clear the mind of all thoughts. Even the thought of willing to clear the mind is still a thought. Again, when the mind falls still, there is the danger of an evil thought appearing which, having nothing to throw it out, might gain control entirely. In that way madness comes. To meditate, one must work with a master who understands his pupils' minds and can lead them without fear of danger."

Mun Yiak himself used the slower method which he claimed was the safer. All day long during his waking hours, when he was not cooking or working in house or garden, he repeated the name Ormithopha (Amitabha) to himself and counted his beads. The Buddha Amitabha ruled over the Pure Land and repetition of his name would lead Mun Yiak to understand what the Pure Land was.

I had read that the Pure Land sect and the Tien Tai were poles apart in doctrine, so I was intrigued to hear what Mun Yiak had said. I had read that the Pure Land was an imaginary heaven of worldly delight very different from the Plenum Void, the emptiness that is the focus of other sects. I had had the impression, too, that mere repetition of this name was a very low-grade form of practice. The idea of this man's style of life at first appalled me. Yannang too, for all his appreciation of simplicity, seemed shaken by this practice. After all, muttering a single word all day and sitting cross-legged before an image fingering a string of beads did not seem to be a very profitable occupation – or so it would appear.

"Where is the Pure Land?" we asked.

Mun Yiak spoke and scribbled earnestly for some time and, eventually, Yannang turned to me.

"It's in the mind!" he said. "Its realisation depends upon one's degree of training and total view of life. The end is an understanding of the void, a state of empty mind and heart in which the universe is apprehended as a whole and through which the freed mind travels at will. The idea of the Pure Land is also the idea of unspeakable happiness."

I asked why Mun Yiak repeated his mantra to achieve this end. He told us that since the empty mind of meditation is defenceless against self-destroying influence, emptiness has to be understood at the cost of retaining some defence. The "power word" provides this defence and its continued repetition is an exercise in the concentration that leads eventually to the final experience of release. Amitabha is in the heart, the Pure Land, likewise, and through mental concentration the cover lifts and the universal spaciousness like a great sea pours in.

But Mun Yiak told us he did not want to reach the Pure Land just yet for he would rather have the power to teach. He told us he was actually senior to Fuk Aw, the Abbot of Ngong Ping, with whom he had studied but he needed to have more knowledge and experience.

"You see there are two sorts of leader, those who contact the world and its worldliness through an endeavour to teach and those who by persistent effort and inner realisation are able to enrich themselves spiritually and, through cosmic pervasion, to touch the hearts of the whole world of humanity as well. Such a person may remain in solitude but his existence needs to be known and understood."

Yannang had pursued our enquiry with great diligence and not without some criticism. "His character writing might be better," he informed me, "and he talks in great circles before he gets to the point. But he speaks to people so rarely that this can well be forgiven him!"

It was midnight and time to rest. We discovered that Mun Yiak had laid some rush matting on the floor of our room, placed a tin covered with padding as a pillow at either end and provided a heavy, plaited coverlet to keep us warm. We protested as it seemed this was his own source of warmth but he assured us he would hear of nothing else. Before turning in, we strolled down the garden; our lungs were stuffy and our noses stale from the musty fragrance of burning joss sticks.

We found a small stone table and benches at the end of the little terraced garden and sat beneath the opalescent moon. After a while the pauses in our conversation became longer until, at last, we sat there saying nothing, listening to the faint noise of the wind on the mountain, the chirruping of an occasional cricket and the croaking of the frogs in the valley. The moon sailed serenely on, occasional puffs of cloud passing across her face. There was nothing to say, nothing to be done.

At length Yannang said, "This is pure happiness for there is no desire, nothing more is wanted, pure happiness. The thinking and being together is the secret of it." He shut his eyes and sat there listening to the sounds of night. The air rang with them, tiny sounds curiously significant.

My own mind was not so peaceful. As we sat there, I could feel the tensions of my distress at leaving Brickhill and the demanding work at Stanley, the stupidities at the officers' mess and the frustration of army life. But there was a deeper unease. I was aware of the dangers of the celibacy I was following in my army life yet, as I sat in silence with Yannang, out of the sorrow of leaving Brickhill and my wonder at the nature of our friendship, there grew a conviction that here was something more significant than passion but which needed both of us to make itself felt. I remembered Plato's *Symposium*, in which he argues that from a love of beauty in things and persons there grows a love of the beauty of ideas until, at last, one comes to the threshold of absolute beauty itself. I felt a sudden apprehension that my mind was darkened by sin. I felt shame at the worldliness of my thinking, the contaminated lives of my soldiers and many of my brother officers and the contrast between a soldier and a monk. The purity of our recent conversation was reflected in the worldly mirror of my other life. Yet it was surpassingly beautiful there on the terrace, so much so that never in all my life shall I ever forget the silence between us and the slight noises of the night.

At three o'clock we returned indoors. The house seemed to be holding its breath, no sound at all, merely an occasional splutter from the wick burning in the open lamp. Before the goddess, the flickering light dancing upon her many arms and peaceful face, shadows deepening in the recess behind her, we paused and stood in a silence that was awesome. Here was our history as it were paused in a breathing space.

Mun Yiak was strolling up and down. He was pleased to see us for he knew we had been sitting under the powerful moon. We asked why he did not sleep. "A monk needs little sleep," he said, "When I feel tired I sit up in meditation for about the length of time a joss stick takes to burn. Then I get up refreshed." He showed us how to 'sit'. We tried to assume the Buddha posture in meditation, folding the legs in such a way that both soles of the feet face upwards cushioned on the opposite thigh, hands folded, eyes closed. Mun Yiak laughed heartily at our absurd efforts to get into this posture. It took a long time to achieve, he told us. When he felt ill he 'sat up' in that way until the feeling left him and he could carry on as usual.

Upstairs we made ourselves comfortable beneath Mun Yiak's coverlet. I was very tired and soon slept – but not for long. I awoke to hear an ominous, high-pitched whining above my head – mosquitoes. Hastily we arranged handkerchiefs to cover our faces and placed our noses under the cover near some source of fresh air. The whining continued but I did not appear to be bitten. It was hot, so we opened the window and, after that, we slept. At about five thirty I heard Mun Yiak chanting the dawn ritual, tapping steadily on the wooden fish to create that peculiar plopping sound that so grips my mind.

Awake early and surprisingly fresh and full of life, I went down to meet Mun Yiak who gave me a wet towel and a bowl of fresh mountain water. Soon I had washed and shaved and awoke Yannang. After breakfast, we set out to climb Castle Peak itself or 'Green Mountain', as the Chinese call it. Going up through the monastery terraces, we came upon many shuttered buildings through which a steep overgrown path led through rank herbage to a dilapidated house of many rooms surrounding a small court. It appeared entirely deserted, weeds and grasses growing around the terraces and hanging in tufts from the walls. Surrounded by damp trees, it was the highest and most inaccessible house in the monastery and a notice reading "No Admittance" hung near the door. It was probably used for meditation for prolonged periods.

On the summit of steep, bare rock we sat and watched the heavy rain clouds and gazed down on the patchwork quilt of the paddy fields stretching away beyond Yuen Lang towards China. All the way Yannang picked flowers, lovely little mountain irises, small camellias, scarlet and pink, and little blue four-petalled plants we called our mountain stars. He arranged them in bunches with ferns to improve them. In the simplicity of our walk there was joy.

My self-criticism had not abated. In the rare air of the mountain, in the company of Yannang and Mun Yiak, I seemed to myself to be a worldly person far from the equanimity of which we had spoken. I felt unworthy of the beauty of the mountain, of the piety of Mun Yiak. Always I had been rather proud of my thinking, my intellectual abilities, book learning and of what I felt to be a wide tolerant viewpoint. Yet, faced by the experience of yesterday, I felt I was immature, undeveloped. I had a long way to go. Yannang's smile and the beauty of the monastery terraces on our return reassured me. There were still great hopes.

Chapter Twenty-Five

Moon and Lotus

Mr Yen was giving a party. He had invited several friends around to take tea and to meet a Mr Patel, an Indian follower of the philosopher Shri Aurobindo, who wanted to talk about Buddhism. I found myself sitting next to a Mr Wong and we got on to the subject of modern physics. He asked me to tell him about relativity and I told him, as far as I could, about the difference between the old idea of particulate atomic structure and the modern theory of relativity. I tried to show that there was a parallel between the essence of Buddhism called *sunyata* or emptiness and the fundamental energy of matter. I was saying that if you cut up a piece of wood, and then divided it again and again, eventually you would end up with the indivisible, the cutting apparatus would not be able to go further. One would be left with emptiness. Mr Wong was intrigued but Mr Yen, overhearing us, wagged his finger at me. "Not quite right," he was signalling and I was itching to go over and ask him where I was wrong.

Another Chinese gentleman, a busy looking businessman, had also heard the conversation. He said to me, "How come that a young officer in the army is so interested in these arcane Buddhist problems? Really we think all this is only suitable for old men who see death approaching and want to understand their lives. A young man like you might be better off sowing your wild oats, as you say. You can leave all this till you are older!" I was reminded of Gunner Barry at Brickhill and his suggestion that I get myself "cleaned out proppa like, Sir!" Perhaps they were right but, for the present, my intuitions were not leading me in that direction. The clean-out would have to wait!

Mr Wong was enthusiastic about our conversation and wanted to talk about such things further. He got Mr Yen to arrange a meeting at the premises of a Buddhist temple I had not seen before. It was dark when Yannang and I walked up Tai Hang Road. There were no street lights and the only illumination came from the flanking houses the top storeys of which were on a level with us so steep was the slope. Between the buildings, we could see the flickering fires and lamps of the squatter folk in the maze of slanting huts that clung precariously to the opposite hillside.

Mr Wong met us at our appointed rendezvous, dressed in a capacious, white Chinese suit, wide flared trousers and a neat jacket done up at the neck by a stiff, little collar. He had an air of assertive confidence that differed from his attitude when in Western dress. Leading us down a steep flight of steps he took us along a dim passageway between tall buildings. A scramble up further steps led us through a door into a tidy room, furnished with the heavy, wooden chairs and tables common in Chinese homes. There is little comfort in such furnishings, no cushions or curved surfaces and a rather stiff, almost Edwardian, atmosphere. Facing the door through which we entered was a wide barred window below which stood a gong and a massive, bronze bell. On one wall, facing the focal point of the room, hung a long scroll, depicting a full moon poised in splendour over a fully opened lotus bloom.

We sipped tea together while Mr Wong told us about his faith. He was a member of an esoteric sect known as the Secret Sect or True Word Sect from the privacy of its practices. This is the most Indo-Tibetan of the sects of Chinese Buddhism and makes use of Tantric practices is a way not usually undertaken by Chinese Buddhists. The doctrines are graded to suit the understanding of the practitioner and much is hidden, requiring personal revelation from a master. The teachings are found in three famous sutras, the Great Sun Sutra, the Diamond Head Sutra and the Resting Place Sutra, the first describing the meditation method and the others consisting mainly of ceremonies and mantric chants for particular occasions.

"We believe six qualities to be the roots of all phenomena and of Buddha nature itself. These are earth, water, fire, wind, space, by which we mean the emptiness between and within things, and finally feeling or perception, that is consciousness. Since these qualities exist in all things and in the Buddhas themselves, it follows that everything, this chair, this table, knife, yourself and myself are all Buddha. Our task is to come to understand this directly in experience. It is a great and wonderful truth to which our minds are usually blind. When we realise that peace resides within all things, then we know we are Buddha. Before we come to understand that, we are only Buddha unrealised. All forms of Buddha spring from the one root we call Vairocana the Great Sun Buddha. Sakyamuni, yourself, myself, all persons, are enveloped, as it were, by this same truth. When we talked the other day you called it energy but terms and words are of little importance. I have studied this for twenty years but I only know my old books, so I was most interested in what you had to say coming from an entirely Western source."

"How in your scheme of things does one come to know Buddha?" I asked him.

"There are two main ways, both of which we practise here with the aid of our master. The first is meditation on the Moon and Lotus Flower and the second involves the correct performance of certain ceremonies. Most of them were invented or elaborated from Indian or Tibetan sources by Kobo Daishi, a great monk of Japan who founded the Shingon Sect on Mount Koya. We are close followers of that tradition."

He drew out a number of beautifully bound books. In one were photographs of a recent Buddhist conference in Japan and another contained photographs of Mount Koya. He poured us out another cup of tea.

"Look," he continued, "you see that scroll over there?" We turned to look at the painting. At first glance it was not remarkable, simply a white disc above an open lotus bloom, not great art at all. Yet, as I continued to gaze at it, I became aware of certain optical peculiarities on the disc. It seemed to shine as might the face of the moon on a cloudless night, seeming almost to pulsate or breathe very slowly, growing into a semi-sphere for a moment, before reappearing as a plain, undifferentiated disc. There were faint suggestions of cream colouring within the white surface which may have been part of a design to produce this effect.

"This picture is our chief subject of meditation. We quieten our minds by gazing upon the moon and allowing the breath to flow gently in and out of the body. After a time the moon becomes spherical; at first for short time but then for longer and longer periods until it is continuously present. We then add the lotus bloom to our contemplation until the two are suspended together against a background of great emptiness. We have then the global moon of purity above the lotus of nature. We then begin the use of certain gestures we call mudras. If I fold my fingers into a particular pattern my hand becomes the bodily symbol of a particular Bodhisattva and of the virtue he or she represents, Amida for purity, Kuan Yin for mercy and so on." And he demonstrated the mudras with his fingers.

I was intrigued to realise that, in this scheme of things, meditation was not only mental but could involve sound and gesture as well. Chanting mantras and performing the mudric symbolism evokes the attributes of the Bodhisattva upon whom one is concentrating.

"If one carries through these movements correctly and in the right frame of mind, then the symbol of the Buddha you are concentrating upon will gradually appear somewhere on the moon."

Mr Wong took a pencil and drew a Sanskrit letter to be pronounced 'holik'.

"Of course, if one has reached this stage there is no need for drawing. Moon and lotus can be produced entirely in the imagination and the rest follows. The highest attainment is when the Bodhisattva himself actually appears."

The ceremonies are likewise designed in the same way. The mind is calmed and a long and complicated chant sung accompanied by movements and the manipulation of certain instruments. I enquired after the use of mandalas, concerning which C.G. Jung has written in his commentary on *The Secret of the Golden Flower*, an ancient Taoist-Buddhist text translated by Richard Wilhelm.*

"Yes, we use mandalas too for meditation, although in Hong Kong that is not a common practice. They represent the totality of the universe and its spiritual attributes in one complex and beautiful circular design. Now, time is running on I am afraid. You must come upstairs and visit our shrine and the ladies are waiting for us over the way."

Upstairs we visited a beautiful little upper chamber where we had to remove our socks before entering. Within the room, tastefully designed as a small temple, wooden columns, entwined with elaborate

---

* It is now known that Wilhelm's translation was full of misunderstandings due to his lack of knowledge of technical Taoist terms. This in turn influenced Jung whose commentary is now largely redundant. The recent work of Thomas Cleary (*The Secret of the Golden Flower*, Harper, San Francisco 1991) gives us a fresh authoritative text demonstrating the subtle links between Ch'an meditation and Taoist alchemy.

carvings of plants and animals, climbed to the ceiling and led towards a delicate little altar, complete with tiled roof and steep eaves enclosing a small gilt image of one of the Buddhas, backed by an elaborate mandala depicting a number of Buddhas in a circle about a central figure. Cleverly disguised lighting brought out the colours with refined intensity. The brass instruments used in the ceremonies stood before the altar on a little table together with a stool for the master. There was also a side chapel containing ancestor tablets belonging to members of the institute and a small altar to Kuan Yin. It was here that Mr Wong himself practised.

He picked up a small porcelain image. "This little Kuan Yin has been with me for years. Once, during the war, a Japanese shell fell nearby and it was thrown to the ground. As you can see only part of the base was broken and the figure was unharmed. Then, when I was hiding in the interior, some robbers stole many of my valuable possessions but again, after they had left, I discovered this little thing lying still unbroken under a table. I find it very curious."

Yannang wanted to know how he felt when he was carrying out the chants. "Can you hear what you are saying or is it automatic? How do you feel when you have finished?"

"Well", smiled Mr Wong, "I have never seen a Bodhisattva or anything like that and I believe that anything that occurs in that way has reality only in the mind. The importance of practice lies in the values and qualities we place upon it. Yes, of course, I hear and know what I am saying. Even after twenty years I must concentrate on the meaning of each word and gesture for, without that, the whole affair would have no meaning. And afterwards? I rise refreshed and go about my work with a quietened mind that refuses to distinguish opposites. I see you are puzzled so let me try to explain."

He paused a moment before continuing, "After all these years I can say I look upon the world in a different way than I used to do. Good and evil are basically all the same to me now. Against a background of disinterested calm both are identical forms of illusion. Placing the problems of life into a cosmic context, I find I am not moved to extreme feeling by good or evil or anything. I am quite happy and I no longer know that sense of random striving that I used to have."

"I understand," Yannang remarked. "There is, of course, all the difference between the simple putting into words of these matters and the true feeling that is the expression of them. It is easy for us to stand here and to discuss them. To actually do them is another matter."

Afterwards Yannang remarked that this way of life must have some good if it resulted in true feelings that were more than just words. Yannang hates empty ceremonial but he seemed content with Mr Wong's interpretation of the meaning of ritual. As for Yannang himself, he was not a stranger to placing the difficulties of life into a cosmic context. He had told me that, when troubled, he would go out at night and look at the stars, reflecting that cosmically everything would be the same in a thousand years.

Mr Wong now led the way along more dark passages and through heavily padlocked doors to another building. His Association of the Mantra Sect owned two houses, one for men and one for women. They all gave us a cordial welcome and again showed us a beautiful upstairs shrine.

Everywhere the Japanese influence was pronounced. Floors were covered with loose rush mats resembling tatami. Many pictures and images came from Japan but there was a Chinese flavour, the carvings and decorations had a more ponderous feel than the refined delicacy of Japanese interiors. It was all spotlessly clean but again lacked the fastidious attention a Japanese shrine would have received. We were treated to some lotus seed soup and presented with fine prints of Kuan Yin by a famous artist before we departed.

At the Cheero Club, Gunner Davis was waiting for me with some friends. They had been bathing with Chinese girls on Stanley beach. Davis smacked his lips. "Good uns they was, Sir," and his companion offered me his finger to smell. "Want to sniff my woman, Sir? Lovely she was."

I did not doubt it. Their eyes held the gleam of their delight and the moon must have cast magic upon the earth that night. As we crossed the pass of Wong Nei Chong and went on down towards Repulse Bay I looked up at the moon. "I seem to have a lot to do with you in one way or another these days," I said to myself.

Chapter Twenty-Six

The White Ship

And when my ship with sharpened prow shall pass
across this silvered surface of candelabra glass
a flying wind shall carry high my song,
the drifting wave my farewell sigh,
and bear upon the wings of air
a small cloud shadow on the glistening sea.

And when across your house's roof this thought shall glide
remember then the mountain and the moon,
the terraced temple that overlooked the sea
and may that self-same breeze's voice
that whispered there, acacia wise, that night
grow again in both our silenced hearts.

Yannang and I sat down at a table at the Peak Café. The town was disagreeable from the heat and we had come up high in search of coolness. Hibiscus flowers and tapering bamboo leaves adorned the bushes and low hedge around us, while far away below lay the dark slopes of the Peak and the blue channel of Aberdeen, with emerald islands shining on the sea. A light breeze fanned our heated cheeks and we relaxed into our chairs, filling lungs with air sweet with the scent of mountain vegetation blown from over the waters. We fell into a long silence while the waiter brought us lemon tea and an ice cream apiece.

"It is a strange occasion," said Yannang. "I find it impossible to discover what I feel." His eyes shone with the bashful twinkle that rose in them whenever he wanted to say something springing from his inmost thinking.

"Most things can be expressed, at least in part," I said. "What do you mean?"

"True – but only poets with a special genius can express some things truly and do them justice. The rest of us can only labour at a wording that is hopelessly inadequate."

There was a long pause. I fell to musing. Bamboo and hibiscus flowers, the last time, how strange, why oh why? Bamboo and hibiscus and the light breeze drifting up from the valleys and trailing pennants from the peaks. Surely again, next week, I shall be here with him, everything as now. But no, not so, the ship, tomorrow – O my dear bamboo and hibiscus with the breeze's voice within you, why is this so?

"You see, I feel kind of lost."

"Lost!" I smiled. "So shall I be in a few hours' time. Is it because I am leaving?"

"Yes," he said, with the release of tension known to those who struggle to disclose a deeply-felt confidence.

"You see, you and I have spent a lot of time together lately. Macao, Castle Peak and our walks together. Suddenly it all stops. Often friends need not meet for a month or so and it makes little difference but we know this is not like that. When the ship sails it will be years certainly before we see each other again. We have known this last meeting must come but, now that it has, the thought of it is very sharp and sudden. It all ends, now, in a few moments and there will be only the dream and an occasional letter. Suddenly it stops. It is a kind of being lost."

He was smiling, as if this was any normal occasion. He talked with precision, only his eyes betrayed the depth of his feeling and they were bashful because of that. I was silent for he was talking as I wished to do myself; he was doing the work for both of us. I waited while the sunlight laced the paving stones with a dance of bamboo shadows.

"This friendship is very curious. We come from continents apart with all the centuries themselves between us. Our language, customs, ideas, all are different but somehow we have achieved a kind of miracle. We understand each other. It is all so easy. Yesterday when you put those 300 dollars into the savings bank for me, it seemed quite an easy thing to do. Suddenly it happened there at the counter. Suddenly I have some money, for the first time in a long while. But I did not realise it then for it was just part of our moving together. It was one of the things we did as if in a dream. Then all at once I realised; it is a big sum for me. Yes, indeed I will use it carefully. But all these things run together, part of our knowing one another."

"Almost like a pattern, as if preordained," I said.

"Almost. What strange kind of Yin Yuen [karmic effect] brought us together, from so far, from such coincidences? Yes, it really is like a miracle."

"You see," I said, "When I read your article in the newspaper that evening - when was it? As long ago as December? How fast the months have flown! It seemed that in the writing there was some quality that appealed to me at once, a kind of restraint, compassion or pathos in so few words - just that last paragraph. Looking at them now they mean little but, at that moment, I resolved to write to you. I remember admitting to myself it was just a chance. There was something there which told me you possessed some quality I needed to know. Perhaps it is compassion, your love of nature, a kind of simple ingenuous charm you have - I don't know - nor do I care so long as it exists."

"So really it is neither our conversations, nor the topics we discussed, nor our ideas that mean so much as our companionship with one another," said Yannang. "You have shown me to myself what my thoughts are! You can express myself to me!"

"But really I am expressing myself to you!" I said laughing.

"It is strange!" said Yannang. 'Strange' in his vocabulary meant anything curious but also rather wonderful. We had both fallen into using the word in that sense. Other words between us had also discovered special meanings. For instance, 'idea' most usually meant those deeply felt things that spring from our inmost character rather than simply thoughts running through our minds.

"It is strange to me too," I told him. "You see I am a much happier person now than when I came to Hong Kong a year ago and it is through my Chinese friends and especially yourself that I have discovered that happiness. There is a quality in your company that brings a calmness to my mind. When we express our ideas to one another, there is a kind of synthesis, a building-up and a reaching out into a wider understanding. We seem to have discovered a true mutual empathy, as if we were mirrors to one another."

The breeze tossed the hibiscus blooms and it seemed as if my mind jumped with them through the last few years.

"At school in my last year, I had a friend whom I idolised, thinking him perfect, wise and beautiful. Really he was not so; he was young, impetuous, hearty and athletically brilliant as a young English schoolboy should be. I expected qualities from him he could not possibly possess. Really I was projecting upon him some personality out of my imagination. Naturally enough no friendship based on such expectation could succeed or develop, so it simply fell apart and I became very distressed and filled by needs I did not understand. Looking back now it seems as if the person I saw in him was actually an idealisation of my own character – or, perhaps, of what I would have liked to have been. In the break-up of that friendship I seemed to lose myself. Then, during my years at university, I found little in life but materialism, although I strove to pierce the wall that seemed to surround me. The interesting thing is that out here, among my Chinese friends, I have found a calmed mind and attitude that has seen reborn in me a sense of values. Indeed, it is through you that I have found myself, that more serene other self, which I appeared to have lost years ago. No European has been able to do this for me."

"Yes, that is true for me too. I have several very good Chinese friends but not one of them has been the same revealer of me to myself as you have been. It is a curious thing this for it seems that each of us had to find the other to fulfil some capacity within us."

Whatever the explanation of our friendship may have been I knew that in our conversation we at last understood each other fully and shared the inestimable value each had brought into the other's life. Maybe we could invoke other explanations but really there was little point in pursuing them. There it was. Somehow out of the obscurities of space and time we had come together. Perhaps love is not too great or difficult a word to use for it.

We walked around Lugard Road, the wind whistling in the needles of a fine horsehair tree as we sat for a while in its shade. Cloud shadows dappled the evening sea and beyond the broken-headed peak of Lantao, the sky glowed orange, wraithlike clouds turning from pigeon grey to soft pink. For the last time, maybe forever, we watched these things, talking quietly as if tomorrow we could see each other again.

Standing before the black, wet rocks where a small waterfall cascaded through overhanging ferns and mosses into the mountain forest below, Yannang turned to me.

"This is a precious time. We shall remember it and value it always. Now, as we stand here, it seems in some way quite ordinary for we are not really worried any more by the passing of time. Yet soon it will have gone and then, indeed, it will be precious. Even as we stand here it becomes so."

I am not good enough a poet to express the living joy and sorrow of those last moments together. The landscape assumed a brilliant, dancing delicacy that maybe transcended its real self. The grasses sighed and, below mountain and cloud, the great harbour spread below us rippling with waves.

"There is a curious sensation of space," said Yannang. "The little boats crawl like insects on the water – you know the kind that run across calm pools on mountain streams. And there are the big ones, so still, sitting deeply embedded in the sea. All that collection of light and colour..."

We fell silent and after a while I remarked, "The big, white ship at the Kowloon wharf is mine. Tomorrow, at noon, she sails for England."

"She is very large, she must go quickly," said Yannang.

"For some days I shall be lost too," I said, "Yet perhaps it is not really being lost for, if we think of it this way, the energies of the seas, rocks and islands are the same as those of our two minds. When we think of one another those energies are disturbed and we can know that somewhere, somehow the other will at some time know and understand the feeling."

"I cannot yet think that way."

"No – in reality neither can I!" We laughed.

"Actually, there is a great difference between what one can say to comfort oneself and what one is capable of feeling. We shall be lost for a time, however we like to think we can feel about it."

Coming down off the Peak we passed the tragic remains of a gun site shelled by the Japanese not so many years before. I thought of the officers and gun crew who had been there then. By a trick of fate I had been spared that kind of sorrow. After a while I said,

"I am thinking of the moment we say goodbye! What shall we do? Shake hands and smile conventionally, I suppose, knowing that there is no more to be said and that nothing more can be done. Perhaps this evening in our conversation we have said all that needs to be said in time."

"That is lucky. We are taking it easily, I think," he said, his eyes shining.

And so it was, after the university compound, the bus ride through the crowded, noisy streets, at last we agreed.

"At the next stop."

"Yes."

"It is a strange goodbye. One of us simply gets off the bus!"

"Life is like a bus ride in which one meets many passengers."

"True – here two bus rides come to an end."

"Yes."

The agonising passing of time, the tension waiting for the bus to shudder to a halt.

"Well – goodbye – here I must leave the bus – both buses."

"Goodbye, John."

I stepped off and turned to move. He glanced once after me still smiling and waved. Then, at the same moment as he looked away, I turned and went. I flicked my screwed-up ticket into the air and, passing into one of the arcades, knew not and seemed not to see or feel where I was going.

Postscript

In Chinese mode: thinking of a friend

Reading a book of Chinese translations
I remember my distant friend,
a bamboo breeze drifts though my study,
moonlight on the terraced temple shines again.
Climbing to those high places
sometimes you picked flowers
and in the monastery monks
disliked our intrusion,
tried to put us off, speaking of one infected
who'd died last night in the visitor's room.

Before the dawn the wooden clappers clacked
and in the shrine room I recall
the candles flickered along the wall
the golden images splendidly sat
there was no time at all in that
and now that all these years have flown
and after midnight I sit here alone
I see again the silvered lateen sails
that down the fishing moon's track trailed
as silently they put to sea
below the hill that sprouted guns.

Wearily I reflect, modern life
differs little from the time of Li Po.
I too seek my mountain cottage,
winter winds strike the oaks and birches
and the rushing stream gurgles past the muddy yard.
Woodfire burns low and by my candle

I read some far-off words.
This is no bamboo mountain
yet here too the natural stillness
creeps from the stones and trees
as in my secret heart I discover
my lone home.

Thinking of you and the passing years
of war and waste, treaties broken
and pledges meaningless,
the rise in prices and the difficulty of travel
passports and regulations,
I am comforted to know that old officials
in your ancient land also knew
the weariness of worldly noise,
that little changes in a thousand years
is proven true.
Time and space are endless
and only a fool finds a comfortable way.

Maenllwyd 1994